P9-DXO-247

Planet Earth

EARTHQUAKE

Other Publications:

LIBRARY OF HEALTH
CLASSICS OF THE OLD WEST
THE EPIC OF FLIGHT
THE GOOD COOK
THE SEAFARERS
THE ENCYCLOPEDIA OF COLLECTIBLES
THE GREAT CITIES
WORLD WAR II
HOME REPAIR AND IMPROVEMENT
THE WORLD'S WILD PLACES
THE TIME-LIFE LIBRARY OF BOATING
HUMAN BEHAVIOR
THE ART OF SEWING
THE OLD WEST
THE EMERGENCE OF MAN
THE AMERICAN WILDERNESS
THE TIME-LIFE ENCYCLOPEDIA OF GARDENING
LIFE LIBRARY OF PHOTOGRAPHY
THIS FABULOUS CENTURY
FOODS OF THE WORLD
TIME-LIFE LIBRARY OF AMERICA
TIME-LIFE LIBRARY OF ART
GREAT AGES OF MAN
LIFE SCIENCE LIBRARY
THE LIFE HISTORY OF THE UNITED STATES
TIME READING PROGRAM
LIFE NATURE LIBRARY
LIFE WORLD LIBRARY

FAMILY LIBRARY:
HOW THINGS WORK IN YOUR HOME
THE TIME-LIFE BOOK OF THE FAMILY CAR
THE TIME-LIFE FAMILY LEGAL GUIDE
THE TIME-LIFE BOOK OF FAMILY FINANCE

This volume is one of a series that examines the workings of the planet earth, from the geological wonders of its continents to the marvels of its atmosphere and its ocean depths.

Cover
Shattered buildings and rubble-strewn, fissured streets of Calitri, Italy, testify to the fragility of man-made structures before the savage onslaught of heaving earth. Similar devastation was visited on 179 villages in a 4,600-square-mile area in the earthquake that struck Italy on November 23, 1980.

Planet Earth

EARTHQUAKE

By Bryce Walker
and The Editors of Time-Life Books

Time-Life Books, Alexandria, Virginia

PLANET EARTH

EDITOR: George Daniels
Editorial Staff for *Earthquake*
Senior Editor: Thomas A. Lewis
Designer: Donald Komai, Raymond Ripper
Chief Researcher: Pat S. Good
Picture Editor: Richard Kenin
Writers: Deborah Berger-Turnbull, Jan Leslie Cook, John Newton, Peter Pocock, David Thiemann
Researchers: Feroline Burrage and Elizabeth B. Friedberg (principals); Therese A. Daubner, Barbara Moir, Oliver G. A. M. Payne, Deborah Lee Rose
Assistant Designer: Susan K. White
Copy Coordinators: Victoria Lee, Brian Miller
Picture Coordinator: Jane Martin
Editorial Assistants: Kathy J. Wicks, Annette T. Wilkerson

Editorial Operations
Production Director: Feliciano Madrid
Assistants: Peter A. Inchauteguiz, Karen A. Meyerson
Copy Processing: Gordon E. Buck
Quality Control Director: Robert L. Young
Assistant: James J. Cox
Associates: Daniel J. McSweeney, Michael G. Wight
Art Coordinator: Anne B. Landry
Copy Room Director: Susan Galloway Goldberg
Assistants: Celia Beattie, Ricki Tarlow

Correspondents: Elisabeth Kraemer (Bonn); Margot Hapgood, Dorothy Bacon (London); Susan Jonas, Lucy T. Voulgaris (New York); Maria Vincenza Aloisi, Josephine du Brusle (Paris); Ann Natanson (Rome). Valuable assistance was also provided by: Wibo van de Linde (Amsterdam); Jeanne Abbott (Anchorage); Tom Ross (Bogota); Helga Kohl (Bonn); Selwyn Parker (Dublin); Martha de la Cal (Lisbon); Millicent Trowbridge (London); Maria Odone (Naples); Robin Raffer (New York); M. T. Hirschkoff (Paris); Mimi Murphy (Rome); Janet Zich (San Francisco); Ed Reingold, Katsuko Yamazaki (Tokyo).

For information about any Time-Life book, please write:
Reader Information
Time-Life Books
541 North Fairbanks Court
Chicago, Illinois 60611

Second printing. Printed in U.S.A.
Published simultaneously in Canada.
School and library distribution by Silver Burdett Company, Morristown, New Jersey.

Library of Congress Cataloguing in Publication Data
Walker, Bryce S.
Earthquake.
(Planet earth; 1)
1. Earthquakes—Popular works. I. Time-Life Books. II. Title. III. Series.
QE521.2.W34 551.2'2 81-16662
ISBN 0-8094-4300-7 AACR2
ISBN 0-8094-4301-5 (lib. bdg.)
ISBN 0-8094-4302-3 (mail order ed.)

THE AUTHOR

Bryce Walker, a former Time-Life Books editor, has lived and traveled extensively in earthquake-prone areas. This book is the culmination of a longtime interest in geology that began when he wrote *The Great Divide* in the American Wilderness series.

THE CONSULTANTS

Keiiti Aki, Professor of Geophysics at Massachusetts Institute of Technology, is a graduate of the University of Tokyo. He is a consultant to the Nuclear Regulatory Commission and the Los Alamos National Laboratory, and is author or co-author of more than 100 publications on earthquake-related subjects.

Bruce A. Bolt, Professor of Seismology at the University of California, Berkeley, and director of its Seismographic Station, has been on the visiting faculties of nine universities worldwide. He is the author of numerous books and papers on earthquakes and related phenomena.

Sidney Horenstein is a geologist in the Department of Invertebrates at the American Museum of Natural History and a faculty member of the Department of Geology at City University of New York. He organized and served as coordinator of the Environmental Information Center of the American Museum.

CONTENTS

THE DREAD POWER OF AN EARTHQUAKE

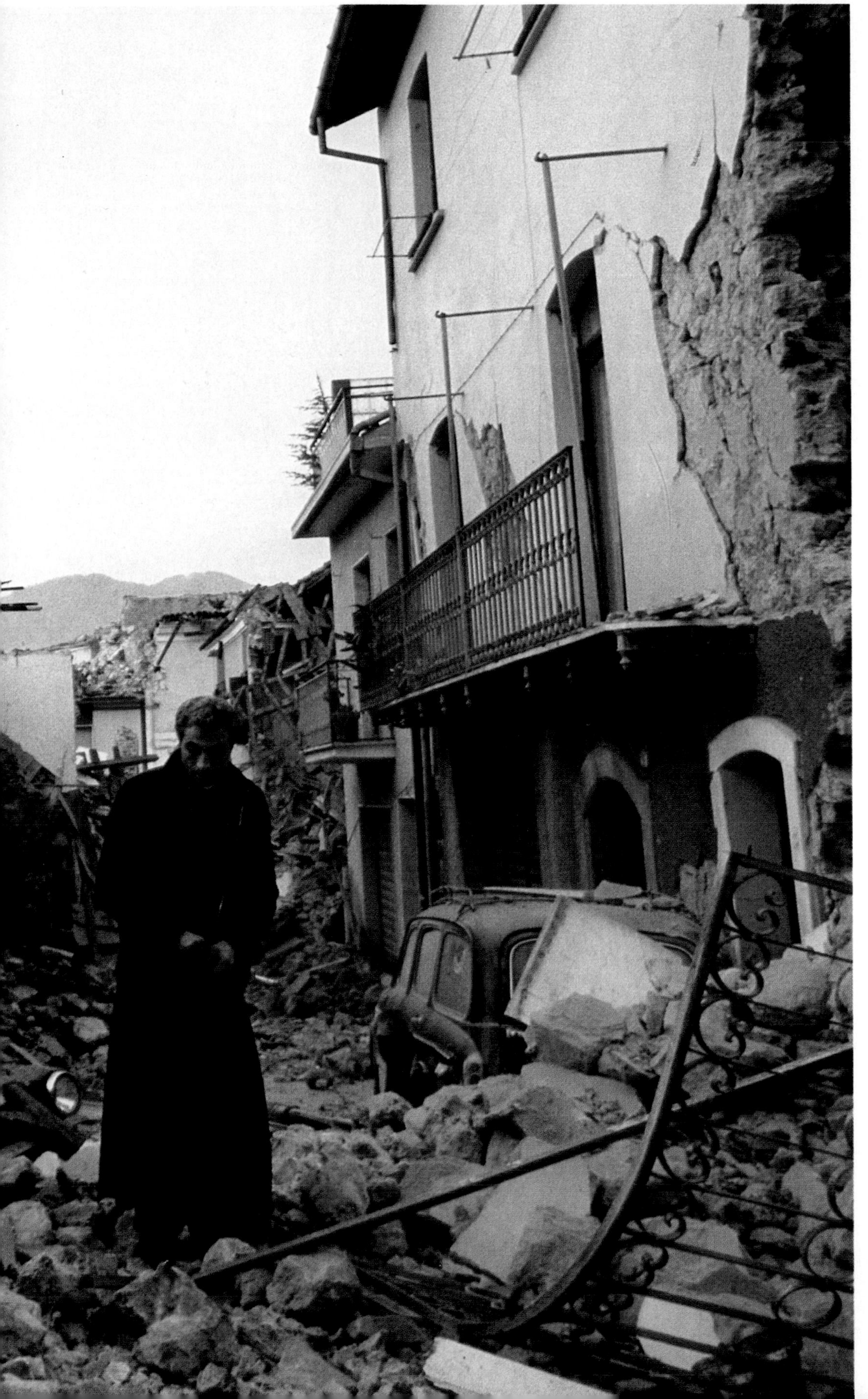

"It is a bitter and humiliating thing," observed Charles Darwin upon witnessing the effects of a great earthquake in Chile in 1835, "to see works, which have cost man so much time and labour, overthrown in one minute." Down through the ages, it has been mankind's common experience to find, as did Darwin, that "the earth, the very emblem of solidity, has moved beneath our feet like a thin crust over a fluid." For the dread earthquake is one of the most insistently frequent of nature's cataclysms.

In a wink of time's eye, the landscape can be altered in fantastic ways, as the pictures on these and the following pages testify. In 1811 and 1812, tremors in Missouri actually shifted the course of the Mississippi River. And the effect on civilization can be catastrophic. Two earthquakes in Tangshan, China, just 16 hours apart in 1976, annihilated hundreds of thousands of people.

For centuries, scientists have struggled to comprehend the place of this terrible force in the natural order of things. Success eluded them until sophisticated instruments made it possible to listen to the innermost mutterings of the globe, calibrate with unprecedented precision the growth of mountains and examine the deepest seas. The discoveries confounded reason: Oceans were opening and closing, continents were being torn asunder in some places and crunched together in titanic collision elsewhere.

The evidence that was assembled constituted nothing less than a revelation. What was once assumed to be a stable ball of static material, whirling sedately through space, is in fact a seething, many-layered conglomeration of molten and solid materials carapaced over with twisting, shifting plates of rock. Man is clinging to the skin of a planet still involved in the elemental forces of creation—ever changing, never at rest.

This knowledge places the earthquake in new perspective, and raises fresh hopes of predicting, surviving and perhaps one day controlling these outbursts. But for today, and many tomorrows, people will continue to live with the inescapable certainty, expressed by historian Will Durant, that "civilization exists by geological consent, subject to change without notice."

Rigid with shock and foreboding, a young priest searches the silent rubble of a street in Lioni, Italy, for a friend missing in a November 23, 1980, earthquake. The upheaval killed 3,000 people and left 300,000 homeless. Shortly after this photograph was taken, the priest's friend was found dead.

A hillside in Teora, Italy, many of its buildings leveled by the 1980 earthquake while structures on the far slope remain undamaged, offers dramatic evidence of the erratic forces that were at work. Such extremes are attributed to many factors, including the age of the buildings and the nature of underlying soils.

Once-fertile farmland in Aomori Prefecture in Japan lies in fissured ruin after a 1968 earthquake. The shaking of a great earthquake can turn certain kinds of subsoil into a heavy liquid, depriving surface features, such as the ridge shown here, of support and causing them to slide, settle and break apart.

A shattered overpass sprawls across severed freeways after an earthquake struck California's San Fernando Valley at dawn on February 9, 1971. Though five overpasses fell, the absence of heavy traffic helped account for the relatively few fatalities. Only 64 died, while 3,200 buildings were damaged or destroyed.

Doors that once opened on a quiet street in Calitri, a hill town in southern Italy, face a yawning chasm that was created by the November 1980 earthquake. An ancient crack in the bedrock gave way with the onslaught of the tremors, allowing surface soil layers under the street to drop nine feet.

Shuddering in an aftershock of the great Montana earthquake of August 1959, Yellowstone Park's 8,257-foot Mount Jackson shrugs off thousands of tons of rock in dusty torrents. Nine hours earlier the main shock had jolted 500,000 square miles, creating one new lake and reactivating 160 dormant geysers.

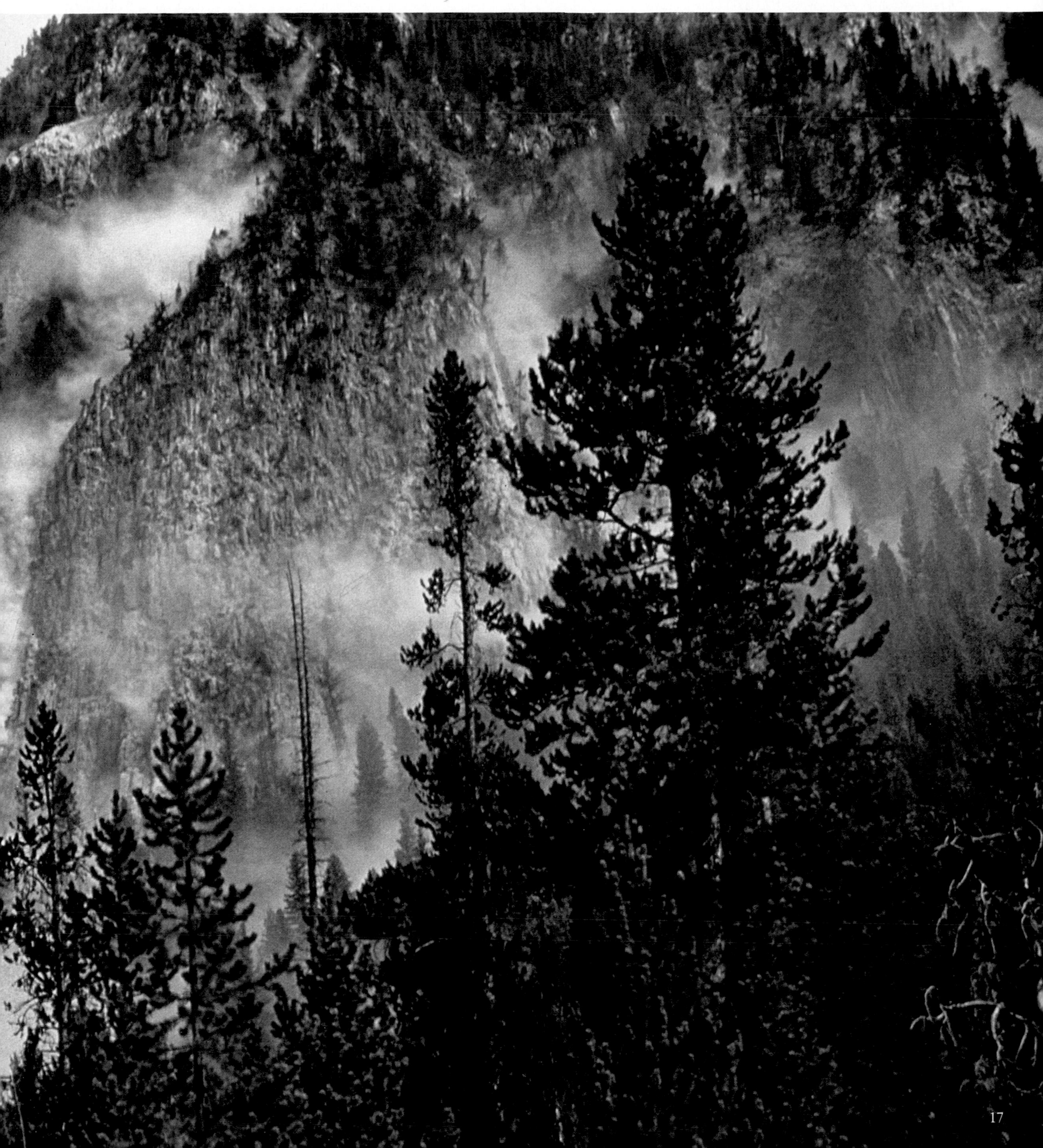

Chapter 1

ALASKA 1964: A WORLD GONE MAD

A station wagon teeters precariously at the edge of gaping fissures that split the ground beneath an Anchorage residential district during the great Alaska earthquake of March 27, 1964. Shock waves generated by the quake were felt 800 miles away.

Anchorage, Alaska, in 1964 was a boomtown—vigorous, roughhewn, optimistic. Its population had quadrupled to 64,000 in scarcely 10 years, and it now held almost one quarter of the residents of the 49th state. Its downtown streets teemed with oilmen, bush pilots, lumberjacks, crab and salmon fishermen, construction workers, geologists, wildlife officials—the professionals of the outdoors who always congregate in a fast-developing frontier settlement. But this was a frontier town with more substantial achievements to its credit: Through its offices, port facilities, railroad terminal and international airport passed an annual commerce of more than $140 million. It was the financial, if not the political, capital of the state.

So rapidly had the city expanded that it seemed in a perpetual scramble to catch up with its own growth. Its architectural style could best be described as pragmatic; it was a hodgepodge of modern high-rise offices, jerry-built shops and taverns, cinder-block houses and tree-filled vacant lots awaiting the developer's bulldozer. Here and there stood clusters of ramshackle wooden cabins left over from pioneer days. When a building was needed, it was put up, and fast; in this atmosphere of flourishing prosperity there was no time or inclination to pause and consider the meaning of occasional, minor tremblings of the ground, or the seldom-heard myths of the Indians and Aleuts that spoke of ancient devastations wrought by shuddering mountains and raging sea waves.

This rough-edged, thriving jumble of human enterprise had imposed itself on a natural setting of unmatched glory. Anchorage sprawled at the head of a deep, fjordlike bay, Cook Inlet, that cut 150 miles northeastward into Alaska's southern coast. Between the city and the sea, along the peninsula bounded by the inlet and the Gulf of Alaska, rose the rugged ranks of the Kenai and Chugach Mountains, flanked by glaciers and clothed in evergreen. To the north in the even more imposing Alaska Range rose the 20,320-foot eminence of Mount McKinley, the tallest peak in North America, easily seen on a clear day. Here was a landscape of outrageous splendor, and Anchorage was dwarfed by comparison. It seemed to cling precariously to the edge of a vast continent of silent and immutable grandeur.

The city's vulnerability was real, as Anchorage was to discover that fateful spring. The serenity of its surroundings was only apparent. For as unchanging as it seemed to the human eye, the landscape of south-central Alaska was in fact involved in a process of gradual but ceaseless geologic transformation. The young and fiercely jagged mountains of the Chugach and Alaska ranges were still in the process of growing, propelled upward by massive subterranean forces working in a kind of slow ferment within the earth.

Along the southern coast of Alaska, these immense forces were imperceptibly but implacably driving the bed of the Pacific Ocean underneath the Alaskan land mass. It was a movement that amounted to only inches a year, but over the centuries critical strain had accumulated at the boundary of the vast slabs as the irresistible force of the shifting ocean rocks encountered the near-immovable object—the North American continent. It was as though a steel spring were slowly being tightened and twisted; somewhere, sometime, a breaking point would be reached, with a variety of possible results. Under certain circumstances the release of energy might be slow and gradual, undetectable except by the most sensitive of instruments. Or it might take the form of the most awesome cataclysm that mankind can experience—a major earthquake.

In the early spring of 1964, beneath the waters of Prince William Sound and all along the seaward edge of the Kenai and Chugach Mountains, the tortured rock deep beneath the surface was nearing its breaking point—under circumstances that ruled out the milder forms of upheaval. On the afternoon of March 27, 1964—Good Friday—Anchorage was just beginning to unbutton from six months of winter. Temperatures hovered at a seasonable 28° F., intermittent snow flurries and rain showers sifted down from a lowering sky. Schools were closed for the holiday, offices had let out early, and although stores were open for business, shoppers were scarce. Most people were at home preparing for the evening meal and the festive weekend to come. It was 5:36 p.m.—the breaking point.

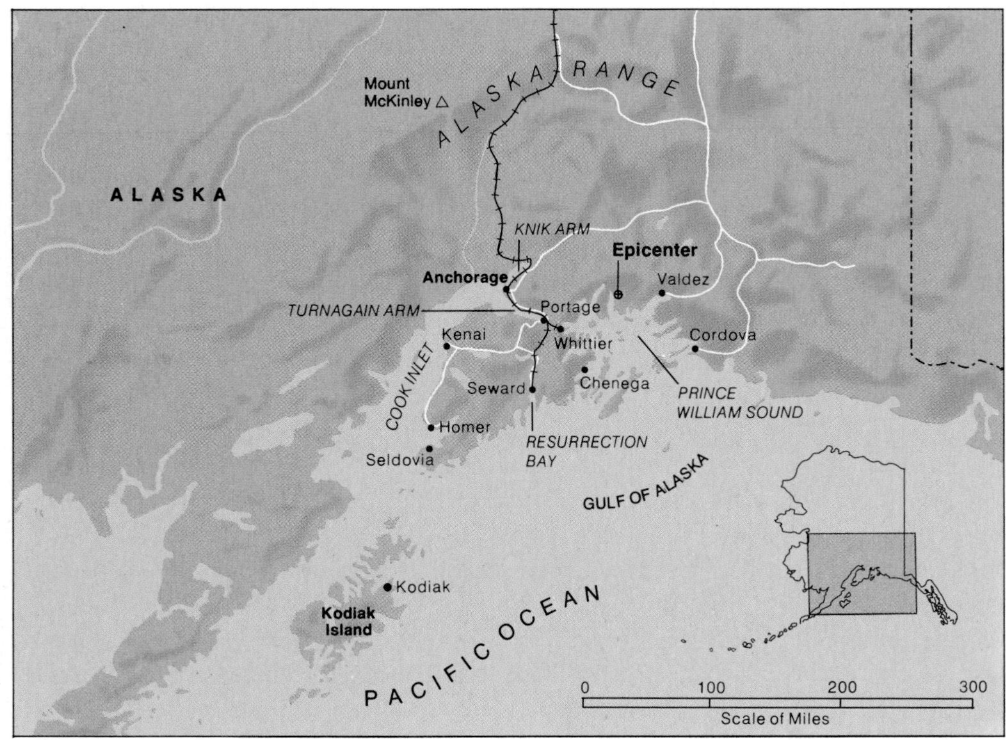

The great Alaska earthquake occurred in a complex geological region of craggy peaks, glaciers and fjords at the north end of Prince William Sound in the south-central part of the state. Massive damage to man-made structures extended over an extraordinary distance, across a crescent-shaped area from the Chugach Mountains in the north to Kodiak Island in the south.

Along the entire south-central coast of Alaska, the earth shrugged like some monstrous animal turning in its long sleep. The convulsion shuddered along the Alaskan land mass with awesome speed and force, cutting a 500-mile swath of destruction from the fishing port of Cordova in the east to Kodiak Island in the west. Rockslides and avalanches crashed down the sides of mountains. Roadways collapsed, bridges crumbled, entire towns were ravaged. For thousands of Alaskans Good Friday, 1964, would be a day of unprecedented terror. But the Alaska earthquake would not be remembered as a great calamity for mankind. The death toll in the state's sparsely settled expanses would be relatively light. Rather, the Good Friday quake would go down in history as an epic geological event. For in this upheaval, so many things happened with such power over so vast an area, things that had never before been observed with precision, that in the aftermath the scientists of the world would find an unprecedented opportunity to plumb the secrets of the forces at work in the depths of the planet.

At first, for perhaps 10 seconds, the ground rocked gently, like a boat at anchor in a safe harbor. Housewife Carol Tucker was browsing through the third-floor chinaware section of the new J. C. Penney department store in downtown Anchorage. Suddenly she saw some porcelain figures jiggling on a countertop. She was not overly worried at first; she had experienced many tremors, perhaps a half dozen a year, and had learned to shrug them off as part of life in the rugged north country. But this tremor was different. Instead of tapering off, the vibrating grew worse—and still worse. The entire building began to shake.

Outside, the ground started to surge underfoot in great undulating waves, shock after shock. And as it did, Anchorage began to fall apart. Whole blocks of houses were sliding about, pavements burst open, and fissures, some up to 30 feet wide, opened and closed like yawning mouths. "The earth started to roll. It rolled for five minutes," one woman said. "People were clinging to each other, to lampposts, to buildings."

In Penney's, mirrors and display cases exploded into shards of glass; chunks of ceiling plaster shook loose and fell. Then the lights went out. Carol Tucker found a stalled escalator and blundered down it, hands clasped to her head to ward off falling wreckage. Suddenly she pitched forward, tearing ligaments in her leg as she fell. Somehow she got down the next flight to ground level. Just before going out the front entrance, for no reason she can name, she paused.

At that moment the building's façade, massive concrete panels five inches thick, began to break off the structure and cascade into the street. A young man crouching on the sidewalk, trying to keep his balance as the earth shook, was crushed to death. A woman driving by was struck and killed inside her car. A parked station wagon was battered flat. Carol Tucker made her way out a back door to the relative safety of the parking lot.

The shocks slammed into Anchorage with particular intensity; it was hit harder than any other city. A new six-story apartment house—mercifully unoccupied—collapsed in a heap. A crevasse gaped open beneath the Government Hill elementary school, tearing the structure down as one wing dropped 20 feet into the depression. A quarter-mile section of Fourth Avenue, the main business thoroughfare, ripped apart; bars, stores, pawnshops and cars along one side of the street dropped 11 feet in a splintered, twisted tangle of devastation—by some geologic freak the quake left the other side of the street intact.

There were other instances of nature's caprice. In northwest Anchorage, a 30-block area slid horizontally in what geologists call a block glide (the term refers not to a city block but to a block of the earth's crust). Structures at the edge of the area were shattered but those near its center survived. A six-story apartment house was transported 10 feet with almost no damage. But along the main shopping street of suburban Spenard, every building taller than one story was smashed. At Anchorage International Airport the 68-foot concrete control tower toppled, killing an air-traffic controller but leaving runways intact.

The cataclysm had its special sounds. As the pitching of her Anchorage home intensified, Betzi Woodman remembered "a roar with the sound of frozen earth breaking and squeaking apart. Lamps swung drunkenly, china came crashing from shelves, furniture slithered across the room. And always the threatening noise underneath." She ran outside. "There was a frantic pitch to the dogs' barking and birds darted about uncertainly." She saw bewildered neighbors emerging from their houses, trying to decide what to do. One of them attempted to get to a car, "which bounced about as though possessed. A sharpening of the quake threw us to the ground, into the wet, cold snow. I found myself shouting, 'Boy, oh boy, oh boy!' It had no meaning, but plenty of feeling."

One of the worst places to be during the earthquake was in Anchorage's proudest housing development—Turnagain Heights, a cluster of expensive homes perched on a bluff southwest of the downtown area, overlooking Knik Arm where it widens into Cook Inlet. There, Robert B. Atwood, publisher of the *Anchorage Daily Times,* had been relaxing in his spacious modern home. At the first strong tremors he ran outside to find a landscape in chaos—trees falling, the ground breaking up into frozen, tilted slabs.

Atwood remembered that he "turned around and looked and saw the house twist and squirm. The earth under it was moving, twisting the two ends in opposite directions. It seemed to elongate the house and then shrink it up and the noise was terrific. The glass breaking, the timbers giving, snapping, cracking, splitting, everything tearing apart—the noise of a dying house. And the earth started opening up; it was then that I discovered I was falling.

"The earth had just opened up and I was going down, it seemed an awful long distance. But when I lit I was in soft, dry sand and I was at the bottom of a rather sharp V which opened up—kept opening up more. And trees, stumps, fence posts and frozen soil like boulders came rolling down on top of me. I had to scramble to stay on top to keep from being buried.

"I clambered up the side of the chasm that I was in and looked around and in every direction I just saw nothing but desolation. Houses at all angles and topsy-turvy and everything silent except for the last snapping and breaking. My house was nothing but kindling. It was out on the beach; it had been about ninety or a hundred feet above the water and it was now at sea level."

The headland, for a distance of a mile and a half, had settled and cracked apart and slid seaward, and more than 70 dwellings had pitched downslope toward the waters of Knik Arm.

One of Atwood's neighbors was Tay Thomas, wife of journalist Lowell Thomas Jr. Her husband was in Fairbanks on business, and she was watching television that evening with her children, six-year-old David and eight-year-old Anne, all three with their shoes off. Their first warning was a rumbling that sounded to her like the roll of distant artillery. Mrs. Thomas grabbed her family and raced out the front door, barefoot, into the snow. A violent tremor threw them to the ground, and a fissure opened under their house, wrenching it apart. Another fissure split the ground on which they were lying, separating Anne from her mother and brother. Tay Thomas reached over and pulled her across the widening chasm. The family was now balanced on a slab of icy turf, about five feet across, that had tilted sharply and was lurching crazily downslope. "It seemed like we were on a ferris wheel going backwards, like we were falling right into the sea," she said later. "Then everything stopped. There was just not a sound. I felt like we were the last people in the world."

Tay Thomas knew they had to get to high ground, above the high-water mark, and quickly: "I thought the water would be coming very fast." Taking David by the hand and urging Anne to stay close, she clawed her way across the huge chunks of still-crumbling earth. For perhaps 20 minutes the trio worked along the base of the cliff, their bare feet numb in the snow, searching for a way to the top. They saw a man peer down from the rim and called out for help. He turned and left. After a few moments the frantic family saw him return with more men and a rope. The Thomases were hauled to safety.

Robert Atwood, the Thomases and most of their neighbors were lucky. But lasting tragedy struck one Turnagain household, that of neurosurgeon Perry Mead. Twelve-year-old Perry Mead III had been baby-sitting two younger brothers and a sister. When the quake hit he got them all outside. Just as they reached apparent safety, a crevasse opened under Perry and his two-year-old brother Merrell, and they plunged from the sight of their brother and sister on

Rushing to safety, three men barely escape being crushed by concrete panels jolted loose from the front of the year-old J. C. Penney department store building, architectural pride of downtown Anchorage. As the shaking of the earth intensified, the entire five-story structure was wrecked in just a few minutes.

firm ground nearby. The bodies of the two brothers were never recovered.

On the other side of town from Turnagain Heights, at the Fort Richardson Army base, destruction was less severe, but no less terrifying. Two residents—a sergeant's wife and her 16-year-old daughter—had rushed into their front yard at the first tremors. There they stood as the ground heaved under them for four awful minutes, until the girl broke into mumbled prayer: "Lord, that's enough now. Please stop it."

From the earthquake's origin east of Anchorage, the shocks ripped along the coast at nearly two miles a second, knocking out roadways, twisting rail lines, devastating port facilities and temporarily cutting communication between the battered communities and the outside world. As landslides cascaded into the sea, they generated gigantic harbor waves that smashed upward against the shore—in some places as high as 100 feet above normal tide levels.

The port of Valdez nestled on a deep-cut inlet on the edge of Prince William Sound, 120 miles east of Anchorage. Overlooked on three sides by mountains, it was called the Switzerland of Alaska. That Friday the 1,000 residents were in a festive mood: A 10,000-ton cargo freighter, the S.S. *Chena,* was alongside the town dock, unloading much-needed goods. Villagers had come to welcome the ship and watch the operation, adding to the waterfront congestion of cargo crates, oil drums, forklifts, deck hands and longshoremen.

About 20 minutes before the 6 o'clock quitting time, a workman aboard the *Chena* felt a sudden lurch, as though the ship were getting under way. He glanced toward the dock and saw the entire structure collapsing into the water. "One second it was there, the next it just wasn't," he said. "It was sucked under all at once, like—well, just like the bobber on a fish line when a big one hits."

By that time the captain of the *Chena,* M. D. Stewart, had reached the bridge of the lunging vessel—he cannot remember how—from the dining saloon three decks below. "The *Chena* raised about 30 feet on an oncoming wave," he later reported. "The whole ship lifted and heeled to port about 50 degrees. Then it was slammed down heavily on the spot where the docks had disintegrated moments before. I saw people running—with no place to run to. They were just engulfed by buildings, water, mud, and everything. The *Chena* dropped where the people had been. That is what has kept me awake for days."

The 28 people caught on the dock had vanished in the maelstrom. None survived. The shoreline had collapsed all along the waterfront, flinging piers and buildings into the harbor along with millions of cubic yards of earth. The water thus violently displaced surged back and forth in Valdez Narrows in the form of the harbor waves that were battering the *Chena.*

"There was an ungodly backroll to starboard," Captain Stewart recalled. "Then she came upright. Then we took another heavy roll to port. I could see the land jumping and leaping in a terrible turmoil." By this time the ship had been washed into the small-boat harbor, and when the wave receded there was no water under the vessel at all. When the water returned, despite the fact that the stern was sitting in broken pilings, rocks and mud, Captain Stewart signaled the engine room for power and, surprisingly, "got it very rapidly." After an agonizing few minutes the waves partially refloated the vessel, and she started to move under her own power. But she could not turn and was simply plowing along, churning through the shallows parallel to the shoreline. At last, an offshore gush of water moved the bow outward. The ship broke free, pushed through the wreckage of a cannery, and moved safely into the bay.

As a result of a massive subsidence, or dropping of the earth, the north side of Anchorage's Fourth Avenue rests in ruins below the relatively undamaged south side. When the quake hit, saloon patrons rushed into the street in terror. "They were flopping and falling down, grabbing onto automobiles," said an eyewitness. "But the cars were rocking and rolling all over the place and they couldn't hold on."

A yawning six-foot-wide crack zigzags down the Seward Highway near the head of Turnagain Arm, 35 miles southeast of Anchorage. Of the 830 miles of primary and secondary roads in south-central Alaska, nearly 200 miles suffered damage, and almost half of the 204 bridges had to be rebuilt.

To the astonishment of the captain, the *Chena* had not even sprung a leak.

In Valdez itself, the ground rolled as though the land had turned to water. The earth rose and fell in billowing undulations—three feet deep from crest to trough by the estimate of one man who watched his six-foot-tall son disappear almost to the beltline as the ground waves passed between them. Long cracks opened up and snapped shut again, sending jets of water and silt 20 feet into the air. Foundations cracked, walls gave way, live power cables thrashed about and muck from broken sewer mains sloshed through the streets. Then the harbor waves that had tossed the *Chena* roared in to swamp the town. As one wave rolled back out to sea, gathering force as it squeezed through Valdez Narrows, it sheared the midchannel lighthouse off its 35-foot-high foundation.

Still the earthquake had not struck its final blow. The massive movement deep under the ocean had churned up a new threat: a devastating series of seismic sea waves called a tsunami or—inaccurately—tidal waves. It was as though the water of the Gulf of Alaska had been stroked powerfully from below by a gigantic canoe paddle. Five hours after the main shocks, when battered residents unversed in the ways of earthquakes might have thought it was all over, the worst of the tsunami swirled devastatingly into Valdez.

The first crest had arrived almost unnoticed 30 minutes after the earthquake. Because the tide was at low ebb and the town was located at the head of the curving inlet, the wave barely reached the normal high-water mark. It was much later—10:30 in the evening—that continuing waves added their power to the rising tides to punish Valdez once more. Noiselessly, the waters poured up Valdez Narrows again and again, at intervals of approximately 30 minutes, until almost 2 a.m., flooding broad sections of the town. Fortunately, by evening most residents had fled into the hills. They spent the night in the open, in subfreezing cold, worrying about missing relatives. At the first light of dawn they straggled back to the somber tasks of recovering their dead and assessing their losses.

The earthquake and its attendant sea waves had totally demolished the Valdez waterfront and had either wrecked or rendered uninhabitable most of the town's large commercial buildings and nearly half its houses. Sixty-eight fishing craft were lost. More than $11 million worth of property had been demolished. And 32 people had died.

The major oil port and rail terminus of Seward, on the Kenai Peninsula 80 miles south of Anchorage, suffered the same sequence of trembling earth and rampaging water, with a fearful addition—fire. As at Valdez, an entire section of Seward's waterfront, three quarters of a mile in length, cracked free and slid out into the bay. The city pier, the boatyard, a cement plant, docks and warehouses were sucked down and submerged. In the nearby freight yards of the Alaska Railroad, 125-ton diesel locomotives were overturned, terminal buildings were broken apart and rolling stock was knocked into a tangled mass.

Able-bodied seaman Ted Pedersen, of the tanker M.S. *Alaska Standard,* was on the dock belonging to the Standard Oil Company, watching over the maze of valves and hoses through which his vessel's cargo of petroleum was being pumped from storage tanks ashore. At the first trembling of the dock, he shouted "Earthquake!" and started to run toward the ship. "All of a sudden a corner of the dock just lifted up 10 feet," he said later. "The ship went up—or maybe I went down. All the hoses parted and there was a spray of gasoline in every direction. The dock just fell in and I saw this big comber wave full of timber rolling in way above me." Pedersen was certain he was about to die. But he was merely knocked unconscious—and he came to a short time later lying inexplicably on a catwalk eight feet above the deck of his ship, a broken leg his sole injury.

The harbor wave generated by the enormous slide heaved the *Alaska Standard* free of the dock and out into open water. Fortunately, the spilled fuel on her decks did not ignite. But on shore, at the site of the shattered dock, a wall of orange flame and black, greasy smoke was rising skyward. Pipes leading to the huge storage tanks had burst open, and their contents had ignited. Soon, entire tanks began exploding, and burning petroleum spewed out in a sheet of fire across the harbor, the flotsam from the shattered dockyards adding fuel to the conflagration.

Hal Gilfilen, a Seward businessman, saw the fire erupt at the Standard Oil tank farm in a "big billowy burst of flame and smoke" that made him think of an atomic bomb. "The railroad track grew cherry red from the fire," he said. And when the harbor wave washed over the rails, the steel "curled and raised like snakes when stepped on."

The Seward harbor wave was as high as a three-story house. It carried boats, timbers, rail track and bridge trusses, even entire boxcars, and deposited them inland in great windrows of wreckage. With the wave came the burning oil slick from the harbor, igniting what was left of the waterfront. "It was an eerie thing to see," said one survivor, "a huge tide of fire washing ashore, setting a high-water mark in flame, and then sucking back."

John and Robert Eads had been locking up their marine yard on Lowell Point, south of town, when the quake struck Seward and the oil tanks exploded. The brothers, with their companion, Carl Christiansen, were watching the holocaust when they spotted the wave. "It sloshed around inside the bay like water in a basin," said John Eads. "We saw it hit Seward and then start back our way" at a speed they thought to be more than 60 miles an hour. The trio ran to a car and a pickup truck to escape, but before the vehicles had gone 100 feet the wave caught them. The truck was tumbled end over end, and the car surfed along the crest—"just like a boat," said Christiansen. Thrown from

A jumble of ruins crossed by bulldozer trails *(below)* is all that remains of 75 homes in Anchorage's Turnagain Heights neighborhood. Before the quake, residents overlooked Knik Arm from a bluff 70 feet above the sea, but seismic waves caused the unstable formation of soft, silty clay to liquefy —transforming a block of land 8,000 feet long and 600 to 1,200 feet wide into a giant washboard *(diagram)* that slid out onto the tidal mud flats.

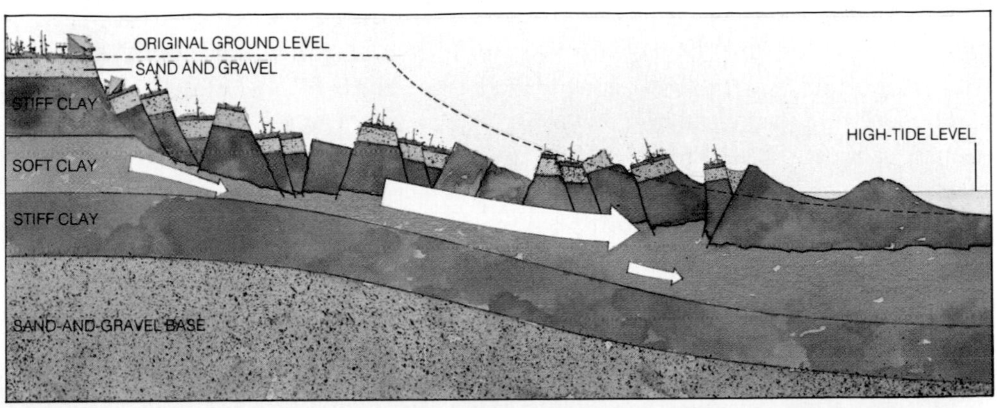

the truck, John Eads tried to stay afloat in the swirling water. The wave carried men and vehicles into the trees 50 feet from the road and 32 feet above sea level. And there, miraculously, it deposited all three companions unhurt.

The fire and wave obliterated most of Seward, including the port's entire industrial area. Twelve people died, and property damage totaled $15 million. Every dock was swept away, the rail yards were demolished, the power plant and 26 huge tanks of petroleum went up in flames.

At Kodiak Island, 200 miles to the southwest, the ground shocks had been frightening but had caused little damage to the main port of 4,800 people, the satellite fishing villages and the U.S. Naval Station. But any feelings of relief were premature, for the real threat to Kodiak Island came from the sea—and the terrible tsunami.

At about 5:45 p.m., fishermen anchored in St. Paul harbor, off Kodiak, noticed a long, gentle swell followed by a sudden ebb. The water receded until less than two feet remained in the harbor. The 160-boat fishing fleet sat on the bottom in the mud. Then at 6:20 a second wave surged through the harbor entrance, cresting at 17 feet above the normal water level. It picked up boats, dock pilings, houses and six-ton harbor buoys and washed them three blocks into the town. It sucked back again, pulling a train of debris into the channel. Ten minutes later a third giant wave arrived, and seven more followed during the night.

Smoke clouds rise from debris near petroleum tanks in Seward. The earthquake opened pipelines and tanks, spewing their blazing contents into Resurrection Bay. An enormous harbor wave sent a rolling 30- to 40-foot-high wall of flame more than 1,000 feet inland.

Captain Bill Cuthbert was on his 86-foot crab boat *Selief* when the waves came in. He was wafted ashore, then out into the channel, then back ashore, four times in all. On his last trip inland he tied his grounded vessel to a telephone pole. Before long a marine radio operator, checking on the vessels in the Kodiak fleet, contacted the *Selief.*

"Where are you, Captain?" she asked.

"By dead reckoning," Cuthbert replied, "in the schoolhouse yard." He was two blocks from shore.

Seventy-seven fishing boats—nearly half the fleet—were sunk or badly mauled by the waves at Kodiak. Two of the island's three crab and salmon canneries were carried off, and the third took three months to repair. Eight people died and property damage totaled almost $25 million.

Other Alaskan communities were left nearly as destitute. Homer and Cordova both lost part of their waterfront. Float installations at Seldovia had been splintered as though, said a resident, "some crazy giant had taken them into his hands and was wringing them to pieces." Chenega, a fishing village built on pilings at the water's edge, had simply vanished under a 70-foot sea wave—every dwelling swept away, along with 23 of the 76 Aleut inhabitants.

The great earthquake of March 1964 spread havoc far beyond the borders of Alaska. The tsunami moved out across the Pacific at speeds of more than 400 miles an hour. The first wave reached Canada's Vancouver Island at 11 p.m., and cascaded 35 miles up an inlet to flood the town of Port Alberni. At midnight the tsunami swirled onto a beach at Depoe, Oregon, and carried away four children who had been camping out with their parents. At 1:45 a.m. the worst of the series of waves to hit Crescent City, California, drowned 10 people, demolished 150 stores and littered the streets with giant redwood logs from a nearby sawmill. The waves raced southward to Hawaii, sending residents fleeing to high ground, and moved onward with diminishing fury to surge against the coast of Japan, 4,000 miles from their source.

Tumbled freight cars, twisted rails, mangled pieces of buildings and uprooted telephone poles litter Seward after the harbor wave's knockout blow. At Kodiak, two crab and salmon canneries were obliterated, and several Aleut fishing villages were swept away.

The sheer physical magnitude of the Alaska earthquake was beyond comprehension. The initial seismic waves were so powerful that they caused buildings to sway as far south as Seattle, Washington. Lengthening and weakening with distance, the radiating waves briefly lifted the ground beneath Houston, Texas, as much as four inches, and Cape Kennedy, Florida, two and a half inches. These movements were too gentle to be felt by the residents and were only revealed by later calculations based on tide levels. And as scientists reset their instruments and watched in fascination, the waves continued to circle the globe. For two weeks the entire planet vibrated like a great silent gong. And that was just the result of the initial convulsion.

In the first three days after the quake, south-central Alaska was jolted by almost 300 aftershocks strong enough to shake the buildings that remained standing—and several of them were strong enough to send residents running into the streets again. Eighteen months went by before the reverberations ceased, by which time the number of aftershocks totaled more than 10,000.

It had been the most violent cataclysm in U.S. history. An estimated 75 per cent of the state's commerce and industry lay in ruins, and thousands of its citizens were homeless. Yet the cost in human lives and injuries was remarkably light. Only 115 people were killed (82 of those were presumed dead; their bodies were never recovered). Of the hundreds who had been injured, most suffered only minor cuts, bruises and exposure. Incredibly, fewer than 50 people were admitted to hospitals. Relief officials later attributed this good fortune to the fact that schools and offices were closed, and the already sparse population of the area was well dispersed.

Alaskans dug out from the wreckage with an alacrity and a gallantry of spirit that fostered a ready, if somewhat rough, humor. They teased one another about living "on the wrong side of the cracks." An Anchorage store owner hung a sign in his window that referred both to his damaged premises and to the long-awaited spring thaw. "Closed," it read, "due to early breakup." At Kodiak, where the tsunami had picked up a general store, wafted it out to sea, then floated it back again to within a few hundred yards of its original foundation, a new slogan became popular: Come to Kodiak and see the tide come in and the town go out.

But gallantry and humor would not be enough to put a shattered state back together. Massive amounts of money were needed, and Alaska was chronically short of capital. Governor William Egan thought the state could raise only about a tenth of the necessary funds, and he telephoned President Lyndon B. Johnson to plead for $500 million in grants. "In no other way," he told the President, "can we rebuild." The city manager of Seward, William Harrison, began a news conference on the problems of recovery by saying: "Fellows, we're in a hell of a mess." Then he broke down and wept.

The President responded immediately with five million dollars in emergency relief funds, and within a few days Congress appropriated $50 million more for reconstruction. Over the next months, hundreds of millions of dollars flowed into Alaska, but it would be years before the scars of the catastrophe healed.

News of the Alaska earthquake reached geologist George Plafker in Seattle, where he was attending a meeting of the Geological Society of America. Plafker at age 35 was an old Alaska hand. For some years he had been working as a research geologist with the Alaskan Branch of the United States Geological Survey—the federal agency whose responsibilities included studying the country's topography and geology, its water, mineral and energy resources, and the hazards posed by earthquakes. He had done extensive work in Prince William Sound, where the Good Friday earthquake seemed to have originated. And he was one of a number of young scientists who were interested in some new and challenging theories of the mechanics of the ever-changing earth.

What intrigued Plafker and his colleagues about the Alaska quake was the immensity of the deformation: Whole cliffs and shorelines had crumpled into the sea, vast inland areas had lifted or dropped, enormous changes had occurred in the levels of the seabed. A precise analysis and measurement of the changes would give modern science its first intimate look at a major reshaping of the land. "From a scientific point of view, it was a great experiment," said Plafker. "It was a time when there was a furor over what was going on in these areas. Everyone was just at the beginning of a whole new approach to earthquakes."

Less than 24 hours after the earthquake struck, Plafker arrived in Anchorage with two colleagues from the Alaskan Branch of the Geological Survey: Arthur Grantz, who had been with him at the Seattle meeting, and Reuben Kachadoorian, who had rushed north from headquarters in Menlo Park, California. The three men split up and fanned out across the vast area affected by the earthquake. For the next week, by light airplane, helicopter and jeep they surveyed what had happened, and their excitement grew. What they saw was described in a later report as "geological effects that were spectacular and perhaps unprecedented, particularly the uplift and subsidence of huge areas."

In a scant seven days after their return to Menlo Park, the three men issued a preliminary report on the earthquake, outlining its effects and the detailed investigations that would be needed. The report became the basic reference for

The Two Faces of Lituya Bay

Lituya Bay lies in the Alaskan panhandle, 150 miles north of Sitka, and it is an enchanted jewel of geography. The seven-mile-long and one-mile-wide inlet is framed on three sides by majestic cliffs that mute the howling winds, and a barrier sandspit and rocky headland at the mouth hold back the combers of the Pacific. Over the bay's waters rests an atmosphere of supernatural calm and beauty.

But the Tlingit Indians, who in generations past hunted sea otter in its environs, know Lituya Bay as a deathtrap. For it is transformed on occasion into a place of raging elements that obliterate everything within reach. According to Tlingit legend, a great and jealous demon *(right)* dwells in the underwater caverns close to the entrance of the bay, and when aroused to fury by the presence of strangers the demon thrashes the land and water in order to capture the strangers and change them into tame bears.

Modern scientists stand in no less awe of Lituya Bay, but they have identified the monster as a large geological fault that runs across the mouth of the bay. When a major earthquake jolts the fault, it causes massive avalanches on the surrounding cliffs and displacements of the bay floor—which in turn result in unimaginably huge harbor waves, far bigger than anything experienced by Seward or Kodiak during the 1964 Alaska earthquake.

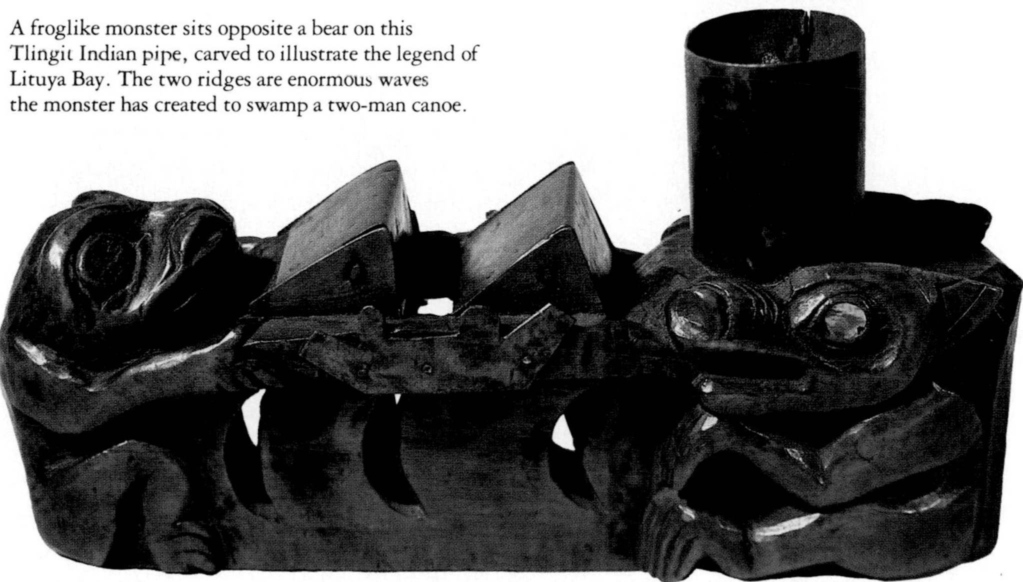

A froglike monster sits opposite a bear on this Tlingit Indian pipe, carved to illustrate the legend of Lituya Bay. The two ridges are enormous waves the monster has created to swamp a two-man canoe.

How great a size these waves have attained in geologic time is unknown. But some idea of their potential can be found in the event of July 9, 1958, when a powerful earthquake shook loose 90 million tons of rock from the cliffs around the bay. Plunging into the confined waters from heights of up to 3,000 feet, the rockfall produced a fantastic wave that swept through the bay and out into the ocean. Because the region is so remote, little loss of property and only two deaths were reported. However, when scientists later surveyed the area they found to their astonishment that the water had surged up to a level of 1,740 feet—the greatest height ever attained by any form of wave in recorded history.

briefing and directing battalions of engineers and scientists from half a dozen government agencies charged with guiding the reconstruction. As they assisted Alaska, the scientists would have an unprecedented opportunity to study earthquake mechanics. To ensure that the hard-won knowledge did not become fragmented and lost, the National Academy of Sciences was enlisted to review all findings of all the investigators and publish a single exhaustive analysis.

Thus for months following the earthquake, the mountains, valleys and waters of south-central Alaska were patrolled by hundreds of foot soldiers of science in pursuit of the secrets of the inner earth. They swarmed through Anchorage, charting the direction in which buildings had fallen and fissures had opened, measuring and analyzing the cracks and damage in buildings still standing, drilling holes to determine what lay beneath the surface and how the underlying materials influenced the damage. They set out seismographs across southern Alaska to measure the aftershocks and assemble a more detailed picture of the earthquake's focus and movement.

The scientists inched along the Alaska Railroad and the highway networks, measuring, mapping and photographing the damage to roadbeds and bridges, making recommendations on repairs, investigating the causes. They climbed mountains to inspect landslides, clambered onto glaciers, flew over lakes and followed the courses of streams and rivers to see what had changed—and why. The geologists and oceanographers crisscrossed the waters of the coast and its inlets to measure the extent of submarine slides and ocean-floor upheavals. Their reports, wrote the president of the National Academy of Sciences later, "constitute perhaps the most comprehensive and detailed account of an earthquake yet compiled."

George Plafker's particular desire, as he prepared to return to the field after helping to write the initial survey, was to measure the warping of thousands of square miles of the earth's surface. Plafker thought he might get some help from a curious measuring device: the barnacles on rocks and pilings. He had often observed the uniform level that barnacle growth assumed along the shore and on pilings and other protuberances from the water, and he thought it might be possible to measure changes in the earth's surface by measuring the changes in the level of barnacle colonies.

Plafker gained a kind of fame for walking around with his pockets stuffed with barnacles. "I wanted to find out how long they would live outside the marine environment," he explained. He discovered that they perished rapidly, and this fact established the utility of his idea. Where the ground had lifted, the barnacles had been raised above the narrow intertidal zone where they thrive. Thus exposed, they died, turned white and formed an easily distinguishable band corresponding to the upward movement of the land. The methods of establishing and measuring the difference and thus the amount of uplift, as refined by Plafker, became standard in subsequent earthquake investigations.

Another novel method of measuring crustal deformation was discovered by David McCulloch of the Geological Survey—in a way that typified the elements of dedication and serendipity that contributed so much to the learning process. McCulloch's assignment was to analyze the damage to the Alaska Railroad and to advise on its reconstruction. While so doing he became interested in the earthquake's effects on nearby lakes and, he recalled, pursued the subject "pretty much on my own." While inspecting Lake Kenai he discovered that bench marks—points of known elevation set by the U.S. Coast and Geodetic Survey—had been placed at opposite ends of the lake. Comparison of the new water levels with the bench marks revealed that the earth beneath the lake had tilted: The lake acted like a giant spirit level and made it possible to calculate the amount of deformation. The discovery prompted a systematic study of the water levels of 17 lakes within 500 miles of Anchorage, each of which was promptly lined with bench marks against which to measure future settling or uplift.

McCulloch's investigation of a puzzling kind of damage to the railroad yielded yet another advance. In addition to the usual damage—from landslides, ground cracks and warping of the surface—there were many areas where the railroad track had been twisted askew by the sideways movement of level ground. The explanation was not new to geology, but the phenomenon had never been observed on such a large scale.

The villain was liquefaction, a process that affects underground layers of very wet soils, particularly sand. Normally these layers are solid enough to provide stable support for the surface. While being violently shaken by an earthquake, however, such a layer takes on the properties of a dense liquid, with two results: Heavy materials on the surface may sink into it, and it begins to flow toward any nearby low spot, such as a stream bed or valley, carrying the surface along with it. It was this movement that had warped the railroad tracks in unexpected places. The researchers also discovered that subsurface flows toward the center of streams from both banks, caused by liquefaction, compressed many bridges and caused them to buckle upward in the middle.

The same process may have been involved in the disastrous Turnagain

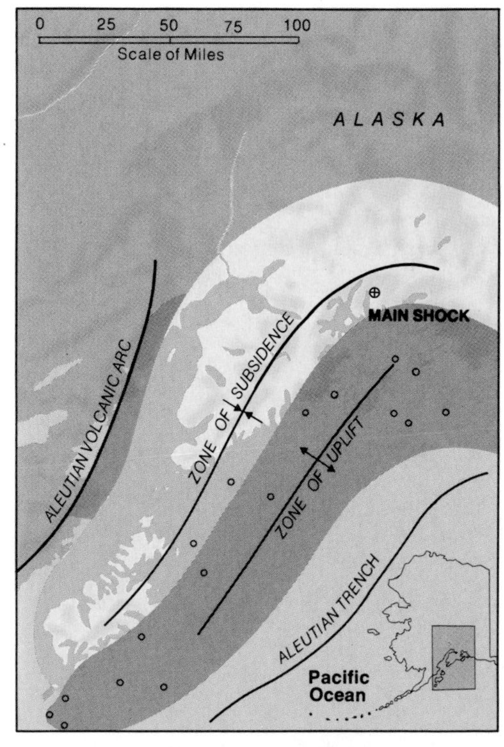

The Alaska earthquake dramatically altered more of the earth's crust than any other seismic event on record. Within the massive S-shaped fault zone an estimated 48,000 square miles of land and seabed subsided *(light-gray shading)* while close to 60,000 square miles were uplifted *(dark-gray shading)*. Following the main shock, there were some 12,000 aftershocks, most of them in the area of uplift, including 17 *(open circles)* that exceeded a magnitude of 6.0 on the Richter scale.

How geologists measured the amount of uplift on Glacier Island in Prince William Sound can be seen in this photograph, taken at low tide, of a sea cliff covered with two bands of intertidal algae, one living *(yellow)* and one dead *(brown)*. The upper growth limit of the live algae approximates the high-tide mark on the cliff after the quake; the top of the dead algae three feet above represents the pre-earthquake mark.

Heights slide in which the Thomas family and others had been caught. The bluff was supported by layers of sand and clay. Earthquake-induced ground failure turned the wet sand and clay into an oozing, putty-like substance along which the bluff began to slide. As it did so, wedges broke off the leading edge and slid toward the sea, carrying houses and people with them.

The observation of causes and effects led to an unprecedented wealth of scientific evidence, from the most minute to the cosmic. As one example of minutiae, the scratches made on the asphalt-tile floor of an Anchorage bedroom by a bureau skidding around during the earthquake were carefully charted and preserved; they confirmed that seismic waves do not travel in only one direction but, by reflection from bedrock, double back on themselves in an eventual maze of multidirectional forces.

Some of the evidence raised new questions without indicating answers. Unnoticed at the time, a magnetometer in Kodiak had recorded several pronounced magnetic disturbances about an hour before the earthquake struck. Scientists could only speculate about the meaning. They were also mystified to find that deep mines and railroad tunnels through bedrock had been undamaged by the earthquake's vibrations.

Still another surprise was the absence of any appreciable effects on the numerous glaciers in the area. Scientists had long theorized that earthquakes were responsible for the sudden advances, or surges, that occasionally occur on many glaciers. To the bafflement of the geologists, none of Alaska's glaciers showed any unusual advance in conjunction with the Good Friday earthquake. Nor, incredibly, did the earthquake produce the expected fissures in the glaciers or any unusual breakage at their fronts.

One fascinating discovery during the study of glaciers involved the enormous rockslides that descended on the ice from the mountain slopes above. Many of these slides were found to have traveled unaccountably long distances across the glaciers, and even to have swooped as much as 80 feet upward on opposing slopes. In some places the passing of tons of rock had made only slight markings in fresh snow on the glaciers and had left intact small bushes growing on the mountain slopes. Investigators at last concluded that the mass of rock had trapped a layer of air between the slide and the surface and had virtually floated along on a cushion of compressed air.

Perversely, despite the wealth of information collected after the earthquake, three vital pieces of information, usually the first and easiest to get, for a time proved unusually elusive. These were its magnitude, epicenter and focus.

The magnitude of an earthquake refers to the size of the seismic waves it generates, and is usually described by using a value from a scale devised in 1935 by geologist Charles F. Richter. A seismograph senses the movement of the earth and translates the motion into wavelike lines on paper. Richter worked out a way to rate earthquakes by measuring the largest wave on the resulting seismogram and converting the measurement into a value on a scale of magnitude. In theory, the magnitude can be determined from one clear seismogram. In practice, so many things affect seismic wave propagation and recording that it takes literally hundreds of seismograms to make a precise assessment.

The problem with the Alaska earthquake was that many seismographs had been unable to record the largest seismic waves. Technicians at the Lamont Geological Observatory in New York State thought that the pens tracing their seismograms might have traveled another foot beyond the edge of the paper had they not been restrained. In addition, the extraordinary length and complexity of the Alaska rupture produced a welter of wave forms that made the seismic evidence difficult to analyze. Of the 800 seismographs in operation around the world, only a few dozen yielded seismograms that could be used in the calculation of the Richter value.

The result was an estimated magnitude of between 8.3 and 8.6 on the Rich-

One awesome effect of the Alaska earthquake can be seen in these before and after photos of Sherman Glacier in the Chugach Mountains. On a hornlike peak—subsequently named Shattered Peak—2,000 feet above the glacier, a 500-foot-thick slab of mountain sheared away, blanketing three square miles of the ice field with rock debris.

ter scale, which is a rough estimate indeed—a Richter scale reading of 8.6 is double the magnitude of 8.3. But the estimate placed the Alaska quake among the two or three mightiest of the century, indicating an amount of energy released equal to 12,000 Hiroshima-type atomic bombs, or about 240 million tons of TNT. Its closest rival in modern times—that is, since the invention of the seismograph in the late 1800s—was a massive tremor that struck Chile in 1960. And that quake had been estimated at 8.5 on the Richter scale.

Similar problems with seismograms made it difficult to calculate the location of the epicenter—the point on the earth's surface directly above the earthquake's first movement. It is normally easy to find the epicenter's distance from a recording station by comparing arrival times of different types of seismic waves whose velocities are known. Once the precise distance of the epicenter from several measuring stations is known, the exact location can be pinpointed. Initial estimates varied sharply because of the unclear seismograms, but were later refined to pinpoint the epicenter at lat. 61° 4′ N., long. 147° 73′ W., at the head of Prince William Sound, about 80 miles east of Anchorage.

The focus of the earthquake is the point beneath the surface where its movement begins. It is determined by precise calculations of the time the seismic waves take to reach the earth's surface, and again the seismic records were not clear enough for precision. The best estimate was that the bedrock had first shattered somewhere between 12 and 33 miles beneath the epicenter.

In addition to the seismic records, scientists had such a profusion of detail about what had happened beginning at 5:36:14 on March 27, 1964, that assembling it in coherent form took years. It was not until 1972, after eight years of work, that the eight-volume, 4,705-page report of the National Academy of Sciences was finished. It presented a clearer and more detailed account of the mechanics and effects of a major earthquake than had ever been available before. "It was," said George Plafker years later, "a great coming together."

The analysis showed that the mechanism of the earthquake was far more complex than anyone had thought. The rupture of the focus, scientists learned, was only the first of a series of events involving six major and separate ruptures, which began within 72 seconds of the first shock. The breaks triggered by the first shock were scattered along a line stretching more than 150 miles to the southwest of the main epicenter. The picture emerged of an interlocking network of shocks, lasting three to four minutes and strung out over a 500-mile arc from the main epicenter to Kodiak Island in the southwest and Cordova in the east. This boundary between two huge slabs of the earth's crust, along which the movement, or cleavage, had occurred, was the fault plane.

The area of the earth's surface deformed by the quake was, Plafker concluded, "larger than any such area known to be associated with a single earthquake in historic time." More than 100,000 square miles of the earth's surface had been heaved upward or dropped downward. For 100 miles inland, north and west of the fault plane, the land had dropped between 2.5 and 7.5 feet. And for 100 miles to the south and east the islands and sea floor had been lifted an average of six feet, with a measured maximum on Montague Island of 38 feet.

Along a line parallel to the fault—from Hinchinbrook Island southwest to the Trinity Islands—a wide area of sea floor had been suddenly uplifted as much as 50 feet, and had thrust up the massive mound of water that became the great Pacific tsunami. The intrusion of the water into the air above it, in turn, caused atmospheric disturbances powerful enough to ripple the ionosphere, 50 miles above the earth.

Surveys of the affected area revealed that another massive movement had taken place—a movement that was undetectable amid the stronger motions of the seismic shocks at the time of the quake. More than 25,000 square miles of land north and west of the fault line had moved laterally seaward—to the south and east. Anchorage had shifted six feet, Valdez 33 feet, Seward 47 feet.

Impressive as it was, the collection of the surveys, measurements and observations was only the beginning of the investigation. Scientists now knew in greater detail than ever before exactly what had happened as a result of the earthquake. But what caused it? What forces were at work in the depths of the earth that could have all these effects? The next step was to reduce the many plausible theoretical explanations to mathematical formulas predicting what would happen on the surface if certain movements took place far below it; by matching the predictions against the measured results of the Alaska quake the scientists could begin to eliminate the untenable theories and confirm the correct ones. Interpretation of the vast collection of details would have been impossibly difficult had it not been for advances in computer sciences. Large-scale digital computers capable of comparing the mass of data to the theoretical explanations of the events had only recently become available.

Even with the help of the computer it was a labor of years. The individual formulas could analyze only a tiny piece of the vast movement that occurred, and the process of proving and assembling the ones that led in the right direction was as detailed and grueling as the gathering of the observations had been. Thus, while the Alaska earthquake was a major advance on the road to describing exactly what happened when an earthquake struck, it was but an early milestone on the still long road to full understanding of the forces at work. It was a route that could not have been traveled before, and it helped usher in a remarkable scientific era.

The next 15 years would see nothing less than a transformation of the earth sciences, a breathtaking succession of leaps in geology. It would be a time when old theories would be put to new tests, and wither away; when young scientists would challenge their elders with new hypotheses, some of which would stand the test of the burgeoning information and gain acceptance. Armed with new knowledge, scientists would make great progress in predicting the cataclysms that beset the planet and in learning how to survive them. Ω

FATEFUL PRANKS BY A GIANT CATFISH

Earthquakes are the stuff of legend, and every society has turned to myth to explain why the earth, mother of all men, should destroy their habitations and claim their lives. Some folklore is stark and chilling. But other legends, particularly those of Japan, are rich with invention—even humor.

According to Japanese tradition, earthquakes are caused by the *namazu,* a giant catfish that lives in the mud beneath the earth. The fish has a penchant for pranks that can be restrained only by the Kashima god, who protects Japan from quakes. As long as he keeps the *namazu* pinioned under his "keystone"—a mighty rock with divine powers—the earth is still. But whenever the Kashima deity relaxes his guard the *namazu* thrashes impudently about.

In October 1855, a ruinous quake rocked the city of Edo (now Tokyo), killing thousands. The disaster coincided with the ritual "month without gods"—the time every October when the deities were said to gather at a distant shrine. To the superstitious citizens of Edo, the gods' absence freed the *namazu* to indulge in his fatal antics. This proof of the ancient myth inspired artists to transform the catfish legend into visual images with a series of popular wood-block prints, or *namazu-e,* a number of which are reproduced here and on the following pages.

The prints and accompanying texts do not simply relate the legend, but seek to cheer survivors of the devastation. The catfish is derided as a rascally good-for-nothing, a coward in the presence of the gods, and the derision extends to profiteering tradesmen and uncaring civic officials.

Many prints offer the comfort of religion: Strong as the *namazu* is, the Kashima deity will subdue him and revitalize the town. A few prints claim a magic of their own; buyers are urged to hang the *namazu-e* in their homes as a talisman against quakes. The result, one print assures homeowners, will be "ten thousand years of happiness."

After an 1855 earthquake has devastated Edo, the seat of Japan's shogunate, grim-faced deities dash back from a conference to restore order in this contemporary depiction of an ancient legend. The Kashima god *(left)* wields his "keystone"—symbol of his power—as houses splinter around panic-stricken citizens; in the text, the gods promise solace and safety.

Whiskers waving, the *namazu* tries to caper his way back into the Kashima deity's good graces by performing a traditional comic drum-dance and chanting a song of apology. The text tells how children were rescued from collapsing houses and how survivors were forced to sleep in the chill night air.

The Kashima god pins down the offending *namazu* with his keystone, thereby giving a stern object lesson to a group of onlooking catfish. These penitent *namazu,* who personify past quakes, offer the lame excuse that they were jealous because other fish were becoming more popular in local cuisine.

When the great earthquake demolishes Edo's red-light district, courtesans and jesters attack the *namazu* unmercifully with everything from knives to knitting needles. But the huge catfish still has friends among the profit-minded carpenters and other artisans *(upper left),* who dash to his rescue.

しんよし原

Chapter 2

PROPHETS OF A NEW SCIENCE

An 18th Century diorama portrays a massive earthquake toppling buildings and spreading panic while a woman unaware of the calamity picks roses in the foreground. The work was probably inspired by a spate of disastrous earthquakes that rocked Europe during that century.

To see death stalking o'er a great city, ready to sweep us all away in an instantaneous ruin . . . this is Fear without remedy; this is Fear beyond battle and pestilence." So wrote a student of earthquakes in the 18th Century. An earth racked by convulsions threatens not only man's survival, but his very sanity; for people have always taken comfort in the stability of the ground beneath their feet. "Solid as a rock" is a phrase that rings with reassurance. But it is a fragile and misplaced confidence and cannot survive the first instant of a great earthquake.

Yet, terrifying though it may be to those who experience it, the trembling of the earth is as pervasive in nature as the falling of the rain or the movement of the winds. The 4.6-billion-year history of the planet is one of unceasing subterranean turmoil that produces more than a million tremors each year—an average of one every 30 seconds day in and day out. To be sure, the vast majority of these quakes are scarcely strong enough to rattle a teacup in its saucer; without sensitive modern instruments they would pass unnoticed. But more than 3,000 a year move the surface noticeably. Hundreds produce significant changes in the face of the land. More than 20 each year cause severe distortions—and when they strike heavily populated areas they are catastrophic.

The human toll in these major quakes can be appalling. Through the ages, fateful circumstance has located many of civilization's densest settlements in the world's most seismically active places—the lands bordering the Mediterranean Sea and the Pacific Ocean, the mountain belts of the Middle East, India and China, and the islands of the Caribbean. Earthquakes and their resultant tsunamis, fires, plagues and deprivations today claim an average of 10,000 to 15,000 lives every year. The figures are even more staggering in historical perspective: Since the keeping of records began—in China more than 30 centuries ago—the number of people known to have died from the sudden quaking of the earth has exceeded 13 million.

No place or time is entirely safe. Though spared the fearsome frequency with which earthquakes strike some parts of the globe, the African highlands, the steppes of Asia, the Amazon rain forest, and the American plains and Eastern Seaboard have all been visited by the horror of heaving earth and crumbling buildings. In the year following the great Alaska quake of 1964, twenty-two major earthquakes occurred around the world. Italy was afflicted four times, Turkey three times, Iran and Chile twice each. In those 12 months, single earthquakes struck Yugoslavia, Greece, Afghanistan, Indonesia, Sumatra, New Guinea, Kenya, Algeria, Japan, Mexico and the Aleutian Islands. The year was far from extraordinary for its seismic activity. This is the way it has been since the beginning of geologic time—when the earth was first formed from a mass of accumulated gases, ice, dust and meteor fragments whirling in space.

Until recent years, mankind could only suffer these natural afflictions in uncomprehending awe. Lacking knowledge, people let their imaginations roam, creating myths and legends to explain the order of the universe—and the agony of earthquakes. Yet superstitions could be constructed only from what was known, and even in the wildest imaginings there gleamed the light of reality.

Primitive peoples ascribed the quaking of the earth to the actions of great beasts similar to the animals with which they were familiar. Before they had any concept of the earth as a sphere, they presumed the ground beneath them to be a platform supported by something—or somebody—and many early explanations of earthquakes embodied that assumption.

The Hindu mythology of India described the supporters of the land as eight mighty elephants and related that when one of them grew weary it lowered and shook its head—as elephants sometimes do—thereby causing an earthquake. To Mongolian lamas the superbeing was a gigantic frog that carried the earth on its back and twitched periodically. Other cultures envisaged the earth suspended in an infinite sea, a concept that suggested to the early Japanese a swimming dragon-serpent that kept the ground afloat. In later versions the serpent was transformed into a monstrous catfish that occasionally gave a high-spirited flip, thereby rocking the earth *(pages 36-41)*.

In time, the mythmakers advanced to the concept of gods, with their intricate human motivations. The inhabitants of one Indonesian island believed that the demon who carried the earth shook with rage if certain sacrifices were not made to him. Members of an ancient Peruvian tribe, the Mainas, thought that when their god visited earth to count the population, his footsteps caused earth tremors; to shorten his task—and the tremors—they ran out of their houses to shout, "I'm here, I'm here," thus incorporating in their mythology the wisdom of evacuating flimsy structures during an earthquake. For their part, the ancient Greeks did not blame earthquakes on Atlas, the god they believed held the world on his shoulders, but on Poseidon, the god of the sea. The myth reflects the reality that much of the seismic activity in that part of the world originates under the Mediterranean and generates accompanying tsunamis.

As societies began to conceive of a single, omnipotent deity, people began to think of earthquakes as instruments of God's wrath. The locales of the Old Testament were seismically active, and earthquakes appear frequently in Biblical narrative. The destruction of Sodom and Gomorrah not only sounds the theme of the earthquake as the vengeance of God, but also illustrates the light modern science can shed on the details of ancient legends. Genesis describes the destruction of the cities by a rain of fire and brimstone from heaven. Geologists now know that the area—today partially submerged under the southern third of the Dead Sea—was rich in bitumen. The oily black substance oozed from beneath the sea, once called Lake Asphaltites because of the large black lumps of the stuff that floated in it, particularly after an earthquake. Much of the stone used to build the cities contained such heavy concentrations of bitumen that it would ignite if subjected to sufficient heat. Associated with the bitumen seepages was the frequent release of natural-gas and sulfur fumes with their characteristic odors.

Thus a geologically plausible picture emerges of a great earthquake ejecting masses of a highly flammable mixture of bitumen, sulfur gas and natural gas over the area. The mixture could have been ignited by hearth fires or by bolts of lightning, with the subsequent conflagration firing even the stone with which the doomed cities had been built.

Yet for all the mythology and religious awe that attended earthquakes, there

A violent earthquake swallows up Korah the Levite and a band of malcontents who led an uprising against Moses, while a wave of fire consumes the rebels' sympathizers in this 18th Century rendition of an Old Testament story. God, according to the Bible, sent the earthquake as a measure of His displeasure with those who questioned the authority of Moses.

were early attempts by men of scientific bent to explain these cataclysms as part of the natural order. Babylonian astronomers believed there was a relationship between the alignment of the sun and stars and the incidence of tremors on earth. And in Classical Greece, Aristotle discussed earthquakes at length in his *Meteorologica,* a volume that sought to explain a wide variety of natural phenomena. He ascribed great power to "exhalations"—his concept of winds produced by evaporation. The heat from the sun, he thought, generated exhalations above the earth, and the earth's "own internal fire" caused similar exhalations below its surface. Earthquakes resulted, he said, when the external winds blew into the earth's interior and built up enough force to shake the ground. "And places whose subsoil is porous are shaken more," he added, in a premonition of geological truth, "because of the large amount of wind they absorb."

Nevertheless, through the ages, the most popular explanation for geologic unrest continued to be divine wrath. The cherished belief that earthquakes were the judgment of God on sinful people gained great force in 1692, when disaster struck Port Royal, Jamaica. The city was England's richest New World possession, having earned that distinction by serving as the lawless pirate capital of the West Indies and a major center for the rum and slave trades. On the morning of Wednesday, June 7, the Reverend Emanuel Heath, rector of the port's largest church, conducted a prayer service "to keep up some Shew of Religion among a most ungodly debauched People," as he dolefully put it. A short while later he was fleeing for his life, with the ground "Rowling and moving under my Feet" as a violent earthquake rumbled through Port Royal.

The city had been built on an unstable ridge, and when the quake hit, two thirds of Port Royal fell into the sea. A tsunami thundered into what remained of the town, and when it was all over, 2,000 people had died. Seldom had an earthquake fulfilled its presumed purpose of punishment with such clarity and precision. "Ever since that fatal day," wrote the Reverend Mr. Heath weeks later, "the most terrible that I ever had in my life, I have lived on board a Ship, for the shaking of the Earth returns every now and then." And, thinking of the "lewd Rogues" and "audacious Whores" who still remained in the place, he added, "I hope by this terrible Judgement God will make them reform their Lives, for there is not a more Ungodly People on the Face of the Earth."

By the mid-1700s, however, the Age of Reason was in full flower in Europe, and scientific inquiry was progressing swiftly. Primed with the previous century's discoveries of physical laws by Isaac Newton and expositions of systematic, rational thought by such men as René Descartes and Francis Bacon, scientists and philosophers were making breathtaking advances in mathematics, physics, chemistry and astronomy. It was a day of growing assurance that no natural phenomenon was without explanation, no puzzle too hard to solve. The major champions of the supremacy of reason were the French *philosophes,* who in 1751 published the first volume of a huge encyclopedia intended to embrace the full sum of human knowledge (the 30-year project, named for its principal contributor, Denis Diderot, filled 35 volumes). It was into this climate of confident inquiry that the earthquake intruded with its customary abruptness.

On February 8, 1750, London was startled by a sudden jolt. The tremor was not that strong, but it rattled windows, shook furniture and sent people hurrying into the streets. It was made particularly disturbing by the fact that in nearly two centuries London had experienced only one minor tremor. "O, that our repentance may prevent heavier marks of His displeasure," cried the evangelist John Wesley. But Wesley's prayers went unanswered. Exactly one month later a second and more powerful shock hit London. This one knocked down chimneys, rang church bells, toppled some buildings and threw the city into a full-blown religious panic. During the next several months, three more tremors shook the British Isles, causing no great damage but vast dismay.

What came to be known as England's "year of earthquakes" posed a direct challenge to the vaunted ability of the thinkers of the Age of Reason to explain everything and anything. By the end of the year close to 50 learned papers had been delivered to London's Royal Society. There were reports on the events themselves, copious speculations about their causes and a valuable history of earthquakes back to the time of Christ.

There was also an enormous amount of misinformation. One writer on the London quakes, a preacher named William Stukeley, had a special knack for misunderstanding. His *Philosophy of Earthquakes* is a compendium of the day's popular misconceptions about earthquakes. He advised that earthquakes usually occurred in calm, cloudy conditions, which were often preceded by strong winds, fireballs and meteors. Stukeley suggested that earthquakes were caused, like lightning, by an electrical discharge between the earth and sky. His review of the available evidence led him to conclude that earthquakes usually strike cities and large towns, most often when they are located near water, but do not affect "bare cliffs and uninhabited beach."

The intense concern aroused by the London earthquakes was raised to fever pitch five years later by a cataclysm that still ranks as one of the worst in history. When it was over, Lisbon, Portugal, a great port and hub of a worldwide empire, had been reduced to rubble. And as Lisbon came crashing down, the very foundations of Western thought and culture were profoundly shaken.

The first shock struck on November 1 at 9:40 a.m., a clear, still Saturday

Arrayed in battle garb, the Roman Marcus Curtius rides his galloping charger into a fiery chasm that opened in the Forum during an earthquake in 362 B.C. According to legend, Curtius acted on the words of a soothsayer, who had proclaimed that the abyss would close only when Rome sacrificed its greatest treasure. The young warrior's offering of his own life immediately sealed the breach.

In a late-medieval fresco from the basilica at Assisi, Italy—the birthplace of Saint Francis—townspeople look on as a grief-stricken mother cradles the head of her son, who was killed when the family's house caved in. Local tradition attributes the collapse to an earthquake, and holds that Saint Francis miraculously restored the boy to life.

morning. It was All Saints' Day, devoted to memorial services for the dead, and many of Lisbon's 250,000 people were in church. Suddenly the city began to shudder violently, its tall medieval spires "waving like a cornfield in a breeze," according to a survivor. In the ancient cathedral, the Basilica de Santa Maria, the nave rocked and the massive chandeliers began swinging crazily. Terrified, the worshippers rushed into the narrow square outside. There they were joined by the congregation of an adjoining church and the residents of nearby houses. The mass of people cowered together in the open, clutching their rosaries and calling on God to protect them. Then came a second, even more powerful shock. And with it, the ornate façade of every great building in the square—cathedral, church, grand private dwellings—broke away and cascaded forward. A billowing cloud of dust obscured everything, and when it cleared, the square was a wasteland of broken stone, a grave for all who had been standing in it.

Throughout the city, buildings weakened by the first shock succumbed to the second, collapsing into the narrow streets and burying both their occupants and the people who had fled outside. A survivor described the gruesome scene: "In some places lay coaches, with their masters, horses and riders almost crushed to pieces; here mothers with infants in their arms; there ladies richly dressed, friars, gentlemen, mechanics. Some had their backs or thighs broken; others vast stones on their breasts; some lay almost buried in the rubbish."

Hundreds of people had rushed down to the River Tagus and out onto a new marble quay along the shore. But there was no escape. With the first shock the river had receded until the sandbar at its mouth was exposed. At about the time of the second shock, the water swept back in a raging 50-foot crest that surged over the quay and up into the city. It pulled back, then returned twice again, sucking debris, ships and bodies into the maelstrom.

Ravaged by the quivering land, swept by the sea, Lisbon now faced another ordeal: fire. The first tremors had knocked over the candles on church altars, igniting tapestries and vestments. In private houses throughout the city, roof timbers and flooring had dropped into kitchen hearths and had been set ablaze. These small fires, at first unnoticed in the confusion, gradually spread and blended into a single holocaust. Fanned by a rising northeast wind, the fire raged for three days before burning itself out. Lisbon and its treasures—warehouses of silks and spices, archives of trade and exploration going back to the earliest days of empire, palaces filled with tapestries, magnificent furniture and paintings by Titian and Rubens—had been almost totally incinerated.

More than 60,000 people died that morning in Lisbon. But the disaster was by no means confined to that city. The shock rippled out across Europe and south into Africa. In the Grand Duchy of Luxembourg an Army barracks collapsed, killing 500 soldiers. From North Africa came reports of Algiers demolished, Tangier horribly damaged and an estimated 10,000 Moroccans killed in the tremors and subsequent tsunami. Throughout Europe and Africa distant lakes and rivers began surging back and forth in response to the seismic waves.

Lisbon had been one of the richest capitals in the world, a bastion of Catholic piety, a repository of art and civilization; its destruction in 1755 struck at the very heart of the century's faith and optimism. It was as though a massive fracture had occurred in the natural order of things, as though the very clockwork of the universe had run amuck.

There were renewed reflections on man's wickedness and God's chastising hand. English Protestants were quick to point out that Lisbon was a stronghold of the Inquisition; that the Portuguese, in their centuries of colonization, had treated their subjects with an almost zealous cruelty. "Think O Spain and Portugal, the millions of poor Indians your forefathers butchered for the sake of the gold," one moralist exclaimed.

If the London tremors had given pause to the foremost thinkers of the Age of Reason, the Lisbon quake threw them into utter disarray. The breathtaking advances in scientific understanding had fostered a philosophy whose tenets—best represented by an informal group known as the Optimist School—had rapidly come to dominate the intellectual life of the time. The Optimists believed not only that human beings were capable of discovering all the laws that governed the universe, but that they would find them to be divinely ordered, harmonious and good—"the best of all possible worlds," as one French writer put it. The Lisbon earthquake confounded the Optimist philosophers because the event suggested a dark, uncaring force that swept humanity and its works away without regard for goodness or mercy.

One writer in particular—Voltaire—seized the opportunity to attack the Optimists with savage sarcasm. In the novel *Candide,* Voltaire's hero observes the Lisbon earthquake and its aftermath while undergoing a series of personal disasters. His conclusion: "If this is the best of all possible worlds, whatever must the others be like?" As the controversy raged on, Optimist writers such as Immanuel Kant and Jean Jacques Rousseau struggled to see the beneficial side of earthquakes. Kant somewhat lamely pointed to the uncovering in certain areas of healthful hot springs and valuable mineral deposits. Rousseau suggested that if people would return to nature and stay out of doors, earthquakes would not harm them. But the cynicism of Voltaire was far more popular, and the self-assured stride of the Age of Reason acquired a permanent limp after the Lisbon earthquake.

While the attention of Europe's philosophers and scientists was riveted on the devastation of Lisbon, one of the centers of the culture of the New World—Boston, capital of the Massachusetts colony—was also jolted into new awareness of earthquakes, though not with such murderous force. Just 17 days after the Lisbon disaster, shortly before dawn on November 18, 1755, a series of sharp tremors hit Boston and reverberated up and down the Eastern Seaboard from Nova Scotia to South Carolina. It was the first noticeable earthquake to

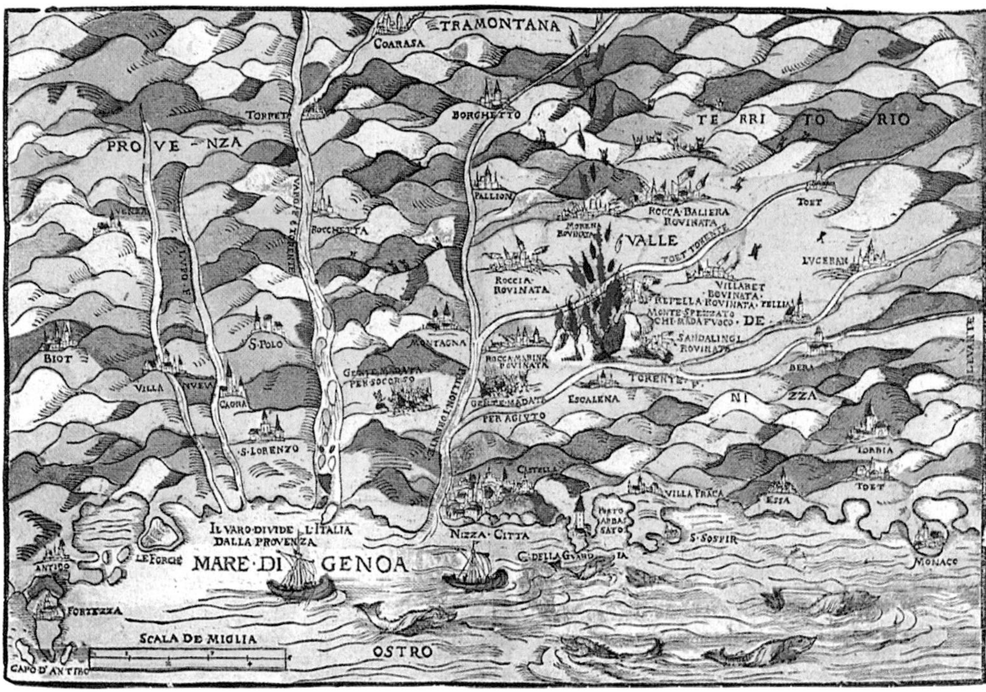

A mountain near the French town of Nice on the Mediterranean explodes in flames and nearby villages fall into rubble in this 1564 map of a combined earthquake and volcanic eruption. One of the earliest known attempts to chart seismic devastation, the map is attributed to Franzesco Mogiol, a Genoese merchant. Beneath the toppled spires of seven towns is the explanation *rovinata*—"ruined."

strike the New World colonists since the same area had been shaken in 1727, and it affected them deeply.

Though no one is known to have died, in Boston 1,500 chimneys were damaged, gable ends fell from brick houses and the famous gilded cricket atop Faneuil Hall's weather vane snapped off. A fissure two feet wide and 1,000 feet long opened in Newington, New Hampshire. Ashlike dust spewed up from cracks in the earth that opened at Scituate, on Massachusetts Bay. "The earth seemed to wave like the waves of the sea," wrote a diarist at Yale College in Connecticut, causing "trembling and fear" among students and villagers alike.

As always after such events, thunderous denunciations of human wickedness rained down from pulpits, and congregations throughout the colonies took to frantic prayer and fasting. The scientific community also had explanations for the earthquake, and one that was very much in vogue in Boston in 1755 involved static electricity. Benjamin Franklin, who had left his publishing business in 1748 to devote more time to science, had proved the existence of electricity in storms with his famous kite experiment. Soon after, he had invented the lightning rod and promoted its widespread use. He believed that electricity had a role in causing earthquakes, and the idea was accepted even by the formidable Reverend Thomas Prince, who had been preaching since the tremors of 1727 that such events were, as he titled a famous sermon, "The Works of God and Tokens of His Just Displeasure." In a 1755 revision of the sermon, Prince suggested that God's displeasure might be electrical in nature, and might be attracted by the forest of Franklin's lightning rods atop Boston's roofs.

Amid all the rationalization and pontification that followed the earthquakes of 1755 there were two men, one in America, the other in England, who were especially intrigued by the events and sorely dissatisfied with the proffered explanations. They also shared an attribute essential to the advancement of science: They did not seek to impose preconceived theories on the facts they observed, but believed in searching out the facts first. Because of that attitude John Winthrop and John Michell would each have a profound impact on the young science of seismology.

John Winthrop IV was one of America's preeminent scientists, an astronomer and a professor of mathematics and natural philosophy at Harvard College. Winthrop personally favored the theory that earthquakes were caused by volcano-like eruptions, but he retained an open mind and was blessed with a faculty for acute observation.

As soon as the shaking had subsided at Boston early that November morning, the professor had leaped from his bed to consult his watch. He compared it with the mantel clock, which had stopped when its pendulum had been knocked askew by the first strong shock. The clock read 4:11, indicating the time the earthquake had started; the discrepancy between it and Winthrop's watch gave the duration—about three and a half minutes.

Winthrop next noted the positions of a brick that had fallen from his chimney and a key that had been pitched from the mantel. Using the speed of falling bodies established by Newtonian physics, he calculated how long it had taken them to drop; he measured how far from their resting places they had landed and was able to determine their lateral velocity. That of the brick was 21 feet per second, he concluded, and that of the key somewhat less, indicating that the forces exerted by the earthquake were different at various heights. He deduced wrongly from the direction the key had traveled that the shock had come from the northwest; modern reconstructions of the quake place the epicenter under the sea off Cape Ann, 55 miles to the northeast. But at least he had the initiative to draw the connection.

Winthrop's most valuable insight into the mechanics of earthquakes came a few days later, when he observed the effect of an aftershock while sitting by his fireplace, feet on the hearth. He was startled to feel and see the bricks jiggling. They seemed to rise up in sequence, one after another, then quickly drop back into place, as though jarred successively from underneath. "It was not a motion of the whole hearth together," he explained, "either from side to side, or up and down; but of each brick separately by itself." The professor described the strange motion as "one small *wave of earth* rolling along."

A wave rolling through the earth: Winthrop had hit upon something important, though neither he nor anyone else at the time realized just how perspicacious this observation was. A century hence, the wavelike nature of seismic motion would become the key to understanding earthquakes.

A few years after Winthrop's brilliant study, England's John Michell completed his own investigations and published the most significant document yet written on earthquakes. Michell's special interest, like Winthrop's, was astronomy, which he pursued avidly in the time left to him after his duties as a lecturer at Cambridge University and rector of nearby St. Botolph's Church. But by 1760, when he published his treatise on earthquakes, he had also become interested in geology and had already contributed important and lasting work on the stratification of the earth's crust.

Michell's paper offered an overall theory of earthquakes, arrived at by reviewing the many accounts stimulated by England's year of earthquakes in 1750 and the 1755 Lisbon disaster. As a general proposition, the author believed that earthquakes were caused by steam produced when water suddenly encountered vast underground fires that burned continuously at various places deep in the earth. But Michell took particular care to analyze the basic effects. Like Winthrop in Boston, he concentrated on the most essential characteristic: the nature of earthquake motion. There were two types, he decided: The first was what he termed a "tremulous" vibration; it was followed shortly by a wavelike undulation of the earth's surface. Michell reasoned that the speed of the earthquake waves could be determined from their arrival times at various distant points, and by reviewing the reports he calculated the speed of the Lisbon waves to be 1,200 miles an hour. It would take far-more-precise instruments and detailed observations to reveal that seismic waves actually travel at widely varied speeds, but Michell was the first scientist even to attempt such a calculation.

Of greater importance to the future of seismology, Michell worked out a practical way to establish the epicenter of an earthquake. He reasoned that by

J. B. van Helmont, a 17th Century Belgian chemist, offered a fascinating variation on the popular belief that a wrathful God unleashed earthquakes on a sinful world. He suggested that an avenging angel struck a huge celestial bell, thus inducing violent atmospheric vibrations that shook the ground when they arrived on earth. Fantasy though it was, van Helmont's idea presaged what modern science knows as seismic waves radiating out from an earthquake's focus.

Port Royal: A Caribbean Atlantis

Terrified colonists huddle in prayer as the earth opens up to consume their fellows during the 1692 earthquake that devastated Port Royal. In this vivid contemporary depiction, the city lies ruined, but in fact a good part of it still stands—locked in layers of sand and sediment deep underwater.

The famed earthquake that destroyed the British colony of Port Royal, Jamaica, on June 7, 1692, was not an especially powerful tremor. Yet by geological happenstance, it not only sent Port Royal vanishing into the sea, but did so in a way that preserved much of the drowned city as a veritable Atlantis and an archeological treasure.

The buccaneers who founded Port Royal built their town on an intrinsically unstable formation: a steeply sloping spit of land formed from a 100-foot-deep accretion of gravel, sand and river sediment. When the earthquake struck, the tremors rocked the peninsula's foundation, and the loose layers above slid seaward, bearing Port Royal with them. Within a few hellish minutes, the town lay under as much as 50 feet of water.

There it remained for more than 250 years, until 1959, when American archeologists began to probe beneath six to 10 feet of silt. What they found was astonishing. Though many buildings had been toppled by the tremors, entire blocks of shops and homes had been carried virtually intact beneath the sea by the gliding sections of land.

Clearing away the overburden, the archeologists explored buildings whose walls stood erect, with doorways and window openings in place. In one kitchen, turtle bones lay in a copper kettle, remains of a meal begun but not finished. In a dining room, stacked pewter plates, glassware and crockery also told of mealtime preparations. A carpenter's shop held a nearly finished bed; an apothecary was stocked with medicine bottles and ceramic jars of salve. Poking through the city, divers found stoppered bottles of rose water; an intricately carved gold wedding band inscribed, "When this you see remember me"; and the booty of some buccaneering raid—a worm-eaten chest and 1,536 silver coins spilled nearby.

Under the best of circumstances, marine excavation is a slow, expensive and risky venture. And in Port Royal it is doubly so. Jamaica is still seismically active, and periodic tremors rumble through the area, jolting divers—and causing new layers of silt to settle over the site.

mapping the direction of the seismic waves observed at various places during an earthquake and extending the lines until they intersected, he could find the origin of the tremor. Oddly, having developed that theory, he did not use it to locate the Lisbon epicenter. Instead he assumed that the tsunami and the earthquake originated at the same place. From reports of the direction of the sea waves, he placed the epicenter on the bed of the Atlantic about 30 to 45 miles off the Portuguese coast, northwest of Lisbon. He was wrong; later calculations based on the technique of mapping seismic waves that he postulated and then ignored located the origin 200 miles southwest of Lisbon. Despite his errors of detail, Michell summed up his theories in a sentence of ringing significance. "Earthquakes," he declared, were "waves set up by shifting masses of rock miles below the surface."

Having satisfied his curiosity about the Lisbon catastrophe, and having achieved prophetic insights into the nature of seismic waves and the origin of earthquakes, Michell returned to the study of astronomy and did no more work in seismology. The excellence of his earthquake paper won him election to the Royal Society, but the paper did not claim the attention of other students of earthquakes and sank into obscurity. Its worth came to be appreciated only long after his death in 1793, when others rediscovered and confirmed his concepts.

Progress in the natural sciences often comes in fits and starts, with grand intuitive discoveries followed by long periods of quiet, methodical research. Michell's paper was such an intuitive leap. And almost a century would pass before another inspired intellect would be focused on the earthquake. In the meantime, the quest for understanding would move slowly, pushed along only by the persistence of dedicated observers.

The techniques of field work were advanced significantly in 1783, when a series of six strong earthquakes hit the Calabria region in southern Italy. The quakes killed 35,000 people and caused massive destruction. But instead of the usual one or two great shocks, the Italian quakes were separate and distinct from one another—occurring between February 5 and March 28—and their effects were localized. While some towns were leveled, others nearby sustained only minor damage. These variations in destructiveness provided the investigators with their most interesting data.

Scores of researchers moved through the countryside assessing the effects of

Under the benevolent gaze of the Holy Mother and Child, Leonardo Rodriguez helps to free his daughter, who was trapped in rubble by the murderous quake that wracked Lisbon, Portugal, on November 1, 1755. According to the inscription on the painting, Rodriguez commissioned the work as an offering in gratitude for the miraculous survival of his child. But elsewhere, death triumphed that day; one quarter of Lisbon's population perished.

French philosopher Voltaire reacted to the Lisbon earthquake by fiercely attacking proponents of the mid-18th Century's so-called Optimist School—believers in a benign and perfectly ordered universe in which everything is for the best. After the quake, Voltaire wrote bitingly: "The heirs of the dead will benefit financially; the building trade will enjoy a boom. Private misfortune must not be overrated. These poor people in their death agonies and the worms that are about to devour them are alike playing their proper and appointed part in God's master plan."

the quakes. The chief physician at the court of the King of Naples produced a 569-page study containing valuable firsthand observations by rescue workers. The Neapolitan Secretary of War, who had lost six members of his family in the disaster, toured the stricken cities and noted that the March 28 tremor was the strongest of the six quakes but was not the biggest killer; he speculated that the destruction and fear produced by the preceding quakes had driven people outdoors, where they were safer. The Neapolitan Academy of Sciences and Fine Letters appointed an earthquake commission, the first such body in history, which tabulated the damage in more than 150 towns and villages. The commission's report comprised 372 pages, complete with maps and drawings of the battered areas. It detailed the geology of the area, the time of each earthquake, the damage and fatalities it caused, the resulting aftershocks and sea waves, and the impact on the survivors of the catastrophes and the subsequent epidemics.

While these investigations produced no new revelations they set a tone of thorough observation that would be the basis of further discovery. They also introduced a new concept to seismology. This was the intensity scale, a systematic tabulation of the effects of earthquakes that made comparisons of their observed strength possible. The first intensity scale was compiled by an Italian physician, Domenico Pignataro, who reviewed the accounts of all the earthquakes in Italy between January 1, 1783, and October 1, 1786. The grand total, including the Calabrian quakes, came to 1,181. According to the descriptions of damage and loss of life, he classified all but the Calabrian quakes in four groups—slight, moderate, strong and very strong; the Calabrian shocks were designated "violent." It was a crude tabulation, but it represented an idea that would become a basic tool of seismologists everywhere.

Thus as the years passed the data accumulated. There was a growing awareness, for example, that earthquakes not only shake the ground, but also cause massive and permanent distortions of the earth's crust. Such shifts of landscape had long been suspected, but never actually documented. Then in 1822, an English travel writer, Maria Graham, experienced a violent earthquake near Valparaiso, Chile. A few weeks after the quake she took a trip along the coast to survey the damage. For a distance of perhaps 100 miles, Mrs. Graham reported to London's Geographical Society, the entire shoreline had been raised by as much as four feet. "I found the ancient bed of the sea laid bare and dry," she wrote, "with beds of oysters, mussels, and other shells adhering to the rocks on which they grew, the fish being all dead, and exhaling the most offensive effluvia." The writer suspected that this was not the first time such an uplift had occurred, for she saw similar layers of shells and beach gravel, now long dry, extending upward from sea level to a height of 50 feet. She thus identified a phenomenon to which geologist George Plafker 142 years later would turn for help in analyzing the Alaska earthquake.

The man who would take this mass of information and use it as the steppingstone for the next leap forward in seismology was Robert Mallet, an Irish engineer who commenced the study of earthquakes almost by accident. Mallet was one of those inspired natural mechanics who rose to fame—and considerable fortune—in the Industrial Revolution. He was scarcely 21 in 1831 when he became a partner in his father's plumbing-fixture factory in Dublin. So brilliant were young Mallet's mechanical designs that within a few years the firm had expanded vastly to become the most important engineering works and foundry in all Ireland. The Mallets designed and built railroad stations, devised central heating and ventilating systems for a wide range of edifices, forged cannon and mortars for the British Army and Royal Navy, built swivel bridges across the River Shannon and erected the famous Fastnet Rock Lighthouse that marks Ireland's southernmost landfall.

Mallet became interested in earthquakes while looking at a new text on the natural sciences that was published in 1830. The book contained a diagram of two stone pillars in Calabria whose upper sections had been twisted by an earthquake. Mallet applied his practical engineering experience in an attempt to explain the nature of the forces that could affect the pillars in such fashion without tipping them over. A satisfactory solution evaded even the gifted Mallet. But his mind was engaged from then on in what would become a lifetime avocation—the study of earthquakes.

During the next 20 years the Dublin engineer assembled an immense library on earthquakes—books, journals, monographs, travelogues, newspaper reports—anything he could find on the subject. From this wealth of material he compiled a remarkable catalogue of seismic events. It was the largest, most systematic compendium of its day, with 6,831 earthquake listings, each giving date, location, number of shocks, probable direction and duration of the seismic waves, along with notes on related effects. Then Mallet plotted the major tremors on a large chart and produced the most complete world seismicity map of the time. It portrayed with unprecedented clarity the definite belts of frequent earthquake activity that garland the troubled globe, and directed the attention of Mallet and his successors to the question of why earthquake activity is concentrated in such a way. The answer would be a long time coming, but it was the right question.

Like Michell before him, Mallet realized that understanding the nature of seismic waves was the first priority of earthquake study. He designed experiments to measure the speed of the waves through the ground. Since Dublin rarely experienced seismic tremors, Mallet had to create his own, by exploding charges of gunpowder underground. To monitor the shocks, he placed a container of mercury one measured mile from the charge. Peering at the mercury's surface, he would set off the gunpowder and start a stop watch. When the shock arrived, the mercury would ripple, and Mallet would note the elapsed time on his watch. His measurements revealed that the shocks traveled at different speeds through different materials; he found a range that varied from 563 miles per hour through sandy soil to 1,135 miles per hour through granite. These calculations were far more precise than those of Michell, who had estimated the velocity of the seismic waves at Lisbon to be 1,200 miles per hour. Though still far from the mark, Mallet had uncovered the important truth that the velocity of the waves was affected by the material through which they passed.

Mallet's most famous contribution, however, was his brilliant on-site study of a major Italian earthquake that devastated a wide area east of Naples in 1857. Two villages were totally destroyed, two more were heavily damaged and more than 10,000 people were killed. The engineer arrived in Italy shortly after the disaster and found the job of attempting an orderly investigation of such chaos to be a major challenge. "When an observer first enters upon one of these earthquake shaken towns," he wrote, "he finds himself in the midst of utter confusion. The eye is bewildered by a city become a heap. He wanders over masses of dislocated stone and mortar. Houses seem to have been precipitated to the ground in every direction of the azimuth. There seems no governing law, nor any indication of a prevailing direction of overturning force."

Using the engineer's most basic tools—a compass, a measuring stick and an experienced eye—Mallet made his way through the Neapolitan countryside. Village by village and street by tumbled street, he measured the cracks in walls, the fall of columns, the overthrow of masonry. Then, from his knowledge of construction, he was able to estimate the forces that had brought them down.

Mallet worked up his data in various ways, creating first an isoseismal, or equal intensity, diagram of the area. Like Pignataro, Mallet devised an intensity scale with four gradations of damage. He then drew lines on a map of the battered region outlining the four areas of more or less equal devastation. The isoseismal lines formed rough circles, the innermost outlining the area of

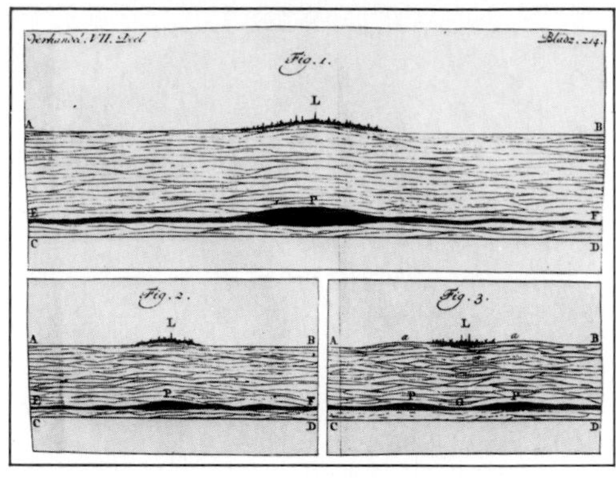

Lisbon rides the earth's billowing crust in this illustration by Dutch theoretician J. F. Dryfhout, who attributed the 1755 earthquake to a subterranean explosion. Dryfhout speculated that mines of gunpowder-like material ran through the earth and that such a mine *(P in Figure 1)* exploded beneath Lisbon *(L)*, lifting it "like a marble bounced on stone." As the city settled back *(Figures 2 and 3)*, the crust began to roll *(A-A)* in response to gases *(P-P)* moving away from the explosion.

strongest shaking and suggesting the earthquake's source. Next, he plotted the direction of the seismic waves and tried to estimate the angles at which they reached the earth's surface—all from his observations of fallen objects such as tombstones and of the patterns of cracks in buildings. Using the technique developed by Michell, Mallet located the epicenter by noting where the lines of travel of the seismic waves intersected. And by applying his study of the upward angles of the waves through the earth, Mallet became the first to estimate the location of the focus—the underground origin of the earthquake motion. His guess in this case was that the focus was 6.5 miles beneath the surface.

Mallet's two-volume monograph on the Neapolitan quake would go unchallenged for 40 years as the most thorough study of a single seismic event. In it he gives his theoretical definition of an earthquake—one that represented a major advance in understanding. It was, he said, "a wave of elastic compression," caused "by the sudden flexure and constraint of the elastic materials forming a portion of the earth's crust, or by their giving way and becoming fractured."

So finally it was understood that an earthquake, whether brought on by the Almighty or by the laws of physics, involved the bending or splintering of bedrock and consisted of a series of seismic waves in the earth. But further comprehension of the mechanics, and especially of the forces that underlie them, would require another advance—this time in the quality of the instruments seismologists use to monitor earthquakes. An apparatus was needed that could record the complicated motions of tremors in such a way that they could be analyzed. When finally one was devised, it was done under the influence of John Milne, a brilliant English geologist working in Japan in the late 1800s.

John Milne towers head and shoulders above all the rest of seismology's founding fathers. Hardy and venturesome as a youth, he traveled to Iceland at the age of 21, and with a chum embarked on an enterprise they titled grandly "The Exploration of the Unknown Interior of the Great Glacier, Vatna Jokul." For several weeks, they trekked around the southeastern wastes of Iceland, with its raging rivers, forbidding marshes and vast ice fields. On their return Milne

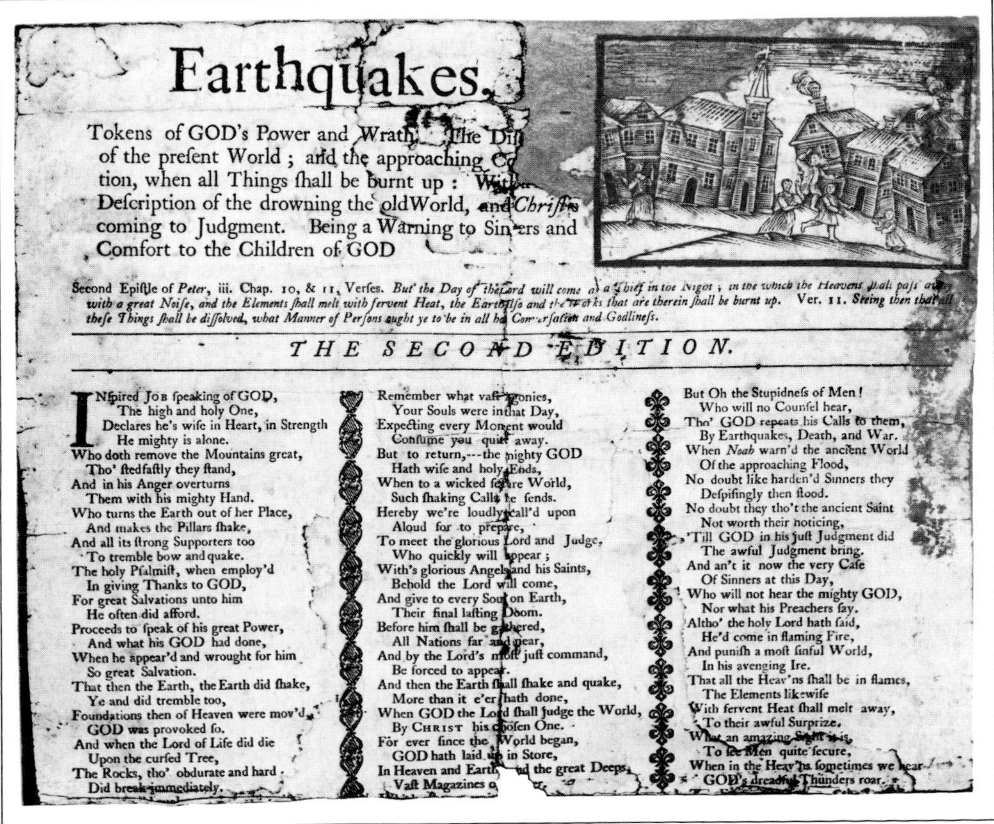

Earthquakes.

Tokens of GOD's Power and Wrath. The Di[illegible] of the preſent World; and the approaching C[illegible] tion, when all Things ſhall be burnt up: W[illegible] Deſcription of the drowning the oldWorld, and Chriſt's coming to Judgment. Being a Warning to Sinners and Comfort to the Children of GOD

Second Epiſtle of *Peter*, iii. Chap. 10, & 11, Verſes. *But the Day of the Lord will come as a Thief in the Night; in the which the Heavens ſhall paſs away with a great Noiſe, and the Elements ſhall melt with fervent Heat, the Earth alſo and the Works that are therein ſhall be burnt up.* Ver. 11. *Seeing then that all theſe Things ſhall be diſſolved, what Manner of Perſons ought ye to be in all holy Converſation and Godlineſs.*

THE SECOND EDITION.

INſpired Job ſpeaking of GOD,
The high and holy One,
Declares he's wiſe in Heart, in Strength
He mighty is alone.
Who doth remove the Mountains great,
Tho' ſtedfaſtly they ſtand,
And in his Anger overturns
Them with his mighty Hand.
Who turns the Earth out of her Place,
And makes the Pillars ſhake,
And all its ſtrong Supporters too
To tremble bow and quake.
The holy Pſalmiſt, when employ'd
In giving Thanks to GOD,
For great Salvations unto him
He often did afford.
Proceeds to ſpeak of his great Power,
And what his GOD had done,
When he appear'd and wrought for him
So great Salvation.
That then the Earth, the Earth did ſhake,
Ye and did tremble too,
Foundations then of Heaven were mov'd,
GOD was provoked ſo.
And when the Lord of Life did die
Upon the curſed Tree,
The Rocks, tho' obdurate and hard
Did break immediately.

Remember what vaſt Agonies,
Your Souls were in that Day,
Expecting every Moment would
Conſume you quite away.
But to return,---the mighty GOD
Hath wiſe and holy Ends,
When to a wicked ſecure World,
Such ſhaking Calls he ſends.
Hereby we're loudly call'd upon
Aloud for to prepare,
To meet the glorious Lord and Judge,
Who quickly will appear;
With's glorious Angels and his Saints,
Behold the Lord will come,
And give to every Soul on Earth,
Their final laſting Doom.
Before him ſhall be gathered,
All Nations far and near,
And by the Lord's moſt juſt command,
Be forced to appear.
And then the Earth ſhall ſhake and quake,
More than it e'er hath done,
When GOD the Lord ſhall judge the World,
By Christ his choſen One.
For ever ſince the World began,
GOD hath laid up in Store,
In Heaven and Earth, and the great Deeps,
Vaſt Magazines o[illegible]

But Oh the Stupidneſs of Men!
Who will no Counſel hear,
Tho' GOD repeats his Calls to them,
By Earthquakes, Death, and War.
When *Noah* warn'd the ancient World
Of the approaching Flood,
No doubt like harden'd Sinners they
Deſpiſingly then ſtood.
No doubt they tho't the ancient Saint
Not worth their noticing,
'Till GOD in his juſt Judgment did
The awful Judgment bring.
And an't it now the very Caſe
Of Sinners at this Day,
Who will not hear the mighty GOD,
Nor what his Preachers ſay.
Altho' the holy Lord hath ſaid,
He'd come in flaming Fire,
And puniſh a moſt ſinful World,
In his avenging Ire.
That all the Heav'ns ſhall be in flames,
The Elements likewiſe
With fervent Heat ſhall melt away,
To their awful Surprize.
What an amazing Sight it is,
To ſee Men quite ſecure,
When in the Heav'ns ſometimes we hear
GOD's dreadful Thunders roar.

Spouting hell-fire and damnation, broadsides like this one exhorted Bostonians to acknowledge God's hand in a spate of minor earthquakes that shook the New World between 1638 and 1755. The colonists took smug comfort, however, that God had "spared New England's happy shore" from severe damage, as another broadside boasted, while dealing death and destruction to a wayward Lisbon.

A raging whirlpool swallows up vessels while lighthouses crumble in this contemporary view of an earthquake that rocked Italy's Calabria region in 1783. Observers said the sea actually appeared to be boiling at times, and the deepwater fish called *cicirelli* were found in large numbers at the surface.

reported at length to the Engineering Society at the University of London on the difficulties of his journey and, more significantly, on the area's rich untapped sulfur deposits. Fresh out of London's Royal School of Mines in 1873, Milne spent another two exciting years exploring the geology and resources of the Newfoundland wilderness and the desert wastes of the Sinai Peninsula before settling down to his life's work: professor of geology and mining at the new Imperial College of Engineering in Tokyo.

It was a plum of a job for a young geologist. The college would shortly be the largest technical school in the world as a suddenly awakening Japan sought to catch up with the industrial West. The college subjected its prospective teachers to a rigorous investigation to make certain of their professional qualifications—then offered a contract that restricted their activities to the academic world and made sure they did not use their position to accumulate undue wealth. Milne's title, and that of his colleagues, was *oyatoi-gaikokujin,* which literally translated as "honorable foreign menial." To Japanese thinking, that was in no way a slur or a contradiction in terms.

Milne arrived to take up his post early in 1876—to be greeted his first night in Tokyo by a small earthquake. Mild tremors of this sort were not unusual in Tokyo. Milne wrote later that there were "earthquakes for breakfast, dinner, supper and to sleep on." Perhaps the very frequency of the quakes made them seem less interesting at first, because four years would pass before Milne focused on what would become his passion. During that time, he was fully occupied by his new teaching position and with studying the islands' geology—especially the volcanoes of central and northern Japan. To the consternation of his friends, he repeatedly demonstrated his indifference to personal safety by climbing forbidding peaks to look down into the seething craters of active volcanoes. In 1880, however, when a strong tremor leveled buildings in Yokohama, Milne called a meeting of scientists, both Japanese and foreign, and organized the Seismological Society of Japan, the first such group anywhere. And from then on he devoted all of his considerable energy to the study of earthquakes.

Milne's first concern was the lack of reliable information. Any serious investigation of Japan's seismicity, he knew, would require an enormous amount of information on the location, frequency and strength of every tremor. To elicit this information, Milne hit on a simple yet ingenious scheme: He sent bundles of self-addressed questionnaire postcards to postmasters and other midlevel government officials in every large town within 100 miles of Tokyo. Milne sent along explicit instructions for filling out the cards, and the conscientious Japanese bureaucrats responded enthusiastically. Each week the correspondents would return one of the cards, with descriptions of all tremors that had occurred during the previous seven days. The result was a veritable flood of information, from which Milne calculated the origin and extent of every shudder, and prepared meticulously detailed seismic maps and isoseismic diagrams of the area.

Milne, of course, realized that these impressive-looking graphics appeared more exact than they were—because they were based on subjective appraisals of damage submitted by a wide variety of observers. What Milne needed was measurements of the motions involved that would be accurate and consistent enough to be analyzed mathematically. For this he would require sophisticated recording devices to measure and preserve a record of seismic shock waves.

Elementary seismometers, which indicated the arrival of seismic waves and gave an idea of their strength, had been in operation for many years. A number of such instruments had been installed at the Tokyo college, and some were rigged to inscribe a permanent record of the seismic waves. But Milne found these seismographs to be either too imprecise or too complicated to be reliable.

So Milne set out to build one of his own. For months he kept the staff at the Imperial College busy designing improved seismographs, which he took into the field for exhaustive testing. Rather than wait for sporadic natural tremors, he created his own seismic waves by dropping 1,800-pound weights from various heights and, like Mallet, by setting off explosive charges. To his chagrin, one of the charges had a more powerful effect than he had anticipated and showered him with "about a ton of earth, flattening me and the instrument alike, and bringing that experiment to an untimely end."

In his quest, Milne drew heavily on the talents of two colleagues—James Alfred Ewing, a professor of mechanical engineering and physics, and Thomas Gray, a professor of telegraphic engineering. It took an entire year of trial and error, but eventually the trio succeeded. And the device they produced revolutionized the young science of seismology.

Not only was the new instrument more sensitive and simpler in concept than

The earth heaves and pitches like the waves of the Mediterranean in this depiction of the Italian seaside town of Reggio di Calabria during the 1783 quake. Scientists were impressed by the variations in damage according to building site; towns that had been built on high ground underlain by rock fared better than those, like Reggio, that stood on sandy clay.

its predecessors, but it was the first to record the movements of the earth in all three of their components: up and down, back and forth, and side to side. Three separate seismographs could be set up, one to record each component of movement, so that their styluses traced their records simultaneously on a roll of smoked paper. A clockwork movement enabled each device to record for 24 hours at a time; in addition, it was designed to stamp the paper with the precise time of arrival of the first seismic wave. In 1893, Milne adapted the machine to make a photographic record on light-sensitive film, thus eliminating the problem of the friction between the pen and paper, which tended to distort the shape of the seismic waves. It was this instrument that became known as the Milne seismograph and within a few years it became standard equipment for seismologists around the world.

These marvelous new capabilities permitted Milne to distinguish between what he called "condensational," or back-and-forth waves, and "distortional," or up-and-down and side-to-side waves, traveling at different speeds and intensities. The advanced seismographs soon opened up another surprising new vista for Milne and his colleagues. The instruments ran continuously, even when he was not dropping weights or setting off explosions, and Milne noticed that the styluses would quiver mysteriously at times when there was no apparent tremor in the immediate vicinity. Some of these jiggles, he discovered, coincided with earthquakes on other islands and even other continents. Studying the records more closely, Milne found that the longer the time between the arrival of the first, condensational waves and the arrival of the larger distortional waves, the farther away the waves had originated.

The precision of his new instruments allowed exact comparisons, and Milne soon found that the relationships were consistent. If the difference in arrival times was a minute and a half, the waves had originated about 450 miles away; a two-minute difference indicated a distance of 600 miles; and an interval of two and a half minutes placed the epicenter 750 miles away. Milne's time-distance principle was capable of infinite application, and this, in turn, affirmed a conclusion of monumental importance, namely that "every large earthquake might, with proper instrumental appliances, be recorded at any point on the land surface of our globe."

In 1891, Milne's attention was diverted from his study of distant earthquakes to the examination of one close at hand—the greatest inland earthquake to strike Japan in recorded seismic history. The devastation in the fertile Neo valley west of Tokyo, especially in the provinces of Mino and Owari, was awesome. In a report for the British Association for the Advancement of Science, Milne described "the contortions produced along lines of railway, the fissuring of the ground, the destruction of hundreds of miles of high embankments which guard the plains from river floods, the utter ruin of structures of all descriptions, the sliding down of mountain sides and the toppling over of their peaks, the compression of valleys and other bewildering phenomena." He reported that almost 10,000 people had been killed, another 20,000 injured, and that nearly 130,000 dwellings had been destroyed. "In an area of 4,176 square miles, which embraces one of the most fertile plains of Japan and where there is a population of perhaps 1,000 to the square mile, all the buildings which had not been reduced to a heap of rubbish had been badly shattered."

The full resources of Milne's Seismological Society were mobilized to record and study every detail of the quake. Milne and a fellow professor, W. K. Burton, went immediately to the Neo valley to photograph the devastation. The result of their mission was a comprehensive and lavishly illustrated volume titled *The Great Earthquake in Japan, 1891.* Even to this day, the book remains notable for its 30 pages of excellent pictures and its exceedingly detailed description of the earthquake's effects.

It was characteristic of Milne's work that he preferred to pursue facts and

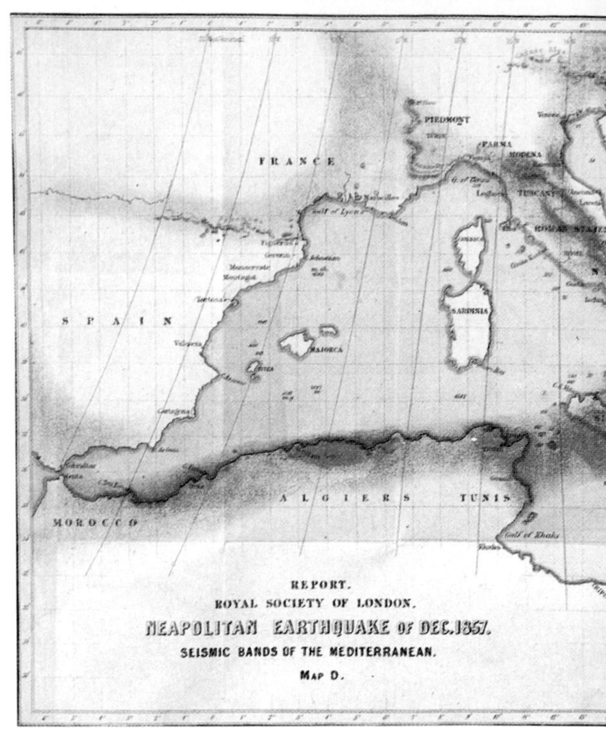

The first extensive map of seismic zones in the Mediterranean region was drawn in 1857 by Irish engineer Robert Mallet, whose lifetime avocation was probing the mysteries of "the viewless and unmeasured miles of matter beneath our feet." Mallet combined personal observations in Italy and an enormous catalogue of historic earthquakes to produce his map, which remains accurate to this day.

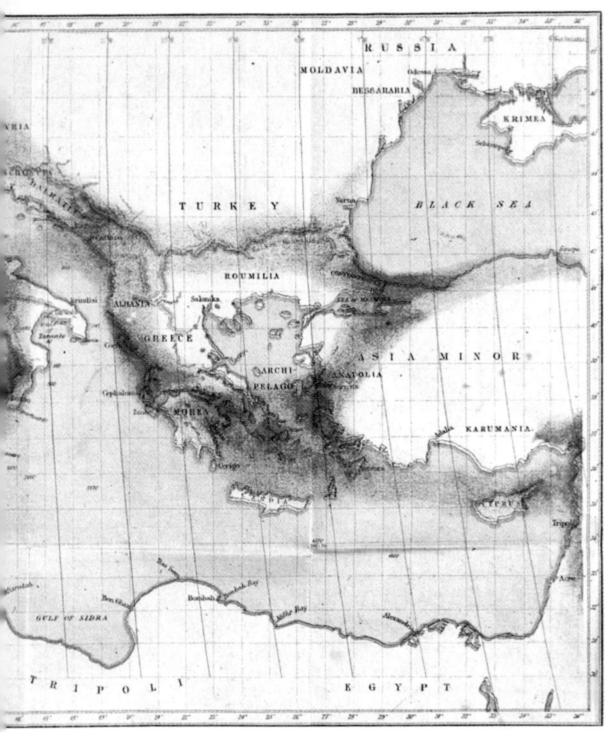

leave most of the theorizing to others. He was criticized for this from time to time, because of the value everyone would obviously place on his most tentative speculations. Nevertheless, Milne persisted in his methods. Thus it happened that in the investigation of the Mino-Owari earthquake it was not Milne but a Japanese colleague, geologist Bunjiro Koto, who drew from the data a conclusion that would electrify seismologists.

Most scholars at the time believed that earthquakes caused faulting—a sudden lateral or vertical movement of bedrock along an existing line of fissures usually far beneath the surface. The Mino-Owari quake was unusual in that it revealed a surface fault line of extraordinary size and clarity. It was nearly 70 miles in length and cut almost completely across the main Japanese island of Honshu. It was this feature that riveted the attention of Bunjiro Koto.

"It strikes across hills and paddy fields alike," Koto wrote, "cutting up the soft earth into enormous clods and raising them above the surface. It resembles the pathway of a gigantic mole." At one point the fault ran between two ancient persimmon trees that had stood, said Koto, "time out of mind" in an east-west line. The earthquake motion along the fault had moved one tree to the north, the other to the south until, "to the great astonishment of the owner," wrote Koto, "they now stand in a north-south line." All along the fault line there were signs of surface shifting—at one place one side of the fault had sunk 20 feet below the other; at another, lateral shifting approached 13 feet.

Koto's study of the phenomenon led him to a conclusion that was revolutionary. "The sudden elevations, depressions, or lateral shiftings of large tracts of country that take place at the time of destructive earthquakes are usually considered as the effects rather than the cause of subterranean commotions; but in my opinion it can be confidently asserted that the sudden formation of the 'great fault of Neo' was the actual cause of the great earthquake." What Koto was saying was that the earth had suddenly fractured along a 70-mile-long plane in the Neo valley and that the fracture had resulted in the release of fantastic amounts of energy; this energy, in turn, had been transmitted throughout the entire region in the form of destructive seismic waves. If he was right, scientists could stop looking for the source of earthquake motion; fault movement was the source of seismic waves, not one of their effects. It would be years before his idea gained acceptance, and it would take another great earthquake with dramatic surface evidence—along the San Andreas Fault in California in 1906—to confirm the correctness of his view.

Leaving the inspired theorizing to others, Milne continued to sift the facts with a curiosity that was itself inspired, reaching into every aspect of the study of earthquakes. He made exhaustive analyses of the existing records and found that earthquakes often occurred in clusters, with intervening periods of inactivity; he believed their frequency was increasing. He even published two papers on how animals behave during and before an earthquake—rejecting reports of strange animal behavior days before an earthquake, but confirming reports that told of odd behavior in the seconds before the first seismic shock was sensed by humans. All this John Milne accomplished in addition to his teaching duties at the Imperial College—by then the Imperial University of Japan—and the writing of three textbooks, one on earthquakes, one on crystallography and one on mining. Few geologists have been so prolific.

In 1895, Milne was totally involved with the life of Japan—cultural and social, as well as seismic. In 1881 he had married a beautiful Japanese woman, the daughter of a prominent Buddhist priest from the northern island of Hokkaido. Milne had become an avid student of Japanese religion and customs, and was a connoisseur of the many variations of the national drink, sake. His second 10-year contract with the Imperial University was coming to an end, but he had the option of renewing it and there seemed little doubt that he would.

Then, on February 17, a personal disaster dramatically altered Milne's life. A

The Japanese village of Itashu lies in splintered ruin in this photograph from Milne's extensive treatise on the calamitous 1891 quake that rocked a 4,200-square-mile area of central Japan, killing almost 8,000 people. With its scores of pictures and its emphasis on the desolating effects of a major quake in a heavily populated region, Milne's work inspired other scientists to study the problem of minimizing casualties and encouraged the construction of more sturdy, quakeproof housing.

The Daily Mirror

THE MORNING JOURNAL WITH THE SECOND LARGEST NET SALE

No. 3,049. FRIDAY, AUGUST 1, 1913 One Halfpenny.

DEATH OF PROFESSOR JOHN MILNE, THE FAMOUS ENGLISH INVENTOR OF INSTRUMENTS TO DETECT EARTHQUAKES AND REGISTER THEIR MOVEMENTS.

A 1913 edition of London's *Daily Mirror* bespeaks the proud regard in which seismologist John Milne was held at the time of his death on July 31. The famed developer of the first practical seismograph —and the force behind a worldwide network of monitoring stations—Milne was accorded the entire front page, with portraits of himself and his Japanese wife, various samples of his seismographic records and a picture of the Milne seismograph.

fire consumed his home and observatory, his irreplaceable library of seismology and many of his precious instruments. Milne and his wife escaped unhurt, but the shock of standing in night clothes and watching years of work destroyed in minutes apparently forced Milne to a reappraisal. In June, after 20 years of instruction to thousands of budding Japanese scientists, Milne resigned from the Imperial University and prepared to return to England. A grateful Emperor paid him the honor, almost unheard of for a foreigner, of a private audience and later conferred on him the Order of the Rising Sun for his service to Japan.

Although Milne was leaving Japan he had no intention of retiring from science. He meant to set up a seismic observatory in England and continue his analysis of distant earthquakes. The spot he chose was the Isle of Wight, which by reason of its subsurface layer of chalk, was well suited to receive seismic waves from around the world. Milne bought a property known as Shide Hill House and began construction of an observatory and an experimental laboratory. Before long, the first seismograph was installed and operating. Milne had resumed his vigil over the heartbeat of the earth.

In time, Milne's Isle of Wight studies became far more than a retired professor's make-work. While reviewing the studies begun earlier in Japan on the distance between seismographs and epicenters, Milne realized that the data offered more information than had been extracted. He reasoned that if three different recording stations each calculated the distance to the epicenter, he could by simple geometry locate the epicenter. Although errors and inaccuracies might prevent the circles from intersecting precisely, the method provided the best way yet devised for locating the origin of an earthquake.

For years, Milne had dreamed of a global network of seismographic recording stations, which would be able to pinpoint earthquakes anywhere in the world. Now, in 1902, his home became the nucleus of just such a system. At his urging, the Seismological Committee of the British Association for the Advancement of Science wrote to similar organizations in 40 countries suggesting that they establish observatories that could maintain constant seismic surveillance of the globe. Foreign scientists were urged to use the Milne seismograph in their observatories, because of the need to standardize readings. Milne's prestige—and the obvious worth of his idea—was such that over the next several years seismic observatories were set up throughout the British Empire from Canada to New Zealand. Before long, more were added—in Spain, Syria, Brazil, Hawaii—until by 1913 there were 40 in all, monitoring every large earthquake in the world and sending their records to the British Association. Milne studied and analyzed them all, issuing to the seismologists of the world detailed reports that came to be known and long remembered as the *Shide Circulars.*

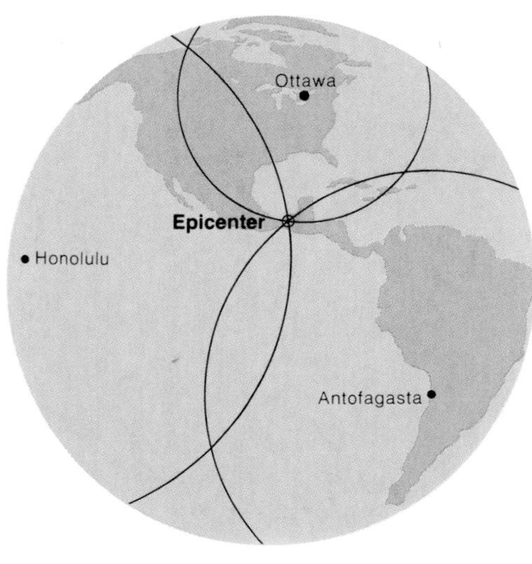

A technique for finding the epicenter of an earthquake was a signal achievement of turn-of-the-century seismologists, who solved the problem with simple geometry. Once they knew how far away a quake had occurred—gleaned from the different arrival times of various seismic waves—they could plot a circle, taking as its radius the distance from the quake to the station. When the distance from three or more stations—Ottawa, Honolulu, and Antofagasta, Chile, in the example above—was plotted, the intersection of the circles marked the epicenter.

In 1912, a visitor from the United States, Mrs. Lou Henry Hoover, marveled at Milne and his network. "It is a quaint conceit," she wrote, "that to the utter quiet of this pretty, tree-encircled old house, with its grassy stone-stepped terraces leading down towards the little valley, should come the earthquakes of the world to be classified and studied. But come they do." And she added, "This is practically a labor of love on Professor Milne's part. He holds no official position."

In the year after Mrs. Hoover's article was published, Milne was ever more frequently ravaged by a kidney disease that incapacitated him with blinding headaches, raging fevers and an increasing weakness and depression. In July he lapsed into a coma and early on July 31, 1913, at the age of 62, he died.

Of the many epitaphs and eulogies, the most fitting came in the dry scientist's prose of Russia's Prince Boris Galitzin, President of the International Seismological Association. "Nearly all the problems of modern seismology have been considered by Milne," Galitzin wrote. "The continuation of his work by others would be the best monument to his memory."

THE SCOURGING OF SAN FRANCISCO

San Francisco had been visited by numerous small earthquakes during its young life, and a few had caused damage. The people nevertheless felt themselves living in a particularly benign part of the world. "A good shake," as one citizen put it, "is not half so bad as a twister or a hurricane." But that was before the morning of April 18, 1906, when the city experienced one of the most fearsome upheavals of all time, a quake equivalent to 8.3 on the Richter scale.

A survivor recalled that the first great tremor came at 5:12 a.m. with "a rumble and roar like cannonading." Buildings danced, chimneys collapsed, church bells clanged wildly. The quake lasted little more than a minute. Then came silence. Reporter James Hopper walked through the shattered town; he saw people with "a hurt expression—not one of physical pain, but rather one of injured sensibilities, as if some trusted friend had suddenly wronged them."

The mammoth tremor, along a great fracture zone later famed as the San Andreas Fault, shook a 375,000-square-mile area. But the worst damage was in San Francisco, much of which had been built on landfill. And quake-damaged buildings were only the first of the city's misfortunes. When fires broke out it was discovered that the water mains had burst. An *Overland Monthly* writer described the conflagration: "It followed the ground, it scaled the heights, it burned through steel and rock and licked up wood as though it were straw."

To experience such an ordeal was to know calamity upon calamity, to see fire consume not only a neighbor's house but one's own and then the whole neighborhood—on and on for three horror-filled days. The human toll was 315 known dead and 352 unaccounted for. Almost five square miles in the heart of the city were destroyed.

Within a few years, the devastated area had been given new life; 20,000 buildings rose to cover the scars. But the days of cataclysm in April 1906 could never be entirely forgotten. Years later playwright William Saroyan would say: "You walk through the streets of the city and feel its loneliness, and you wonder what memory is troubling its heart."

A mother and son survey the spectacle of San Francisco in ruin after the double disaster of earthquake and fire in 1906. Photographer J. B. Monaco, whose own house stands on the far hill, photographed his family in this overview of the calamity that cost 250,000 San Franciscans their homes and livelihood.

A boiling cloud of smoke rises into the sky above San Francisco from a tremendous fire that started on Hayes Street four hours after the 1906 quake. Known as the "Ham-and-Eggs Fire," this particular blaze was kindled by a woman who had sought to restore normality to her shaken life by cooking a bit of breakfast on a stove with a faulty flue. The match she struck wrote history: The resulting fire incinerated much of the city's business district.

Cable car lines lie twisted into huge zigzags and deep fissures slash through Union Street in this photograph taken by renowned photographer Arnold Genthe. A police sergeant named Jesse Cook was one of few awake at 5:12 that fateful morning of April 18; he saw the earthquake's tearing approach and said, "It was as if the waves of the ocean were coming toward me, and billowing as they came."

Soldiers patrol Market Street, where the ornately towered Call Building, its top stories already ablaze, would shortly become a burned-out hulk. To forestall a breakdown of law and order in the ruined city, Brigadier General Frederick Funston had called out the troops on his own authority, without stopping to consult with Mayor Eugene Schmitz. Ordered Funston: "Shoot instantly any person caught looting or committing any serious misdemeanor."

Water from a ruptured main gushes uselessly onto Van Ness Avenue as fire starts down the hill. San Francisco's reservoir system contained 80 million gallons of water, but so great and widespread was the damage to mains and hydrants that frustrated firemen were unable to make much use of it.

Fire fighters carrying dynamite hurry across Market Street on their way to blow up the Monadnock Building, which stands in the path of the fire. The desperation measure was intended to create barren tracts over which flames could not leap. Too often the explosives spread the fires they were intended to halt; on the first night, an overpowerful detonation hurled burning debris into the air over Chinatown—and every building was destroyed.

At the height of the fires, a stream of San Franciscans flows down Market Street to the Ferry Building and the docks, where the refugees hoped for passage to safety. Greedy flames attempted the same journey but were quelled by firemen, who pumped water directly from the Bay to secure the city's life line.

On foot and in carriages and wagons, San Franciscans crowd Market Street to view the still-smoldering ruins of the the city's business district. In the distance, atop Nob Hill, is the famed Fairmont Hotel, its handsome marble façade intact but its interior severely damaged. An unknown photographer captured this image from the Ferry Building's 235-foot tower.

Refugees patiently queue up for food at a tent city, one of dozens set up by relief agencies. Red Cross workers performed heroically, serving hundreds of thousands of meals daily, and Americans from every walk of life sent help: New York City merchants dispatched trainloads of food and drugs, and in Los Angeles retired boxing champion Jim Jeffries raised $600 selling oranges on a streetcorner.

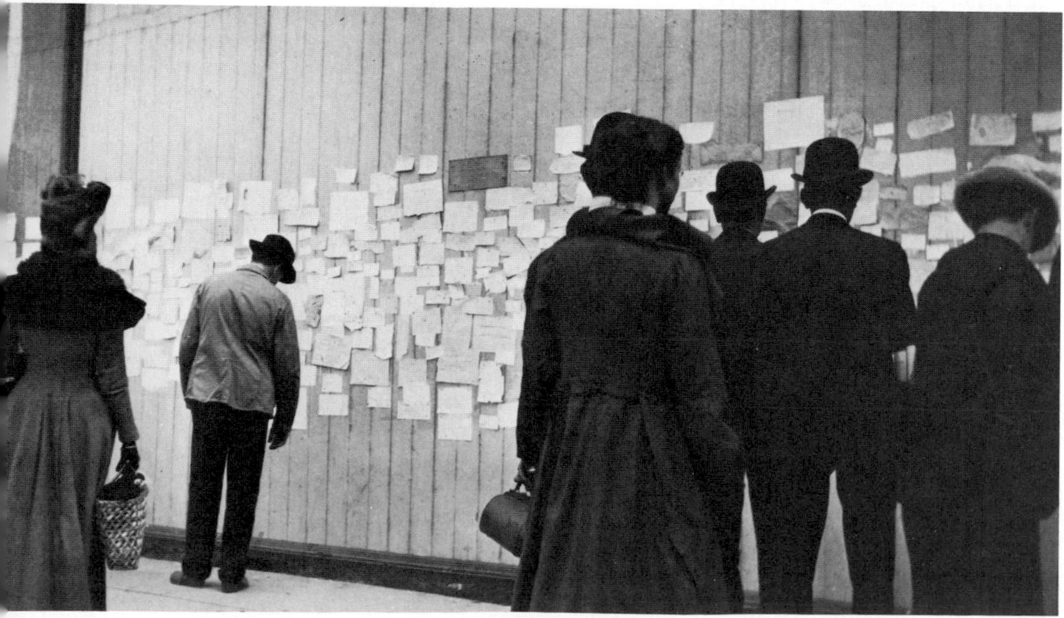

San Franciscans anxiously scan a billboard, seeking news in the messages about missing friends and family. All mail was makeshift; people seeking to communicate out-of-town wrote letters on whatever came to hand—scraps of cardboard, old envelopes, even shingles—and postal workers handled them free, without stamps, as if they were registered mail.

Scavengers poke through safes hauled from the wreckage of a building. Many safes were so hot that a rush of air would incinerate their contents; bankers prudently waited days before opening them.

Surrounded by chaos, reporter Henry Lafter pounds out his account of the earthquake. *McClure's Magazine* published it as "My Sixty Sleepless Hours."

The Juvenile
WILL BE HERE JULY 1ST
AL FRANK WILL OPEN HERE WITH A
COMPLETE STOCK OF FURNISHING GOODS
HATS, TRUNKS AND VALISES.
UNDER THE NAME OF
NEW HOME
OF THE
EMPORIUM
The Emporium
The Emporium
DEPARTMENT
The Emporium

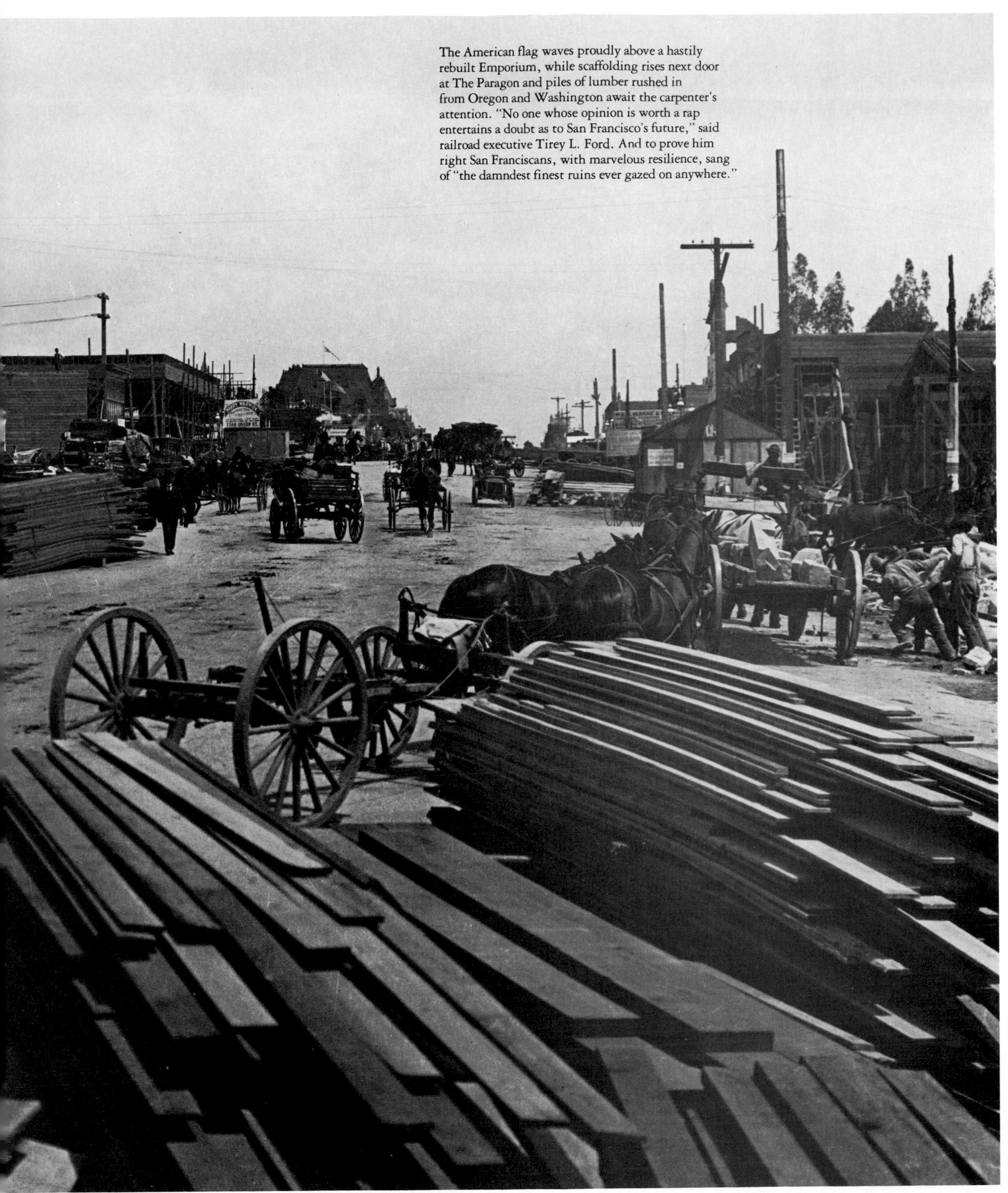

The American flag waves proudly above a hastily rebuilt Emporium, while scaffolding rises next door at The Paragon and piles of lumber rushed in from Oregon and Washington await the carpenter's attention. "No one whose opinion is worth a rap entertains a doubt as to San Francisco's future," said railroad executive Tirey L. Ford. And to prove him right San Franciscans, with marvelous resilience, sang of "the damndest finest ruins ever gazed on anywhere."

Chapter 3

SECRETS OF THE SEISMIC WAVES

Pen in hand, a scientist at the U.S. Geological Survey laboratory in Menlo Park, California, analyzes a seismogram tracing the arrival of seismic waves from a small local earthquake. An indecipherable mass of scribbles to the uninitiated, the tracings tell seismologists much about the earthquake, everything from where it occurred and how powerful it was to the direction in which the ground shifted.

Under the brilliant stars of the Iranian desert night, an exhausted young American Peace Corps field officer stretched out on his cot and twirled the dial of his portable radio. It was late in the evening of August 31, 1968, and for the past eight hours the Peace Corps officer had been working desperately to help survivors of Iran's worst earthquake of the century. Striking northeast Iran in midafternoon, the massive tremor had demolished five villages, heavily damaged many more, had claimed 12,000 lives and left 60,000 people homeless.

Now, preparing like everyone else in the area to sleep in the open for fear of aftershocks, the weary Peace Corpsman tuned his receiver to Radio Teheran to hear details of the disaster. The earthquake had begun at 2:47 p.m. local time, the broadcast announced. The initial rupture had taken place eight miles beneath the earth's surface, and the seismic waves had first reached the surface near the small town of Firdous. The magnitude of the quake on the Richter scale was 7.3, putting it in the ranks of the world's major earthquakes. As he drifted toward sleep, the young man was jolted back to wakefulness when he heard that all this information—indeed, the first reports that there had even been an earthquake—had reached Teheran not from the devastated area itself, a few hundred miles from the capital, nor from any official or unofficial Iranian source, but from an agency of the United States government then headquartered at Rockville, Maryland, 5,600 miles away on the other side of the globe.

The source of the information was the U.S. Geological Survey's National Earthquake Information Service. There, just as a spider waits for vibrations in its web to signal the arrival of its prey, the scientists of the Earthquake Information Service maintain constant watch over their far-flung strands of telemetry for the tremblings that announce an earthquake.

They have posted a sign on the door to their main instrument room—moved since 1968 to Golden, Colorado—dubbing it the "War Room," in testament to the frequency with which it takes on the crisis-laden atmosphere of a military headquarters. One of its walls is taken up with an imposing bank of recording drums, each one turning continuously, night and day, displaying readings from 12 key seismograph installations across the continental United States. Other machines, marvels of electronics, process seismographic data relayed from a variety of American and international networks reaching into every earthquake-prone corner of the world. All told, something like 650 stations report regularly to Golden, and as many as 2,500 more contribute information when called upon. All of this material—around 60,000 seismic readings each month—goes into the center's computers where it is digested, stored, and made instantly available to scientists studying earthquakes.

When a major earthquake strikes, with great loss of life, as in Iran in 1968, Guatemala in 1976 or Italy in 1980, there is an immediate need for accurate information. Police and other government agencies in the stricken area may flash the first news of an emergency (though in remote areas, such as the Iranian desert, there is often no word at all). But until the epicenter and magnitude of the event are known, disaster relief agencies have no way of telling where the worst devastation is likely to be found or how widespread the damage is. Such calculations are best made some distance from the tremors, for a great earthquake will usually overwhelm regional seismographs over a wide area, as was the case in Alaska in 1964. Moreover, if the necessary calculations are to be made accurately and quickly, they require the computer-assisted analysis of a multiplicity of seismograms. The global reach and swift response of the remark-

A seismologist working at the National Earthquake Information Service in Golden, Colorado, monitors a bank of 21 Helicorders that translate earth tremors detected by distant seismometers set up around the United States into traces on revolving rolls of paper. The seismic data are transmitted by both ordinary telephone lines and satellites.

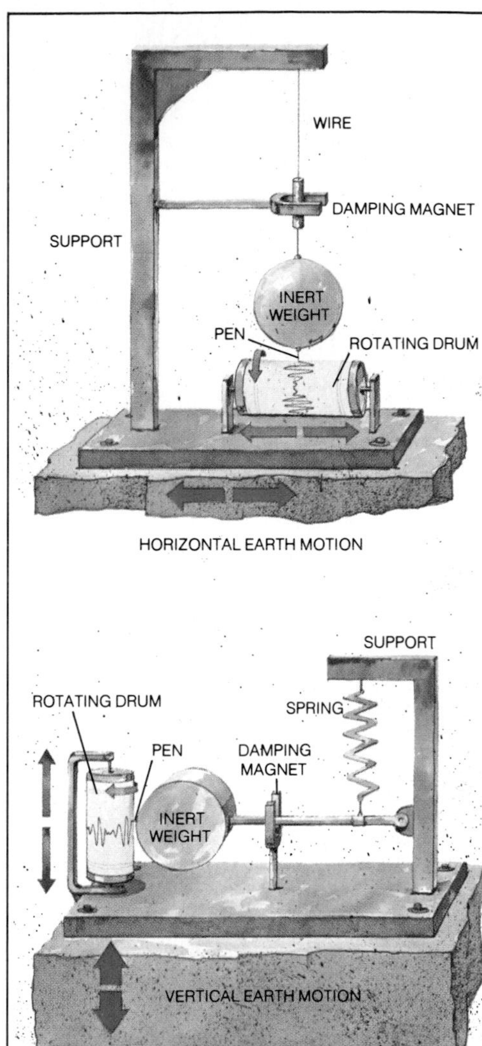

There are two kinds of seismographs, one used for recording horizontal earth motion *(top)*, and another for vertical earth motion *(bottom)*. Both are based on the physical principle that the inertia of a heavy weight suspended on a wire or spring will tend to keep it motionless, while its support structure anchored in the earth moves with seismic waves. The difference in motion between the support structure and the inert weight is recorded on a rotating drum by a stylus.

able international venture centered at Golden have made it the world's foremost collector of earthquake data—and the strong ally of any earthquake-ravaged country, whether a relatively undeveloped nation like Iran or a sophisticated industrial society such as Japan.

Seismic waves from a major quake anywhere in the world will trigger an alarm in the instrument room at Golden. Within minutes telephones begin to ring and telex machines start chattering as other stations relay their preliminary data to Golden for transfer to the center's computers. Within an hour, the time of origin and the approximate magnitude and epicenter of the quake will be calculated. Then the center alerts government agencies, scientists and news organizations in the United States and the area of the earthquake to the potential disaster. It was this communication to Teheran that provided the information heard by the young Peace Corps officer in Iran.

Yet as critical as this service is to the people affected by a cataclysmic earthquake, it is not the Golden center's main activity. Most of the agency's time is spent collecting and disbursing to scientists around the world basic facts about significant earthquakes. Hour after hour, as seismological data are fed into the computers, the scientists on duty calculate the magnitude, focus and epicenter of each earthquake recorded. This information is published immediately in the form of a bulletin called the "Preliminary Determination of Epicenter." Every month the center issues an average of 500 such bulletins. This is just the beginning: When all the readings have come in from stations around the world, the scientists at Golden publish a much more comprehensive "Earthquake Data Report" for each seismic event. In computer print-out it averages 280 pages of figures depicting every known observation of an earthquake from every possible recording station.

The basic document in all this activity—indeed, in all earthquake study—is the seismogram. It is the literature of the earthquake, and from its jagged tracings a trained seismologist can pry a wealth of knowledge. By reading and analyzing the waves, seismologists can calculate not only the earthquake's power, duration and surface location, but the precise distance below the surface of its origin, the direction and magnitude of the movement along the fault that generated the seismic waves, the orientation and extent of the fault, the physical properties of the material through which the seismic waves passed on their way to the seismograph, even details of the structure of the earth, from its core to its outer surface. It is all there on a piece of paper—or, increasingly, on a piece of magnetic tape.

Whatever its source and whatever the material to which it is applied, energy writes a distinctive signature with the wave forms it generates. Seismologists cannot observe an earthquake in progress deep within the planet, but their knowledge of what happens has been burgeoning since they learned to record and analyze the waves it sets in motion in the earth.

The nature of a wave depends on the kind of force that produced it and the medium through which it travels. A sudden snap of one end of a rope causes a ripple to move down its length; the harder the snap the larger the wave and the farther it travels. A bowl of jelly quivers when tapped; the quivers are waves spreading out from the point of impact. Two hands clapped together apply sudden force to the air, producing waves whose frequency—the number that occur each second—is high enough to register as sound on the human ear. The ripple along the rope or across the surface of a pond is an up-and-down undulation, but the sound waves from a handclap travel in a straight line, first compressing, then expanding the air in their path.

The farther the waves travel, the more complex their behavior can become. As they move from one kind of material into another, their line of travel can be bent, or refracted, as light waves are refracted in passing from air to water. Encountering a substance too dense for their strength, they may be reflected back on themselves, as with a sea wave striking a cliff. Two separate waves of the same shape and size may amplify each other, producing a wave form bigger and more powerful than either of the originals.

No single analogy can illustrate the complex nature of seismic waves, which are produced by an immensely complicated event and propagated through a bewildering variety of substances. The sudden force that generates them is not an actual blow, but a wrenching snap, as billions of tons of bedrock, twisted and strained out of shape by the accumulated forces of centuries, rupture along a fault plane and lurch back toward an alignment that relieves the stress. This movement was first described by the man who led the investigation of the San Francisco earthquake of 1906, Harry Fielding Reid. He called it "elastic rebound," and it is fundamental to earthquake mechanics.

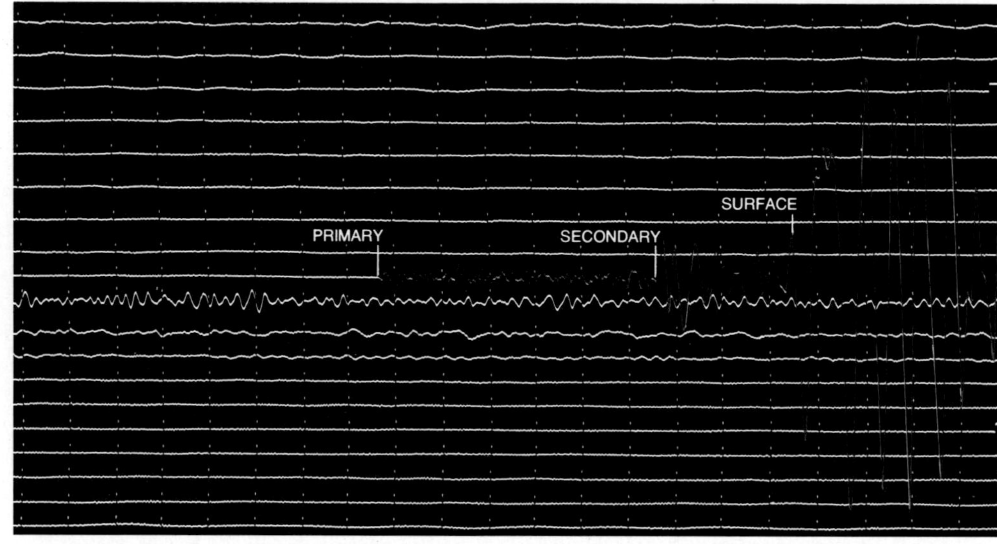

A typical seismic wave pattern can be seen on this section of a seismogram, recorded on May 28, 1976, in Palisades, New York, showing ground motion during an earthquake in Central America. Three basic types of waves appear on the tracing: primary and secondary waves, and the slower but larger waves that travel along the surface of the earth.

With its layered panoply of materials, the earth responds to the impact of an earthquake by vibrating in a maelstrom of wave forms of all frequencies, sizes and velocities. If the frequencies were audible it would be as though a full-sized symphony orchestra were blaring out all the notes of all its music at once, every instrument playing fortissimo in every possible key, producing utter cacophony. When depicted visually on a seismogram, the earthquake's tumult of conflicting and overlapping seismic waves presents an apparently bewildering hodgepodge of zigzag lines.

The confusion is worst near the epicenter, in the surface region directly above the quake's subterranean origin, the focus. Here vibrations from the initial rupture smash through the earth's crust in a bunched, chaotic mass, some bouncing back into the interior, some spreading out along the surface. Furthermore, as the rebounding waves reflect and refract among the underlying strata, some of their energy shoots back up to the surface, subjecting it to double and triple punishment. Often, the returning waves superimpose themselves upon the originals, and if the wavelengths coincide they amplify each other and the ground heaves with a violence much greater than that produced by any single wave sequence. That is why most seismographs situated near the epicenter are often either thrown off scale or hopelessly muddled.

The waves spread out from the focus at different velocities, moving away from one another as they go. When they are recorded far enough away for the jumble to have sorted itself out a bit, seismologists can readily identify the types of waves generated by all earthquakes *(above)*. The simplest of the many forces produced by a quake compresses the particles of rock in front of the movement and expands those behind it. As the rock particles adjust to this motion, a series of pulsations moves out in all directions at a speed of about four miles per second. The fastest of all seismic waves and the first to appear on a

PRIMARY WAVE

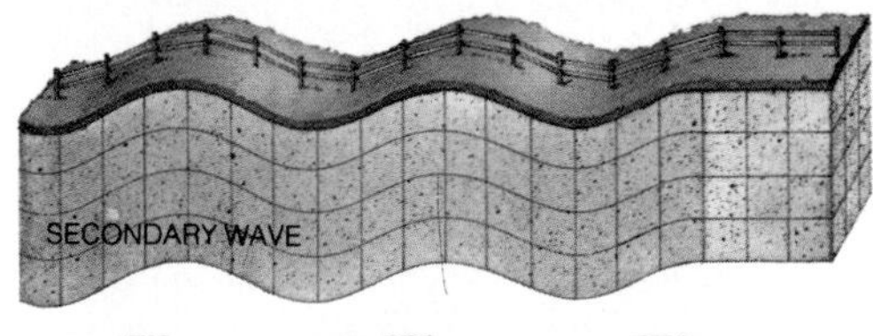

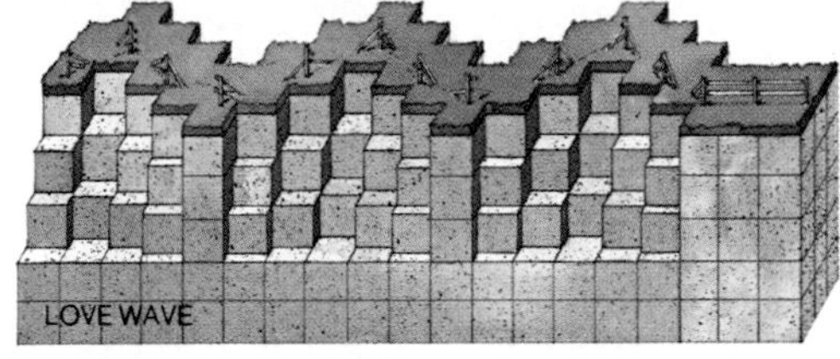

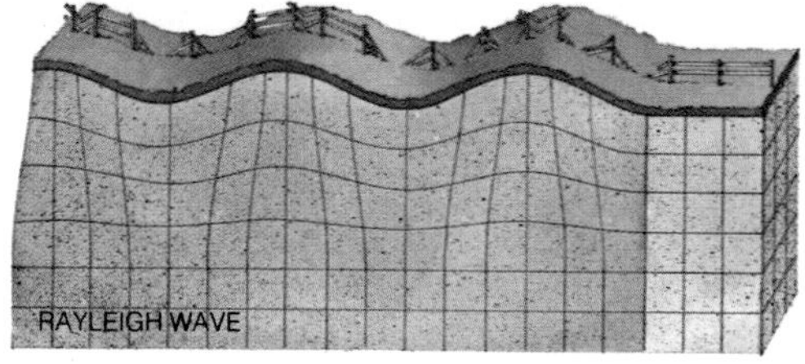

How the earth vibrates during an earthquake is demonstrated by these diagrams. Primary waves punching out from the quake's origin alternately compress and stretch the material they travel through. Secondary waves produce an up-and-down and side-to-side oscillation like the snapping of a rope. The long waves that travel along the surface are more complex: One type, known as Love waves, whips back and forth horizontally; the second type, called Rayleigh waves, churns along like an ocean breaker, rotating the rock and soil in an elliptical pattern.

seismogram, they are called primary, or P, waves. These are the movements that John Milne with his pioneer instruments classified as condensational. P waves can travel through any material—the solid granite of a mountain, the molten lava of a volcano, the water of lakes and oceans, even the air. The express-train roar that people sometimes hear at the onset of a major earthquake consists of P waves in the audible range of frequencies that have broken through the surface to agitate the air.

The twisting and shifting of the bedrock also affects the material surrounding the fault, creating a transverse wave that, instead of driving the rock particles forward and backward in the direction of its path, vibrates them up and down and from side to side. Because of the energy expended in sideways motion, these waves travel more slowly than P waves, at about two miles per second, and show up on the seismogram as a later, stronger and more ragged tracing; they are called secondary, or S, waves. They cannot travel through liquid, because the molecules of a liquid do not resist shearing; in a solid the molecules moving sideways drag the adjacent molecules along, but in a liquid they do not. The velocities of P and S waves change considerably in different materials, but the ratio between their speeds almost always remains the same.

When these so-called body waves, moving outward through the earth from the earthquake's focus, encounter the surface some are transformed into surface waves. Even before the existence of these surface waves was confirmed by seismograms accurate enough to differentiate them from S waves, their characteristics had been predicted mathematically by two British scientists. Working with complex equations quantifying the behavior of wave propagation in elastic materials, John William Strutt, Lord Rayleigh, predicted in 1885 a surface wave that would have a rotating, up-and-down motion like that of breakers at sea, and subsequent study of seismograms revealed exactly that kind of motion. It is probable that Rayleigh waves caused the disturbances (geologists call them seiches) in Europe's lakes and harbors after the Lisbon cataclysm of 1755, and the ripple that lifted Cape Kennedy after Alaska's Good Friday earthquake.

But Rayleigh's theory did not explain all the motions observed on the surface during earthquakes. In 1911, British mathematician A. E. H. Love worked out a mathematical model of another kind of earthquake surface wave that moved transversely, whipping the surface from side to side without agitating it vertically or longitudinally. Again, the mathematics were borne out by closer analysis of seismograms. It was soon learned that the Rayleigh and Love surface waves have lower frequencies than the body waves that spawn them and usually travel more slowly—Rayleigh waves at 1.7 miles per second, Love waves at somewhat less than two miles per second. But they persist for great distances, sometimes circling the globe several times before subsiding.

The ephemeral signature of an earthquake can flicker across any one point on the earth in seconds (although the oscillations from a great quake may last for weeks), and then it is gone. The energy involved is evident only through the destructive aftereffects; the event cannot be preserved as it happens, nor can it be reproduced in the laboratory for study and analysis. Only the seismograph can capture the complex, transitory shudderings of an earthquake in a permanent record. And the extent and value of the information have increased over the years in tandem with the advances in precision and versatility of the seismograph—the instrument that saw its first productive service under the intensely watchful eye of John Milne.

As marvelous as they were for their time, the seismographs that Milne, Gray, Ewing and others developed at the end of the 19th Century fell far short of meeting the demands of a science that was asking ever more complex questions. The early machines measured only a portion of the broad band of wave sizes and frequencies. Another shortcoming was the tendency of the seismograph's pendulum to keep swinging indefinitely once a strong motion had started it. Without a way to control the pendulum's motion the seismograph was unable to record accurately the other kinds of waves that arrived later.

A substantial improvement came in 1898, when Emil Wiechert introduced a damping mechanism that restrained the seismograph pendulum and greatly increased its accuracy. But the machines were cumbersome; they depended on weights large enough to remain at rest despite the energy transmitted both by the shaking of the instrument's frame and by the mechanical linkage that inscribed the seismic waves on paper. One of Wiechert's seismographs was weighted by 17 tons of iron ore—taking a seismograph into the field to study aftershocks or man-made explosions was virtually impossible.

It was entirely appropriate that the man who made the next advance in the technology of earthquake science was Russia's Prince Boris Galitzin, who as president of the International Seismological Association had eulogized Milne so effectively. Galitzin in 1906 introduced a design that did away with the need for mechanical linkage between the pendulum that revealed the earth's movement and the recorder that transcribed it. He mounted a coil of wire on the pendulum and suspended both between the poles of a magnet fixed to the earth. When the earth shook, it moved the magnetic field around the coil, generating an electrical current in the wire. The greater the movement, the more powerful the current. Now the recorder could be separated from the seismometer by running a wire from the coil to a convenient recording site and connecting it to a galvanometer, an instrument that translated the electrical current back to mechanical force, which in turn moved the recording device.

It was a development with profound implications for seismology. With the movement converted to electrical current, designers could use smaller weights in more easily portable machines. And the ability to transmit the signal meant that several seismographs could be monitored simultaneously at a central location. The tedium and delay of traveling periodically from site to site to check instruments was thus dramatically reduced.

While the pendulums in seismographs could be smaller after the introduction of Galitzin's electromagnetic system, it remained a principle of electromagnetism that the amount of electrical energy created in the circuit was related to the size of the coil mounted on the pendulum. Too small a weight would not generate enough current to operate the mechanism. Another 16 years passed before two scientists working at the California Institute of Technology not only found a way to miniaturize the seismograph, but also realized Milne's ideal of an instrument of stark mechanical simplicity.

Harry O. Wood and J. A. Anderson, who were among the first seismologists to measure the earthquakes of Southern California, attached a small cylinder, weighing about one gram, to the side of a tautly stretched vertical tungsten wire. Horizontal movement of the ground caused the cylinder to rotate around the wire, and the twisting of the wire acted like a spring, returning the cylinder to its original position. They fixed a tiny mirror to the site of the cylinder and reflected a beam of light from the mirror onto photosensitive paper attached to a recording drum. When ground movements shook the seismograph, the moving light beam exposed the shapes of the wave motion on the photographic paper. Although the entire unit was only about a foot high, it proved remarkably sensitive to surface waves and was marvelously practical: There was virtually nothing in the mechanism to wear out or adjust. Its utility was such that it would soon become the standard instrument used to calculate Richter magnitude of earthquakes.

But it had one shortcoming. If the device was placed on its side, gravity would drag the cylinder downward, preventing its oscillation. Thus the seismograph measured only horizontal ground movement—the compressional effect of P waves and the side-to-side whipping motion of S and Love waves; it did not

The messengers who galloped into the Chinese capital of Loyang one March day in 138 A.D. discovered that the news they carried of a devastating earthquake 400 miles to the northwest had outpaced them. It had, in fact, traveled with the speed of the tremors themselves. Although no one in the capital had felt much of anything, an ingenious "earthquake weathercock" *(right)* had detected the quake and indicated its direction.

Though knowledge of the Chinese device was lost in later years, 18th Century Europeans regularly monitored delicately balanced objects or bowls brimful of water. Then scientists began to develop more sophisticated instruments *(overleaf)* for measuring and recording the movements of the earth.

One device replaced water with mercury, which has greater density and is less subject to spillage from minor disturbances. Such seismoscopes, as they were called, detected earth movements and the approximate direction of their origin. The first European pendulum-based measuring devices, seismometers that recorded the strengths of tremors, came into use in the mid-1700s.

A suspended mass, such as a common pendulum, remains momentarily stationary even when the ground below it moves, and thus can be rigged to measure the amount of movement. Some seismometers incorporated variations such as a horizontal pendulum, with a mass on a pivoting arm or suspended on a spring to register vertical displacement.

Seismometers increased in sensitivity and precision until the late 1800s, when British scientists developed seismographs, which not only registered the amplitude and direction of tremors but made a permanent record around the clock. Forerunners of an array of modern instruments, these seismographs began to provide scientists with the consistent data they needed to refine their understanding of earthquake dynamics.

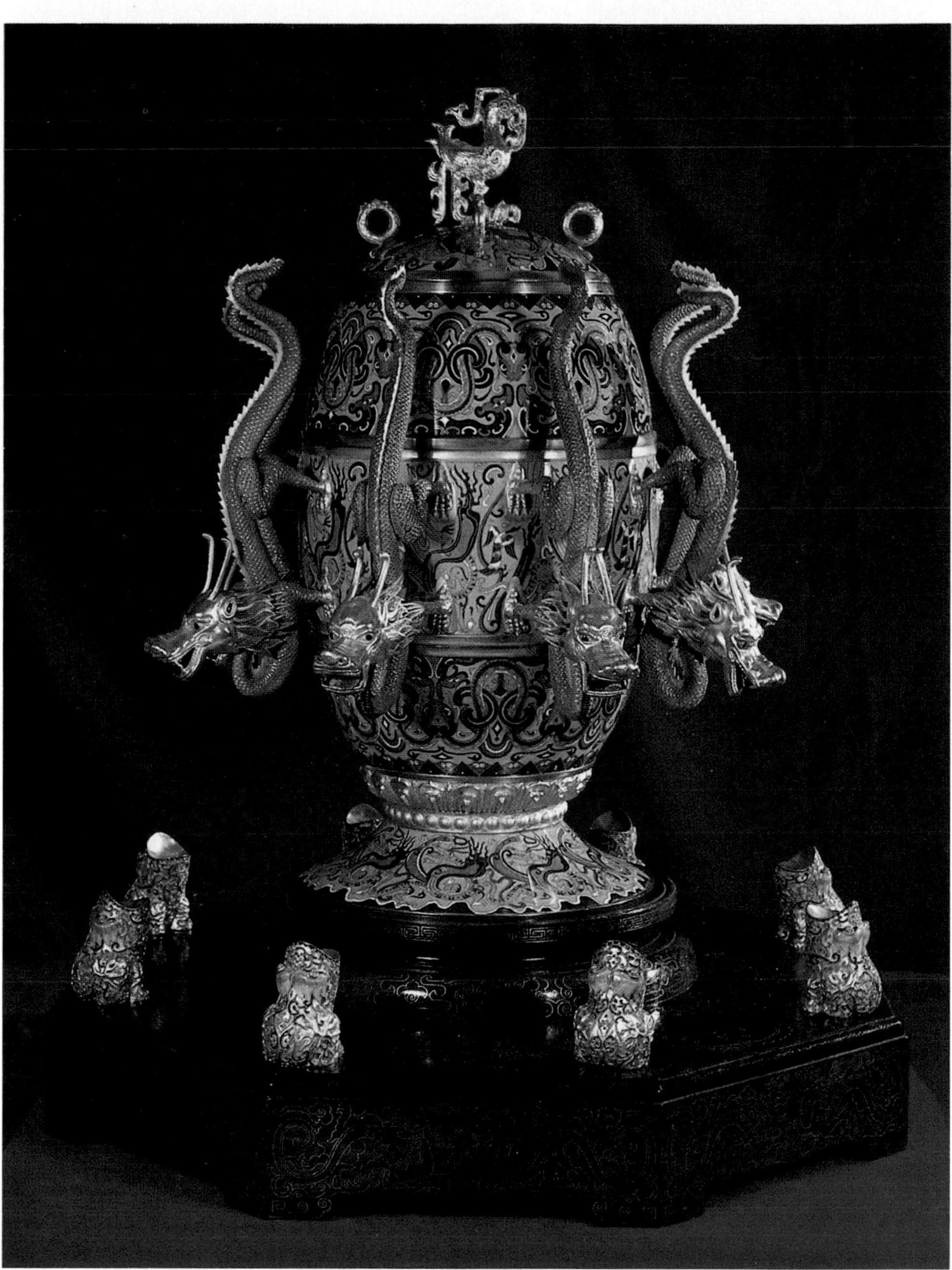

Ornate dragons perch on a cloisonné model of the "earthquake weathercock" invented in 132 A.D. by the Chinese astronomer and mathematician Chang Heng. Eight dragons held in their mouths bronze balls; an internal mechanism, activated by even a slight tremor, opened the mouth of one dragon, releasing the ball to sound an alarm as it clanked into the open mouth of a metal toad below. Imperial watchmen determined the direction of the quake from the orientation of the empty-mouthed dragon.

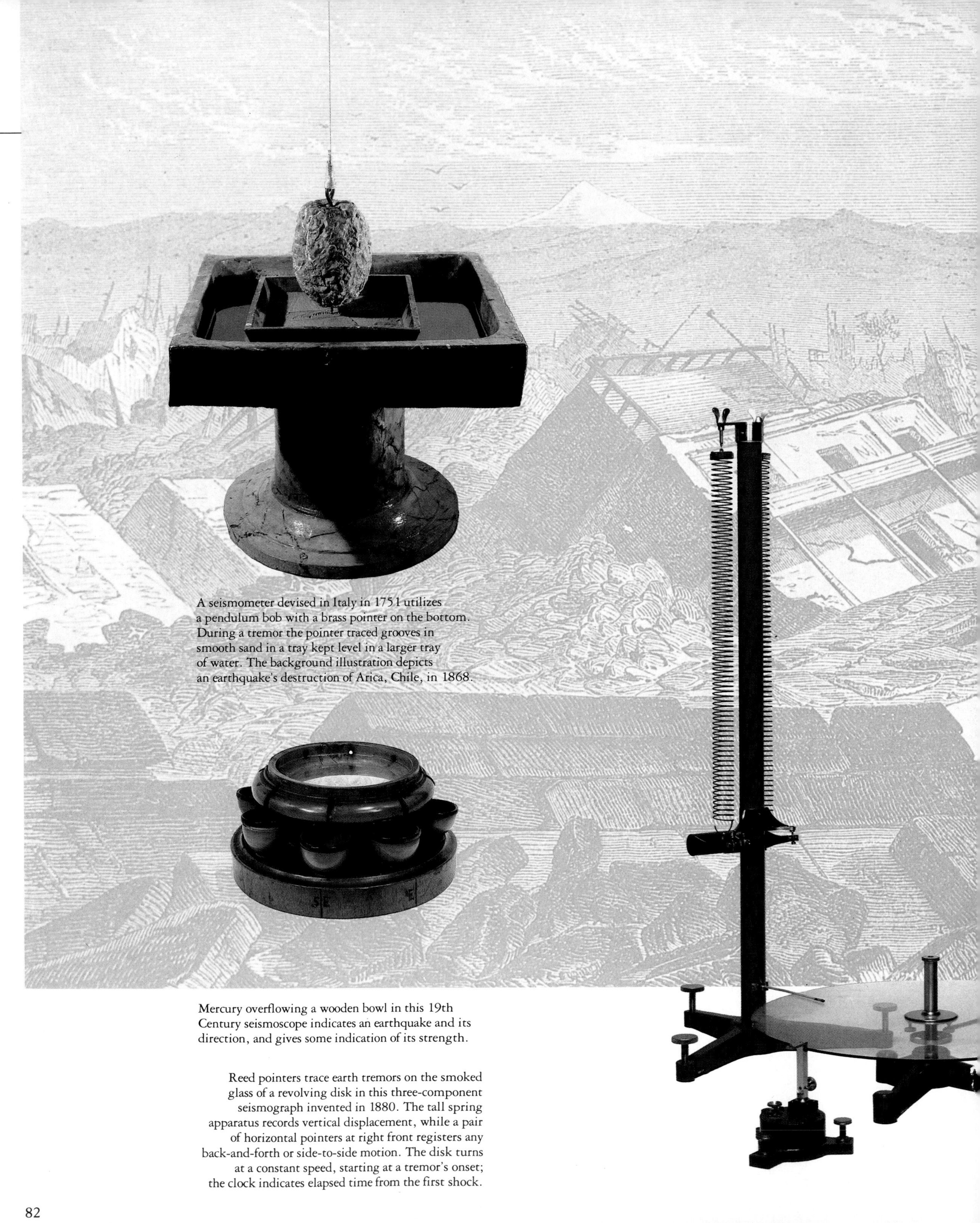

A seismometer devised in Italy in 1751 utilizes a pendulum bob with a brass pointer on the bottom. During a tremor the pointer traced grooves in smooth sand in a tray kept level in a larger tray of water. The background illustration depicts an earthquake's destruction of Arica, Chile, in 1868.

Mercury overflowing a wooden bowl in this 19th Century seismoscope indicates an earthquake and its direction, and gives some indication of its strength.

Reed pointers trace earth tremors on the smoked glass of a revolving disk in this three-component seismograph invented in 1880. The tall spring apparatus records vertical displacement, while a pair of horizontal pointers at right front registers any back-and-forth or side-to-side motion. The disk turns at a constant speed, starting at a tremor's onset; the clock indicates elapsed time from the first shock.

A photographic system made this 1899 seismometer the most accurate of its day. Light from a lamp in the recorder *(left)* shines through a hole in the tip of the horizontal pendulum hung from the post *(above);* in a quake, a pinpoint of light traces seismic waves on a drum covered with photographic paper.

An early portable seismograph, this 1917 model measured tremors induced by explosions touched off by ore prospectors. Minute movements of a pendulum in the long tube turned a mirror at the top, shifting the path of a light beam reflected onto photographic paper in the three-legged recorder.

MODIFIED MERCALLI INTENSITY SCALE OF 1931

I Not felt except by a very few under especially favorable circumstances.

II Felt only by a few persons at rest, especially on upper floors of buildings. Delicately suspended objects may swing.

III Felt quite noticeably indoors, especially on upper floors of buildings, but many people do not recognize it as an earthquake. Standing motor cars may rock slightly. Vibration like passing of truck. Duration estimated.

IV During the day felt indoors by many, outdoors by few. At night some awakened. Dishes, windows, doors disturbed; walls make cracking sound. Sensation like heavy truck striking building. Standing motor cars rocked noticeably.

V Felt by nearly everyone, many awakened. Some dishes, windows, etc., broken; a few instances of cracked plaster; unstable objects overturned. Disturbances of trees, poles, and other tall objects sometimes noticed. Pendulum clocks may stop.

VI Felt by all, many frightened and run outdoors. Some heavy furniture moved; a few instances of fallen plaster or damaged chimneys. Damage slight.

VII Everybody runs outdoors. Damage negligible in buildings of good design and construction; slight to moderate in well-built ordinary structures; considerable in poorly built or badly designed structures; some chimneys broken. Noticed by persons driving motor cars.

VIII Damage slight in specially designed structures; considerable in ordinary substantial buildings, with partial collapse; great in poorly built structures. Panel walls thrown out of frame structures. Fall of chimneys, factory stacks, columns, monuments, walls. Heavy furniture overturned. Sand and mud ejected in small amounts. Changes in well water. Persons driving motor cars disturbed.

IX Damage considerable in specially designed structures; well-designed frame structures thrown out of plumb; great in substantial buildings, with partial collapse. Buildings shifted off foundations. Ground cracked conspicuously. Underground pipes broken.

X Some well-built wooden structures destroyed; most masonry and frame structures destroyed with foundations; ground badly cracked. Rails bent. Landslides considerable from river banks and steep slopes. Shifted sand and mud. Water splashed (slopped) over banks.

XI Few, if any, (masonry) structures remain standing. Bridges destroyed. Broad fissures in ground. Underground pipelines completely out of service. Earth slumps and land slips in soft ground. Rails bent greatly.

XII Damage total. Practically all works of construction are damaged greatly or destroyed. Waves seen on ground surface. Lines of sight and level are distorted. Objects are thrown upward into the air.

This intensity scale used to describe earthquake effects was devised in 1902 by Italian seismologist Giuseppe Mercalli *(above)* and updated in 1931 by American researchers. The 12 levels of intensity are based on eyewitness accounts, but are of limited value, since damage varies widely depending upon the distance from the earthquake's epicenter, the character of the ground and the type of building construction.

completely record the vertical roller-coaster motion of S waves or the churning, comber-like effect of Rayleigh waves.

During the next seven years several attempts were made to produce an instrument that would record accurately in the vertical as well as horizontal dimension, but without success. Then in 1930 a graduate student at the California Institute of Technology, Victor Hugo Benioff, conceived of a device that was later credited with opening a new era in instrumental seismology. Benioff improved on Galitzin's electromagnetic sensor by applying to it the principle of the standard telephone. Instead of using the movements of the earth to generate an electric current, as Galitzin had, Benioff used them to induce minute variations in an already established current, just as a telephone converted sound waves to an electrical signal. The result was a far more sensitive seismograph that permitted the accurate recording and analysis of the tiniest movements of the ground, both vertical and horizontal.

This sophisticated seismograph was only the first of many contributions that Benioff would make during a distinguished career at Caltech. Indeed, scarcely two years later he made a breakthrough in another problem area—the recording of very long wave motions. Every earthquake generates waves that range in period—the time that elapses between two successive crests—from thousandths of a second to thousands of seconds. Most advances of the 1920s and early '30s had resulted in better measurements of the waves at the smaller end of the spectrum. In 1936 Benioff extended the measurements to the longer end.

He achieved this with an unusual instrument that he installed in a vault in the hills near Pasadena. It consisted of a thin quartz rod, 60 feet long, one end of which was rigidly secured to a cement post while the other rested loosely within an electromagnetic sensing device on a second post. When one post moved in relation to the other, the free end of the rod activated the sensor. Benioff had designed it as a strain meter, to measure the extension and contraction of the earth's crust. But it worked equally well as an ultralong period seismograph, registering waves whose crests arrived as much as 60 feet apart. Such waves moved an ordinary seismograph so gently that it did not detect them. But when they raised one of the widely separated posts of Benioff's strain meter, the long rod accentuated the relative motion of the posts and the sensitive recorder captured the wave form. The instrument greatly facilitated the study of the longer waves typical of very distant or very large earthquakes.

Thus by the mid-1930s, a handful of brilliant scientists had worked a stupendous evolutionary change in the techniques of seismology. In a little more than a generation, the state of the art had progressed from a few crude machines to an array of devices capable of recording every twist and turn of tortured rock in an earthquake. But what did the seismological readings mean? It was up to other scientists to discover the mathematical Rosetta stones that would unlock the secrets of the hieroglyphics inscribed on the seismograph.

When Charles F. Richter, a 27-year-old graduate student working on his Ph.D. in theoretical physics, arrived at the Seismological Laboratory at Caltech in 1927, his first job was the routine measurement of seismograms to determine the epicenters of each earthquake recorded. A few years later, plans were made to publish an annual catalogue of Southern California's earthquakes using the data collected at Caltech. The catalogue would be dealing with 200 to 300 earthquakes of varying strength that occur in the area each year, and Richter was concerned about the misinterpretation that would result from what he called "outrageous discrepancies" in their descriptions. His sense of scientific objectivity was offended by the limitations of the only method then used to describe and compare earthquakes—the intensity scale that dated back to the earliest days of seismology.

The scale was based on observation, pure and simple. A scientist would merely go into the field and estimate the damage. He would look for cracks in buildings, overturned furniture, land slumps and ground fissures. He would survey the impressions of the people present when the ground shook. He would then compare these details and accounts with the descriptions in a standard intensity scale, which described 12 gradations of earthquakes of ascending intensity; the higher the number, the more severe the event.

The intensity scale remains a valuable yardstick, both for understanding past earthquakes and for assessing ground conditions and the ruggedness of architecture. But as a precise calibration of an earthquake it leaves much to be desired. It is not even a measurement; it is a description of effects. And the description varies with the skills of the observer, while the effects vary for dozens of reasons that have nothing to do with the power of an earthquake. The collapse of buildings, a key factor in determining an intensity-scale rating, may say as much about the contractors who put them up and the materials used as it does about the strength of the vibrations that brought them down.

Richter's studies of seismograms revealed another, even more serious shortcoming of the intensity scale. He noted that an earthquake that produced a relatively mild seismogram, when it occurred near a densely settled area, could result in effects that gave it a high ranking on the intensity scale, while another that made a more dramatic seismogram but had its epicenter far from civilization could get a low rating. A science that was striving for mathematical exactitude needed a more objective measure of the size of a seismic event. And Richter realized that the solution was right in front of him, on the seismogram.

At first the idea seemed almost too simple. He observed that the seismograms for any two earthquakes, no matter what the distance to the recording station, showed a constant ratio between the largest surface waves recorded. The key to this comparison was the maximum amplitude—the highest crest or deepest trough of an individual wave—on the seismogram. Richter reasoned that if the ratio was the same at any distance it must also be the same at the earthquake's source, and if so, it could be used to measure, directly from the seismogram, the relative sizes of earthquakes. But he found that the ratio varied too much from earthquake to earthquake to be useful; the amplitude of a great earthquake was as much as 10 million times that of a small one. He decided to compress the range by taking the logarithm of the ratio to base 10. Thus an increase of one in the rating would indicate a tenfold increase in the seismic wave amplitude. The result was a compact scale that could be calculated directly from the seismogram to give an objective, quantitative description of the size of the earthquake.

In order to make his measurement readily distinguishable from intensity scales and to emphasize its essential difference from previous comparisons of earthquakes, Richter needed a special term; he borrowed one used by astronomers to describe the measured intensity of distant stars—magnitude. His scale of magnitude had no upper limit, but in practice no earthquake larger than 8.9 has ever been recorded. "That is a limitation in the earth," said Richter, "not in the scale."

As useful as the Richter scale was to the seismologists at Caltech, it could not immediately be used elsewhere. For one thing, the scale was based on the seismograms recorded by the Wood-Anderson seismograph and could not be calculated directly from the tracings made by many other seismographs in operation around the world. The waves measured in setting up the scale had been recorded within a few hundred miles of the shallow earthquakes that typify California's seismic activity. But seismograms recorded at distances of more than a few hundred miles did not yield the same direct comparisons that Richter had observed in California, and earthquakes originating deep in the earth generate no surface waves at all. Modifications of Richter's methods were needed before his scale could be applied universally.

Nevertheless, the problems were worked through one by one in the 1940s, and the worth of the scale improved. Different types of seismographs may enlarge or reduce the ground motions relative to California readings, but they all measure the same thing: the size of the tremors. Therefore it was possible, though far from easy, to work out the mathematics that would standardize seismograms from different machines and areas of the world for the purpose of calculating a Richter value.

After 15 years of research and refinement, the Richter scale was in constant worldwide use as the basic yardstick of the earthquake. In fact, the Richter scale became the first thing mentioned after the location of the epicenter in virtually every news report of an earthquake anywhere in the world. And no one was more surprised at the utility and acceptance of the scale than Richter himself. His objectives when he began work on the project had been limited, and he often deprecated his achievement. "A rather rough and ready procedure," he once characterized it. "The most remarkable feature about the magnitude scale was that it worked at all."

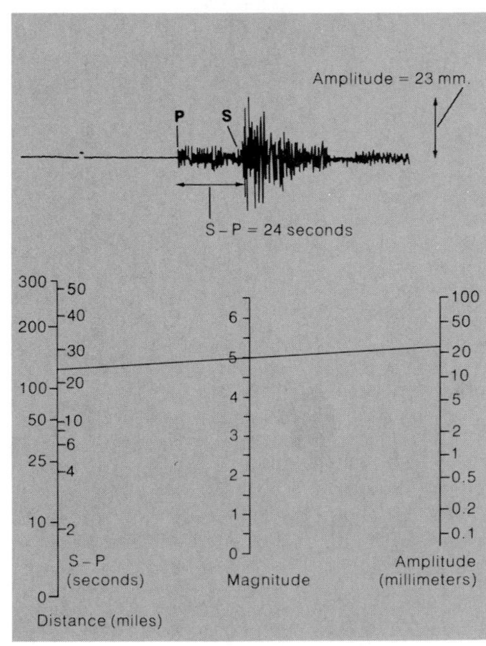

Seismologist Charles F. Richter, seen here studying a seismogram, devised a scale of magnitude in 1935 to measure the relative sizes of earthquakes. On the graph above, the distance to the focus of the earthquake, in terms of the time between arrival of P and S waves, is 24 seconds. The maximum amplitude is 23 mm. Connecting those two points on the distance scale *(left)* and the amplitude scale *(right)* gives the earthquake's magnitude: 5.0.

By the 1950s an unprecedented treasure trove of seismic data was being accumulated all over the world. But collecting enough data for a detailed study of a specific earthquake was still a labor of months. And then much of the material would be from differently scaled machines or instruments that had not been uniformly calibrated, or would have incorrect times because a clockwork mechanism had been set improperly or was out of adjustment.

What seismologists needed was a single worldwide system of sophisticated, synchronized instruments connected by a modern communications network. And in the late 1950s just such a system came into being—not as a tool of scientific inquiry, but as an implement of international politics. The United States was then in the process of negotiating a nuclear test ban treaty with the Soviet Union and was vitally interested in monitoring underground nuclear explosions. But it was apparent that existing seismological networks were unequal to the task. And so the U.S. government established its own seismological network.

A standard package of six seismographs governed by precise chronometers that could be calibrated by radio signal was designed and distributed to 120 stations in 60 nations around the globe. Most of the packages were assigned to existing laboratories in Allied nations. But some were placed in remote and previously unmonitored locations, such as Antarctica, for truly global coverage.

It took several years and the expenditure of more than $10 million to execute the plan. The result was the World Wide Standardized Seismograph Network, or WWSSN. Enough stations were operating in 1964 to be of significant service in the analysis of the great Alaska quake, and the network was virtually complete by 1967. Ironically, the network failed in its primary task. Although it could detect large nuclear blasts, it could not pick up clearly enough the small underground tests that were by the mid-1960s providing data for nuclear weapons research. These were generally masked by the planet's ceaseless natural seismic activity. The Defense Department lost interest in funding the project, and thereafter its budget was underwritten as a cooperative venture by the National Science Foundation and various individual seismological observatories around the world.

The WWSSN did not replace the work of the many existing local and national seismographic networks; they continued as before, pursuing their individual lines of research with their different kinds of equipment. But the worldwide network did make possible for the first time the rapid assembly of a global seismic profile of any significant earthquake, accurately timed and recorded on instruments of uniform calibration. Had it been entirely in place in 1964, for instance, calculation of the Alaska earthquake's precise epicenter, focus and magnitude would have been simplified.

While the WWSSN was being assembled, other seismograph stations and networks around the world were installing better seismographs and, more important, accurate clocks. As Milne had demonstrated half a century before, pinpointing an epicenter depends primarily on the precise recording of the time that elapses between the arrival of P and S waves. The seismographs themselves need not be recorded on the same scale to be of use for that function—the time is the thing. As a result of all this activity, the quantity and quality of data about earthquakes quadrupled during the 1960s. And it is no coincidence that the same decade saw an avalanche of theoretical advances, based on and confirmed by the data, that revolutionized the earth sciences.

One of the continuing mysteries that taxed scientists was how to evaluate the actual power, the full strength of an earthquake. If they were ever to explain the source of the massive forces that produce earthquakes, they had to know exactly how much energy was involved in a seismic event. For all its usefulness, the Richter scale of magnitude did not measure the total earthquake—only the size of its seismic waves. To be sure, magnitude had a direct relationship to the amount of seismic wave energy released. But much of the force of an earthquake is not converted to wave form at all; it is expended in lifting great blocks of the earth's crust, in crushing rock along the fault planes and in producing heat as the shifting masses of rock rub against one another.

Many seismologists are hopeful that the answer to a complete measurement of earthquake energy can be found—once again—on the seismogram; they believe that it can reliably be used to calculate a quantity called the seismic moment. Introduced in 1966, seismic moment was defined as the figure obtained by multiplying the rigidity of the rock times the area of faulting times the average amount of slippage. These factors cannot be measured by direct observation; the length of the fault, for instance, has been clearly visible at the surface in only about 50 earthquakes in this century. And even then, what can be seen is only the top of a complex fault system that might extend for miles, in various kinds of configuration, below the surface.

But the technological advances of the 1960s gave scientists new ways to calculate the dimensions of the earthquake mechanism. The latest seismographs could measure seismic waves with lengths of hundreds, even thousands of miles and periods of an hour and longer. When the instruments were included in the worldwide network of standard seismographs they began furnishing reliable data on the very long period waves from around the globe. The advent of large-scale computers made possible an analysis of the long period waves that showed a consistent relationship between their wavelength and the combined factors of fault length, amount of slippage and bedrock rigidity. This was the seismic moment, and further analysis showed that it could be used to calculate the total amount of energy—measured in units of work called ergs—released by the earthquake. The new measurement often produced a completely altered perception of large earthquakes; when estimated in this way the 1964 Alaska earthquake was shown to have released 25 times as much energy as calculations based on the Richter magnitude had indicated.

In the decade of the 1970s, still greater strides were made in decoding the secret language of the seismograms. For example, seismologists learned to read from them in what direction the earth moves after it shatters, the orientation of the fault plane and the sequence of progressive ruptures along the fault plane. If the initial motion of the fracturing bedrock is toward, rather than away from, a seismograph, then the first P wave to arrive at the station will be recorded as an upward pulse. If the motion is away from the instrument, the first P-wave tracing will be downward. Comparisons of the records from a ring of stations around the earthquake, each showing the direction of rock motion, give seismologists a clear picture of the overall direction of the faulting. The orientation of the fault can also be determined from the seismic records of the aftershocks as the twisted and fractured rock settles back into an approximation of its original alignment, adjusting itself to the aftermath of the quake. By precisely determining the time and focus of each aftershock and charting its relationship to the focus of the main shock, the plane along which the rupture propagated and the sequence of shocks can be estimated.

The role of the computer in all this can hardly be overestimated. While Milne painstakingly calculated the distance from the seismograph to the epicenter using the difference in arrival times of P and S waves, computers can determine these distances in a split second. And Milne's method of triangulating the location of the epicenter using three different calculations and then drawing intersecting arcs on a map is now done far more accurately using reports from hundreds of stations, again by computer. Seismograms themselves are increasingly becoming computerized. For convenience in storing and analyzing masses of data, many seismic stations are installing digital seismographs that, instead of tracing a line on paper, record sets of numbers that define the wave patterns and amplitudes of earthquakes. The computerized seismograph is also useful for measuring earthquakes in the field; just as the Wood-Anderson seismograph and others made the massive size of the instruments of the early 20th Century unnecessary, so the computer-assisted seismograph opens up a vast range of possibilities for measurement outside the laboratory. Portable digital recorders are especially useful in measuring the aftershocks of

Among the 20th Century pioneers of seismology in the United States was Jesuit Father Francis Anthony Tondorf, seen here in 1925 reading a seismogram at Georgetown University in Washington, D.C.

major earthquakes and the seismic activity accompanying volcanic rumblings.

The seismogram does not speak only to the particulars of earthquake mechanics. From the beginning, as scientists peered ever more closely at the cryptography of the seismic waves, they picked up fascinating hints of other vistas—information not just about what was happening during an earthquake, but about the basic structure of the earth itself. An early glimpse of this new knowledge came to light in Yugoslavia at the turn of the century as the relatively primitive seismographs of the time began to record odd changes in seismic waves that had traveled great distances through the earth.

It is a measure of the newness of seismology as a science that so many of its pioneers—Winthrop, Mallet, Milne—took up the study as a passionate avocation while engaged full time in a more firmly established branch of inquiry. So it was with Andrija Mohorovičić, a brilliant Yugoslav meteorologist who in 1892 won appointment as observatory director at the Main Technical School in Zagreb. Within a few years Mohorovičić had built the observatory into a regional center for meteorology and geophysics—and began turning his attention to the arcane young science of seismology.

In October 1909 a minor quake shook Zagreb, and Mohorovičić seized the opportunity to make an intensive study of the event. He collected seismograms from 29 stations at distances of up to 1,500 miles from the epicenter, and the more he studied them, the stranger their message seemed. He found evidence of something that had escaped other seismologists: two distinct groups of both P and S waves. What is more, the two groups appeared to be traveling at different speeds. Stations within 125 miles of the quake recorded one group of P and S waves first; at that distance, a second group of P and S waves overtook and passed the first group. Mohorovičić calculated the velocity of the slower P waves at slightly more than 3.8 miles per second and that of the faster P waves at about 5 miles per second; the S waves varied from 2.5 to 3 miles per second.

Researchers had known for some years that the speeds of both P waves and S waves changed according to the type of material they were passing through and that the rate increased with the material's density. But there had never been any indication that there were different kinds of P and S waves or that they had different velocities. Mohorovičić concluded that the only explanation for his evidence was the presence of a layer of material under the earth's outer crust that

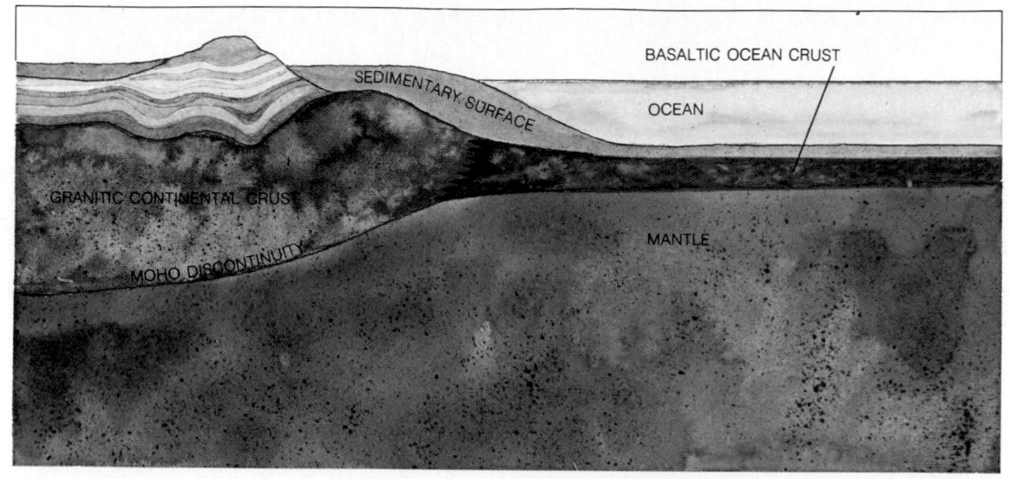

At the abrupt border between the earth's crust and the denser mantle lies the Moho Discontinuity, an interface that bends, or refracts, seismic waves and changes their speeds. The discontinuity's location varies: The Moho is about six miles beneath the basaltic ocean floor, but beneath the granitic continents the depth varies between 20 and 40 miles.

was so dense that it affected the path, and therefore the speed, of the waves.

Mohorovičić reasoned that the P and S waves all started outward from the earthquake's focus at one size and one velocity for each type; but at a depth he calculated to be about 30 miles, they encountered a boundary between the outer crust and the inner layer of dense rock. Today, seismologists know the depth to be closer to 20 miles where Mohorovičić measured it, but his explanation of the phenomenon still stands. At the boundary the waves were split into two groups. One group continued through the earth's outer crust at initial speeds. But the other group was bent, or refracted, and propagated along the top of the denser rock below the boundary, attaining a higher velocity. Though they had farther to travel, the much-faster-moving wave forms eventually caught up with and passed the slower-moving waves in the crust above them. Thus, at distances greater than 125 miles from the focus, the faster waves reached the recording stations first, by a steadily increasing margin.

In a stunning revelation, the seismograms had drawn for Mohorovičić a map of the upper boundary of the earth's mantle, a layer of dense rock underlying the lighter crust. In testimony to his achievement (and to the difficulty of pronouncing his name) the boundary was later named the Moho Discontinuity. Subsequent calculations based on his theories showed that the thickness of the crust varies from 20 to 40 miles under the continents and diminishes to as little as four miles under the oceans. Mohorovičić's discovery was all the more remarkable for having been made with the primitive seismographs then available. And it was among the first clear indications of the rewards of having a multiplicity of seismic records available for a single earthquake.

Two years after the earthquake that had spurred Mohorovičić to his discovery, a 22-year-old graduate student at the University of Göttingen in Germany, Beno Gutenberg, tackled the seismological mystery of the "shadow zone." Studying seismic records from around the world, scientists had identified a 2,700-mile-wide belt—circling the earth on the side opposite the focus of an earthquake—in which the P waves emanating from the tremors virtually disappeared. The P waves could travel straight through the earth to its opposite side, but were not to be found in the shadow zone. Various explanations were offered for the phenomenon. But the one that struck Gutenberg as most plausible derived from the work of two men: Richard D. Oldham, an Irish geologist who was a colleague of John Milne's, and German geophysicist Emil Wiechert. Independently, they had postulated the presence in the center of the earth of a large, dense, at least partially molten core. They had theorized that P waves striking the edge of such a core at certain angles would be refracted, much like bullets hitting the surface of a lake; some would ricochet outward, some inward, but within a certain range of angles none would continue in a straight line and all would be deflected away from the area known as the shadow zone.

Gutenberg's contribution was a mathematical one. Accepting the work of

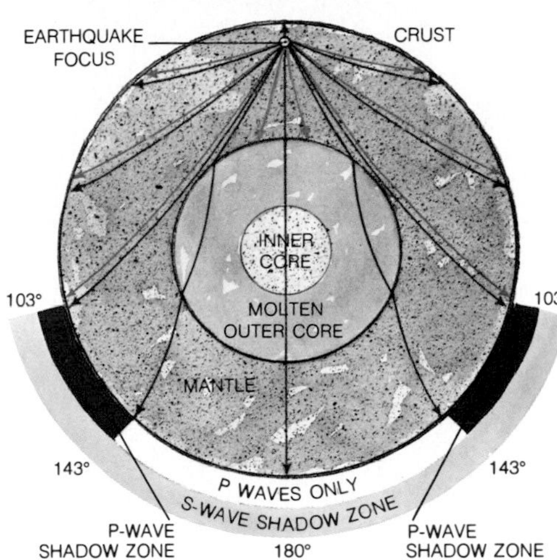

This cross section of the globe shows how the earth's core either blocks or deflects primary and secondary seismic waves, creating wave-free "shadow zones" on the opposite side of the world from a quake. The molten outer core entirely blocks S waves *(blue lines)*, which cannot travel through liquids, creating a huge 154-degree shadow zone. P waves *(red lines)* can traverse liquids, but at each interface between liquid and solid they are refracted in a characteristic pattern, creating a smaller shadow band around the earth.

Oldham and Wiechert as a starting point, he embarked on an exhaustive series of calculations designed to show how the paths and travel times of P waves would be affected by the presence of a dense core at various depths. In effect, he created several mathematical models of the earth and calculated the behavior of P waves in each. Then he searched the seismograms for confirmation of one of the models. Eventually he found that the seismic evidence coincided with the mathematics of a core 1,800 miles below the surface—an estimate whose accuracy has been refined only slightly. Further analysis along the lines of Gutenberg's research indicated that the core's outer edge must be molten.

Gutenberg went to Caltech as a professor in 1930 and was the director of its Seismological Laboratory from 1947 to 1958. He worked closely with Richter in the development of the magnitude scale and was given major credit for the work that expanded the usefulness of the scale to global proportions. Gutenberg's was a life of distinguished service to seismology, but his entry in the authoritative *Dictionary of Scientific Biography* describes his location of the Gutenberg Discontinuity as "his most elegant piece of research."

The laborious work of Mohorovičić and Gutenberg in the first dozen years of the 20th Century revealed the three main divisions of the structure of the earth. The seismograms had delineated an outer crust extending to the Moho Discontinuity, the 1,800-mile-thick mantle below it and the central core, about the size of the planet Mars. And still the seismograms had more to tell.

But further advances would have to await better tools than were available to Mohorovičić and Gutenberg during this period—the improved seismographs of the 1920s and '30s, the worldwide networks of recording stations of the '60s and the assistance of the computers that began to accelerate the process of discovery at about the time of the Alaska earthquake of 1964. All these factors added new detail to man's understanding of the earth.

The earth's core, scientists now know, is not actually a single molten mass. There is an inner core and an outer core, and a transition zone dividing a solid inner kernel from its surrounding sea of molten rock. The mantle, too, has an upper section and a lower one, and some concentric envelopes of elusive discontinuities. New ones are being detected all the time. P waves sometimes rebound from mysterious interfaces at depths of 160 miles, at 250 miles and also at 400 miles. At one layer in the upper mantle, just below the crust, the P and S body waves suddenly lose velocity, indicating that here the rocks become less rigid and may begin to ooze, like taffy.

It is these regions of the upper mantle, the part just under man's feet, that command the special attention of today's seismologists. For here, at the juncture of the mantle and the crust that rides on top of it, lurks the driving force behind most earthquakes. The discovery of what happens in the upper mantle, confirmed through some inspired research during the late 1960s and the 1970s, has utterly changed the concept of the forces that cause the earth to quake. Ω

THE GRAND DESIGN OF A PLANET IN FLUX

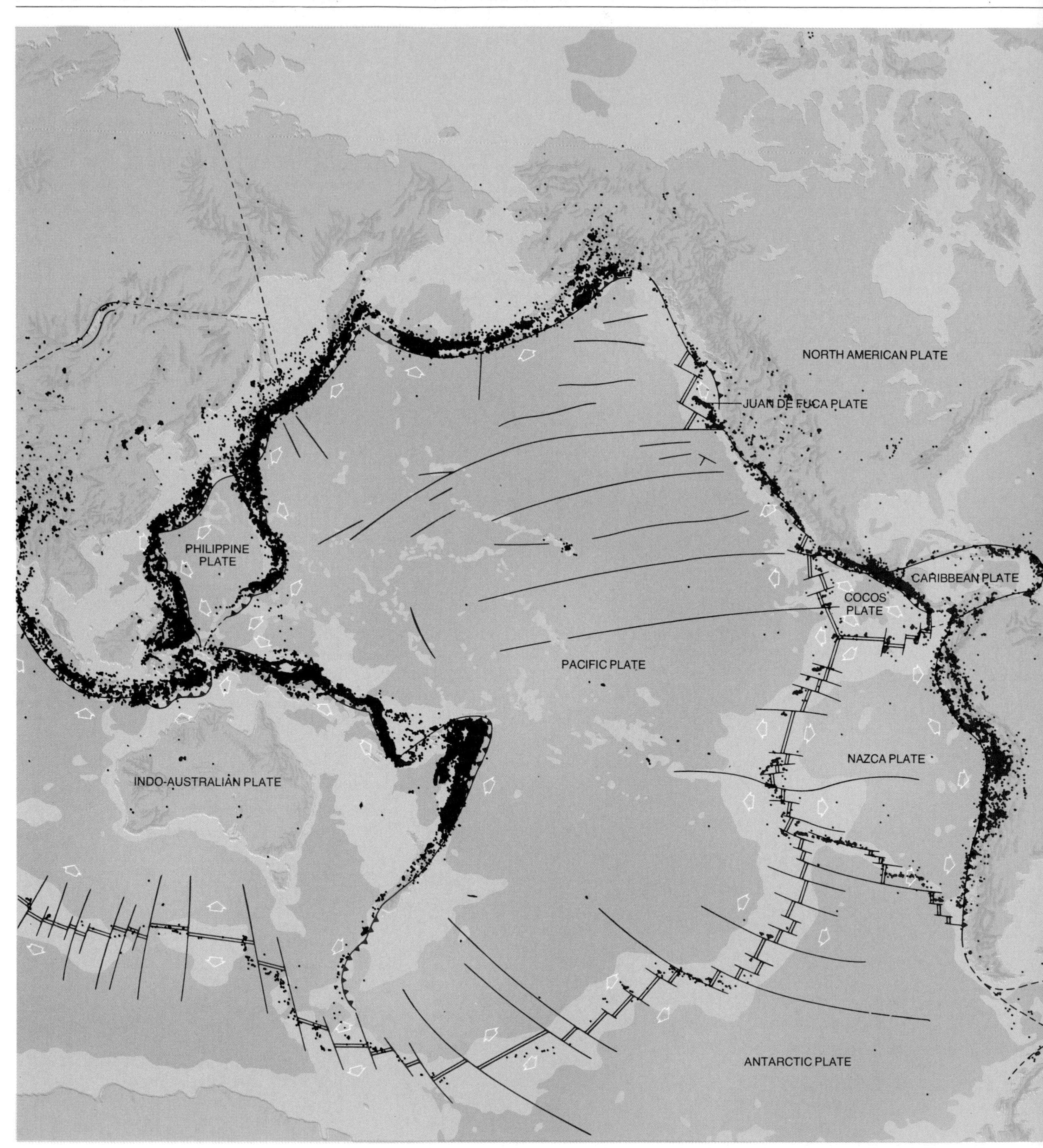

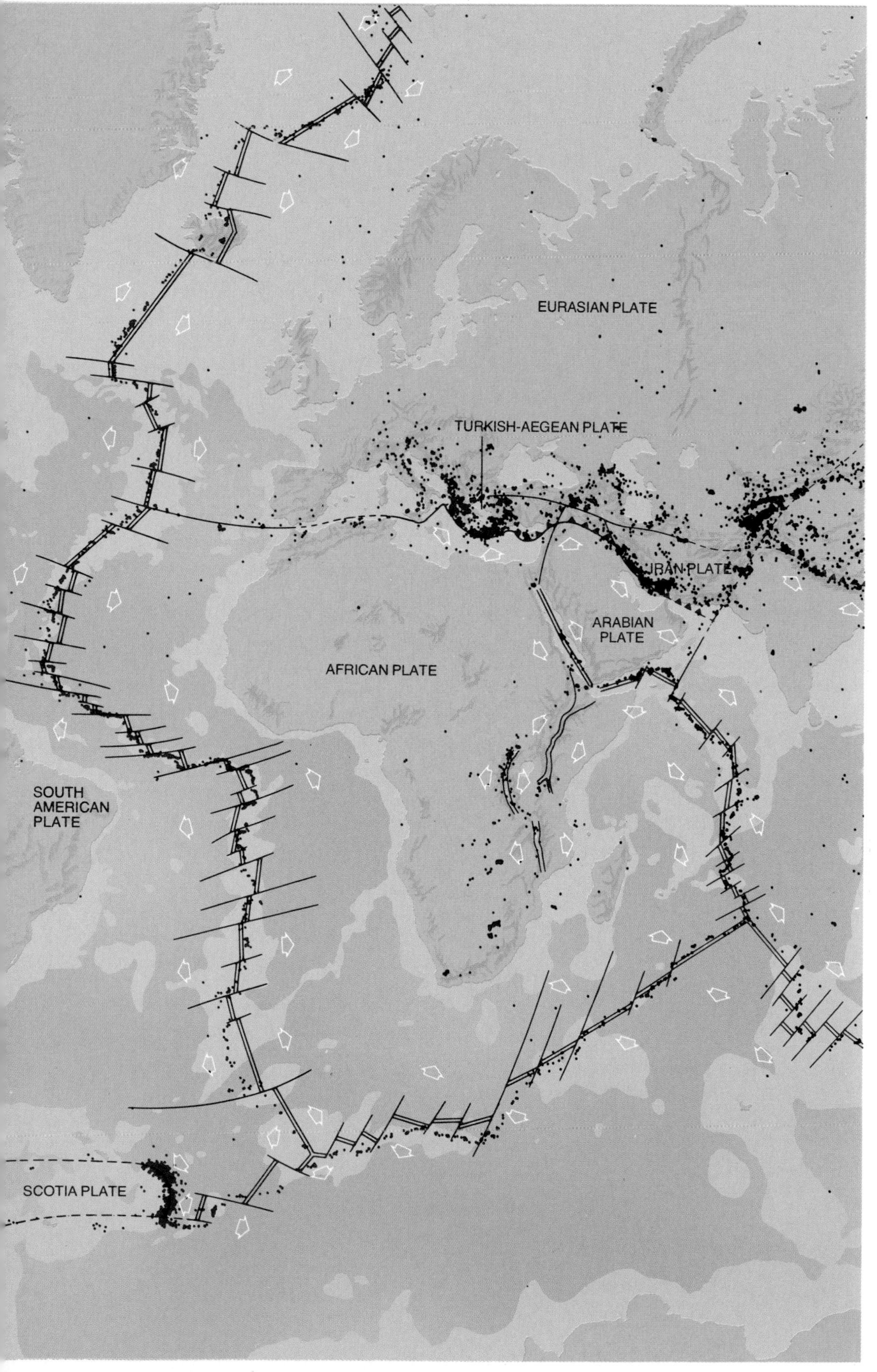

Until the 1960s, when the theory of plate tectonics revolutionized the earth sciences, seismologists trying to explain earthquake mechanics resembled nothing so much as the proverbial Indian blind men who struggled to describe an elephant from whatever part of the beast they could touch. They had no conceptual framework to which they could relate, and every earthquake seemed like an isolated phenomenon.

But then, after countless earthquake epicenters were plotted on maps, the grand design of a planet in flux gradually took shape. The vast majority of tremors occurred along well-defined belts that girdled the earth. This fact, combined with other geological detective work, led to the conclusion that the earth's rigid outer layer, the lithosphere, is broken into many tectonic plates. Seven major ones carry the continents and ocean basins. Powered by forces originating in the earth's molten interior, these plates move ponderously about, at a speed of up to four inches per year, riding on a layer of softer, more malleable rock called the asthenosphere. As the giant plates move, they pull apart or collide along their borders, unleashing awesome, earth-deforming tremors.

Earth scientists have identified three distinct types of plate borders: divergent rifts, where new ocean floor is created by basaltic magma rising and spreading out from the earth's interior; convergent zones, where two plates meet, either colliding head on or one diving beneath the other; and shear borders, where the plates grind slowly past each other. And each border is now known to experience strain that builds up within the bedrock until relieved by an earthquake. Even the few maverick earthquakes that occur thousands of miles from a plate border can generally be explained by the enormous ripple effect of backup pressure generated by a colliding front end.

Many of the exact details of earthquake genesis remain a mystery—for now. But, as Canadian seismologist John Hodgson says, "Whether we can see the fault break, or whether the earthquake focus is hundreds of miles within the earth, no one now doubts that the origin is tectonic."

A map of earthquake epicenters *(red dots)* outlines the borders of the major tectonic plates of the earth's crust, which move about *(arrows)* in relation to one another. The thickest concentration of dots occurs along those island arcs and continental coastlines where tectonic plates converge *(serrated lines)*. More moderate patterns occur where the plates pull apart, as in the midocean ridges and associated fracture zones.

Tremors of Creation in Midocean

THE TRIGGERING MECHANISM: SLIPPAGE ALONG A FAULT

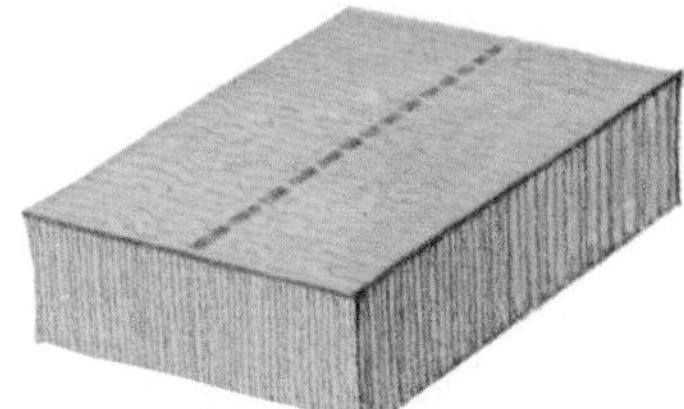

CRUSTAL BLOCKS AT REST

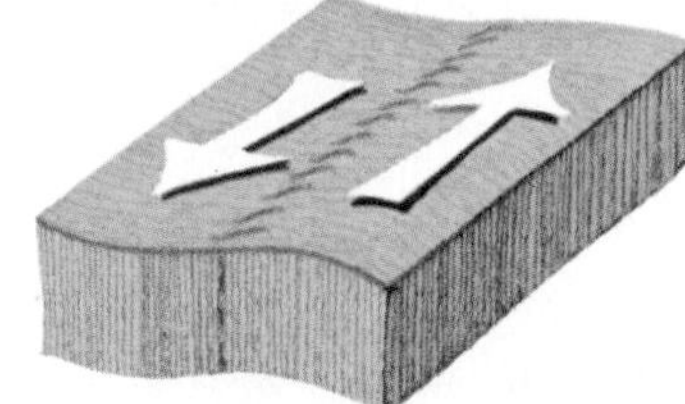

DEFORMATION DURING STRESS BUILD-UP

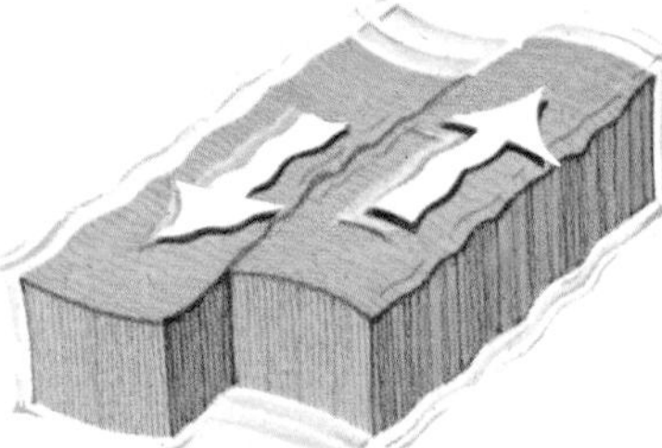

THE INSTANT OF RUPTURE

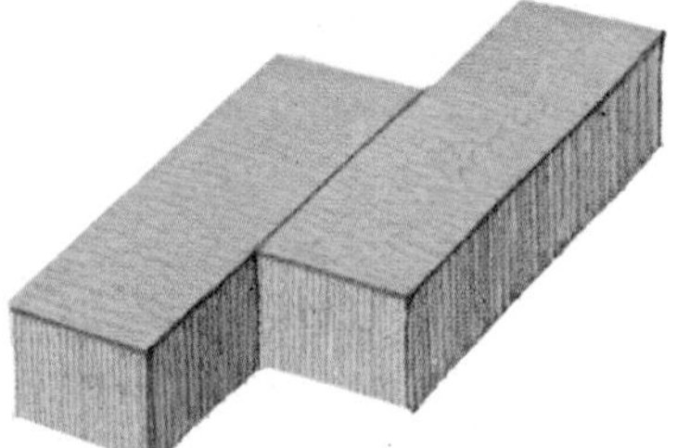

REBOUNDING TO A NEW EQUILIBRIUM

From the most insignificant tremor to the most catastrophic blockbuster, virtually all earthquakes are caused by the same phenomenon: the slippage of masses of rock along earth fractures called faults. This explanation, depicted above, was first developed by American seismologist Harry Fielding Reid after the 1906 San Francisco quake.

Reid based his conclusions on three geodetic surveys conducted in the San Francisco region over a 55-year period before and after the quake. The first two surveys showed Reid that roads, fences and streams crossing the San Andreas Fault zone had gradually bent. The third survey, just after the quake, indicated that the same roads, fences and streams had been dramatically offset—in some places by as much as 21 feet.

Reid realized that rocks possess elastic properties, and in time, along a fault, this elasticity allows rocks to accumulate strain energy. For years friction contains the strain and holds the rocks in place. But eventually, as in a rubber band stretched beyond its breaking point, strain overcomes frictional lock and the fault ruptures at its weakest point. Suddenly the pent-up energy is expended in the form of seismic waves—the earthquake—that radiate outward in all directions from the focus. The rupturing lasts from a fraction of a second for minor earthquakes to five minutes for a major one.

Reid coined the perfect name for his theory: "elastic rebound"—because of the way rocks spring back to a new equilibrium after the strain is released.

The creation of new ocean floor at remote midocean ridges is accompanied by almost continuous earthquake activity. But except by scientists, these earthquakes go largely unnoticed because they are of generally low magnitude and cause no harm to humans.

Along the jagged crests of the towering undersea ridges and up and down the steep sides of narrow canyons in between, hot viscous material called basaltic magma rises from the underlying asthenosphere. The magma relentlessly seeks out paths in the surrounding rock. Cooled by the ocean water, it solidifies as it rises and adheres to the sides of the ridge.

Thus, new ocean floor is constructed—with attendant quakes. As the fresh magma leaches into older faults and cracks, strain builds up in the surrounding rock until it is relieved by a moderate earthquake—or sometimes by swarms of micro-earthquakes in the top six miles of lithosphere. As the new sea floor inches away from both sides of the ridge toward a subduction zone at an ocean trench thousands of miles away, it continues to harden and grow heavier.

LITHOSPHERE

RISING MAGMA

This panoramic view of an oceanic plate shows basaltic magma rising through a funnel in the lithosphere to form new ocean floor and cause earthquakes in a narrow area along a midocean ridge. Hardening and solidifying, the new crust gradually creeps away from the ridge toward a subduction trench, where it is absorbed in the earth—a grand cycle estimated to take 200 to 300 million years to complete.

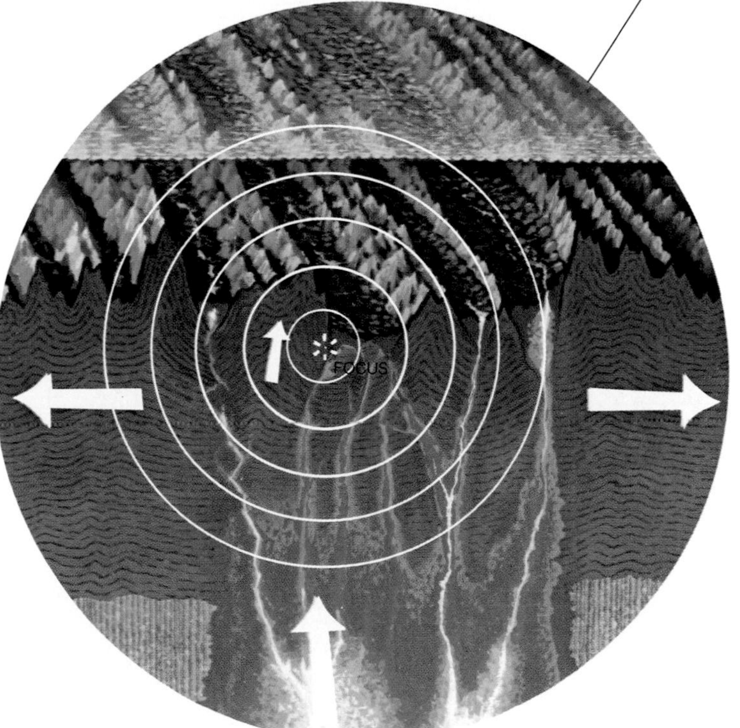

Thin sheets of magma, or dikes, percolate upward into cracks in the newly formed ocean floor along a jagged ocean ridge. As the thin rock on both sides of the ridge spreads laterally, tensional forces generated by the upwelling magma force a weak zone to fracture, triggering an earthquake.

Subduction Trenches: Scene of the Mightiest Quakes

LITHOSPHERE

ASTHENOSPHERE

Almost 90 per cent of the seismic energy released by tectonic plate movement comes from earthquakes in subduction zones, the deep ocean trenches lying off island arcs and continental coastlines where one tectonic plate plunges beneath another. As the cold, rigid slab of lithosphere descends into the asthenosphere, it endures enormous deforming stresses that keep it seismically alive to tremendous depths.

Most of the world's great earthquakes occur under the trench itself, where the oceanic plate grinds beneath the plate carrying the island or continent. These ruptures, generally no more than 30 miles deep, propagate upward, and often touch off other lower-magnitude tremors in a system of overlapping cracks in rock called imbricate faults.

As the slab sinks into the asthenosphere, it endures still further deformation in a remarkably well-defined seismic area called the Benioff zone, after one of its discoverers, American seismologist Hugo Benioff. Here, at depths of 70 to more than 400 miles, heat and compressional forces cause deep-focus earthquakes in the still-brittle slab.

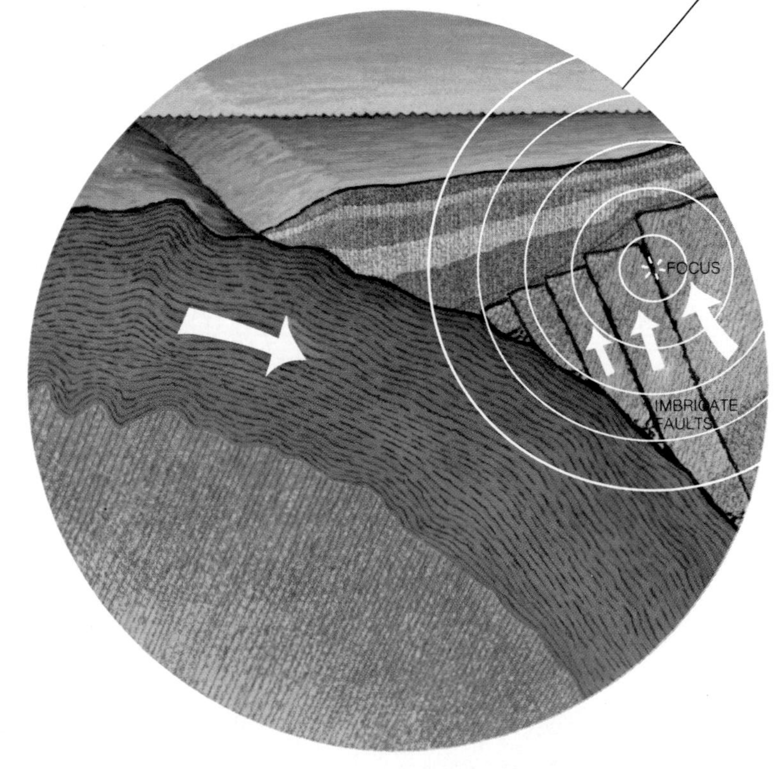

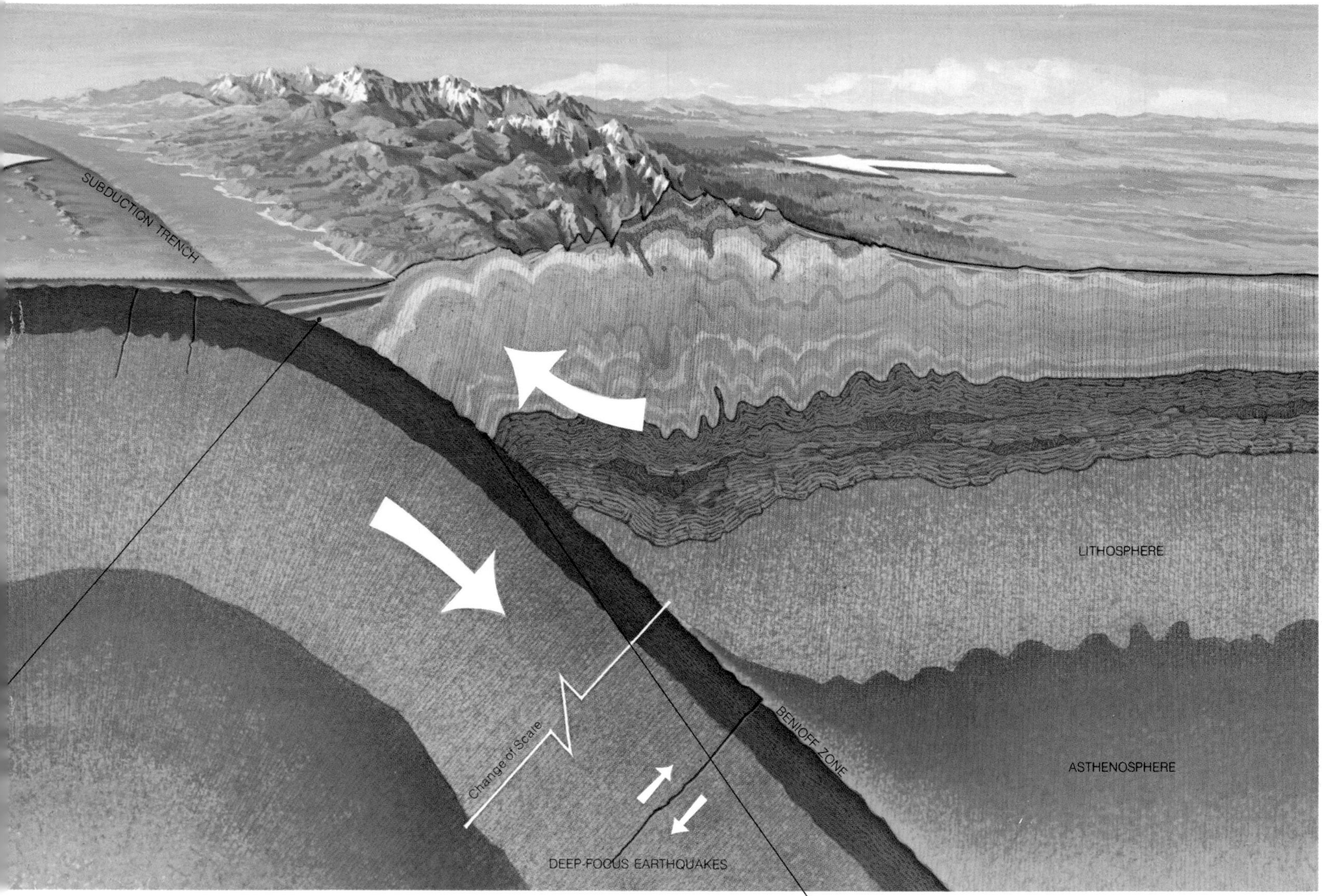

SUBDUCTION TRENCH

LITHOSPHERE

Change of Scale

BENIOFF ZONE

ASTHENOSPHERE

DEEP-FOCUS EARTHQUAKES

Bending into a deep ocean trench, an oceanic plate plunges beneath a converging continental plate toward the earth's interior, where it is consumed and recycled. This tectonic process, called subduction, accompanied by intense earthquake activity, is a journey that takes approximately seven million years.

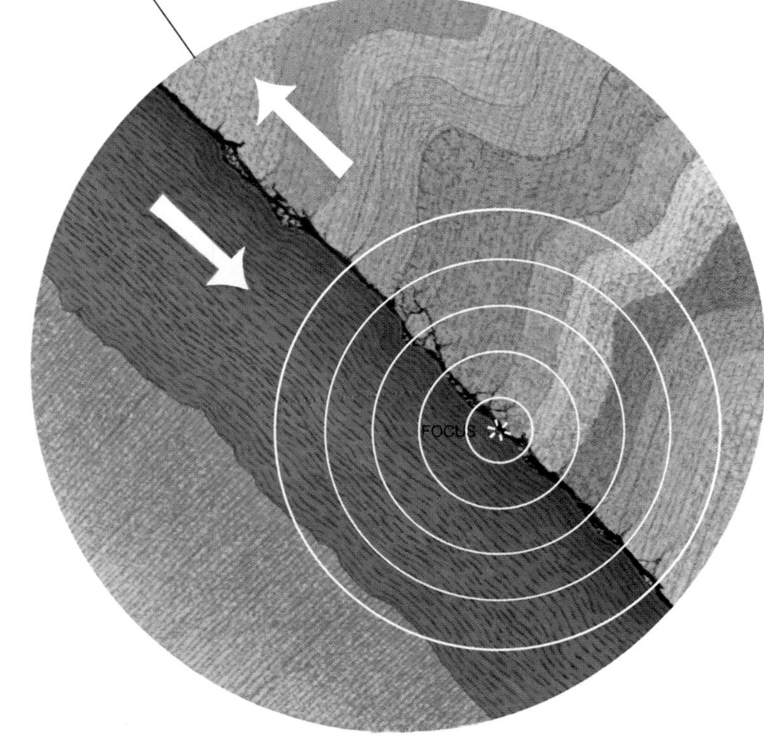

Above the subducting slab of lithosphere, earthquakes occur in imbricate faults—a complexity of weak, layered areas in the continental plate. These secondary earthquakes are a direct consequence of the major slips along the tectonic plate boundaries.

The bending and jamming of the converging plates generates tremendous stress along the plate boundaries beneath the trench, resulting in a major vertical slip and a correspondingly great earthquake. Ocean trench quakes have been recorded at 8.9 on the Richter scale and are among history's most awesome, heaving the sea floor sometimes by scores of feet.

Transform Faults: Nature's Giant Shears

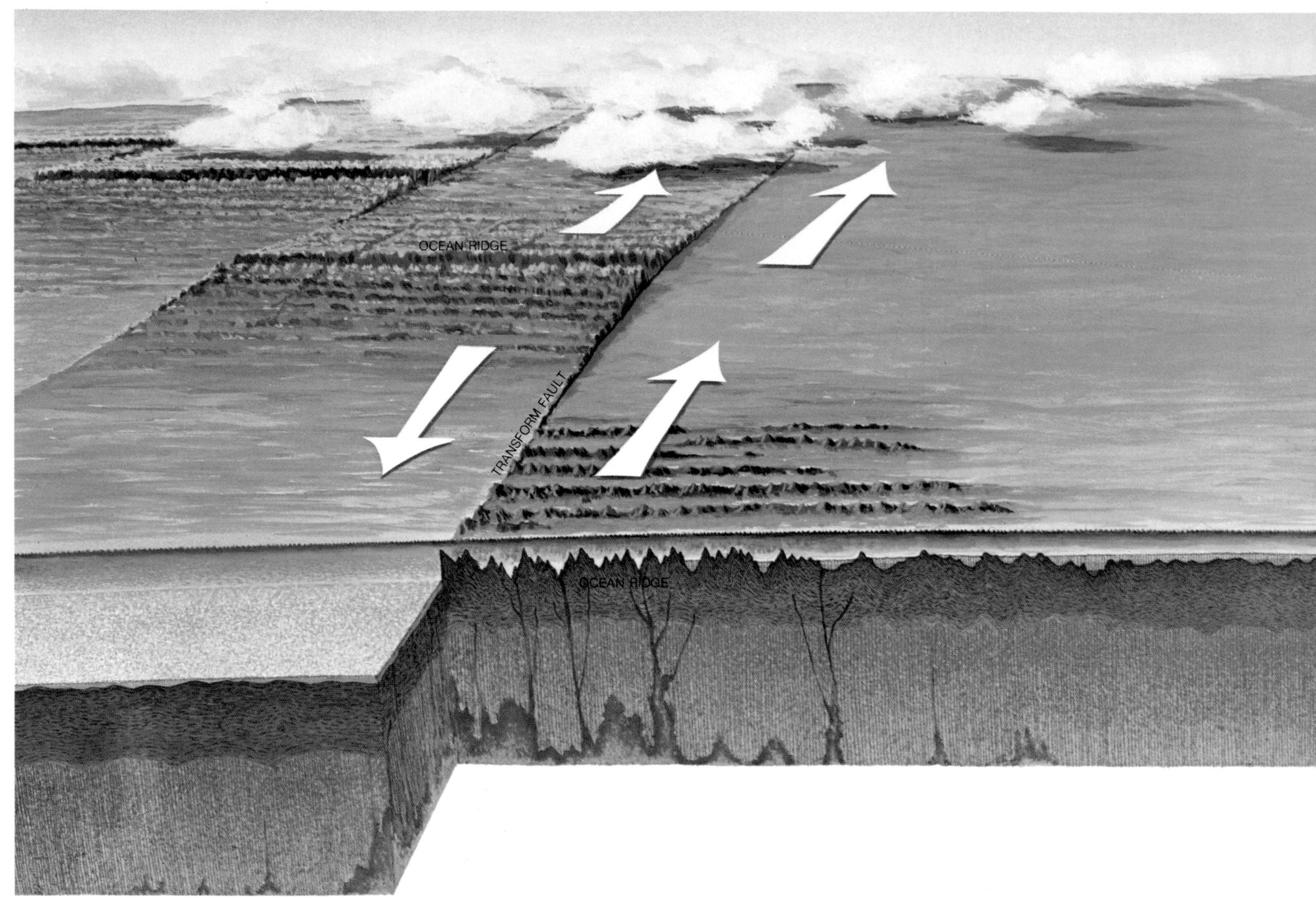

The ocean ridges where upwelling magma creates new ocean floor are frequently offset by zigzag patterns of faults, or fracture zones, at right angles to the crests. Scientists are not sure what forces caused these zigzags in the otherwise linear undersea mountain ranges. But they do know them as the sites of numerous submarine earthquakes.

Because new ocean floor spreads out from both sides of an ocean ridge, a shear effect is created in any deformed, or fractured, area where one segment of the floor is moving in a direction opposite to the adjacent section. A similar earthquake-producing shear occurs when two great tectonic plates are sliding past each other, as in California and parts of South America and Turkey.

The scientist who first focused attention on these linking, seismically active areas, Canadian geophysicist Tuzo Wilson, called them "transform faults" because the fault line suddenly stops or changes direction. The earthquakes associated with them are generally shallow, occurring in the top 10 miles of lithosphere, and are usually less powerful than subduction trench tremors.

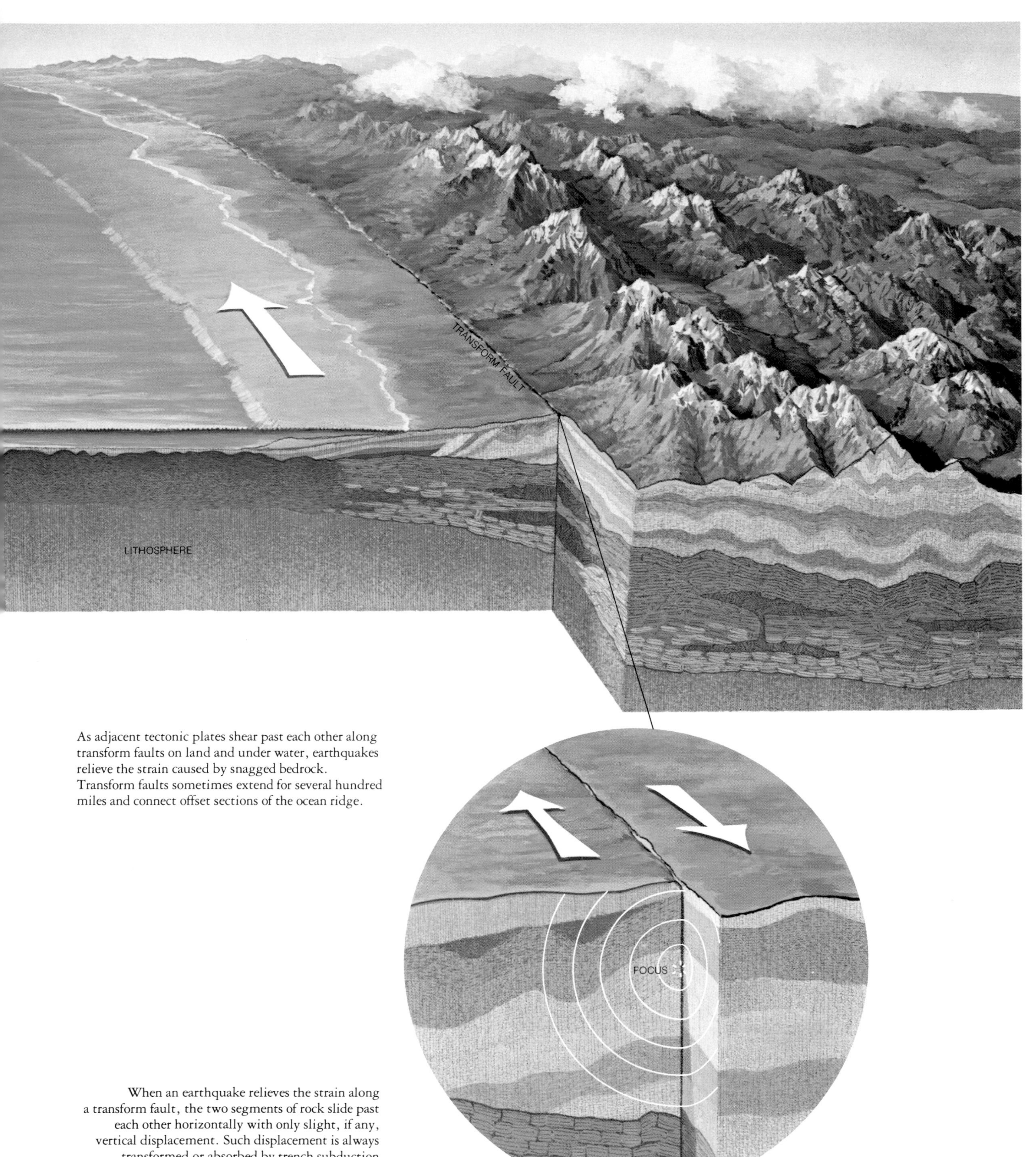

As adjacent tectonic plates shear past each other along transform faults on land and under water, earthquakes relieve the strain caused by snagged bedrock. Transform faults sometimes extend for several hundred miles and connect offset sections of the ocean ridge.

When an earthquake relieves the strain along a transform fault, the two segments of rock slide past each other horizontally with only slight, if any, vertical displacement. Such displacement is always transformed or absorbed by trench subduction and sea-floor growth—important facts that persuaded scientists to accept the theory of plate tectonics.

Reverberations from Colliding Continents

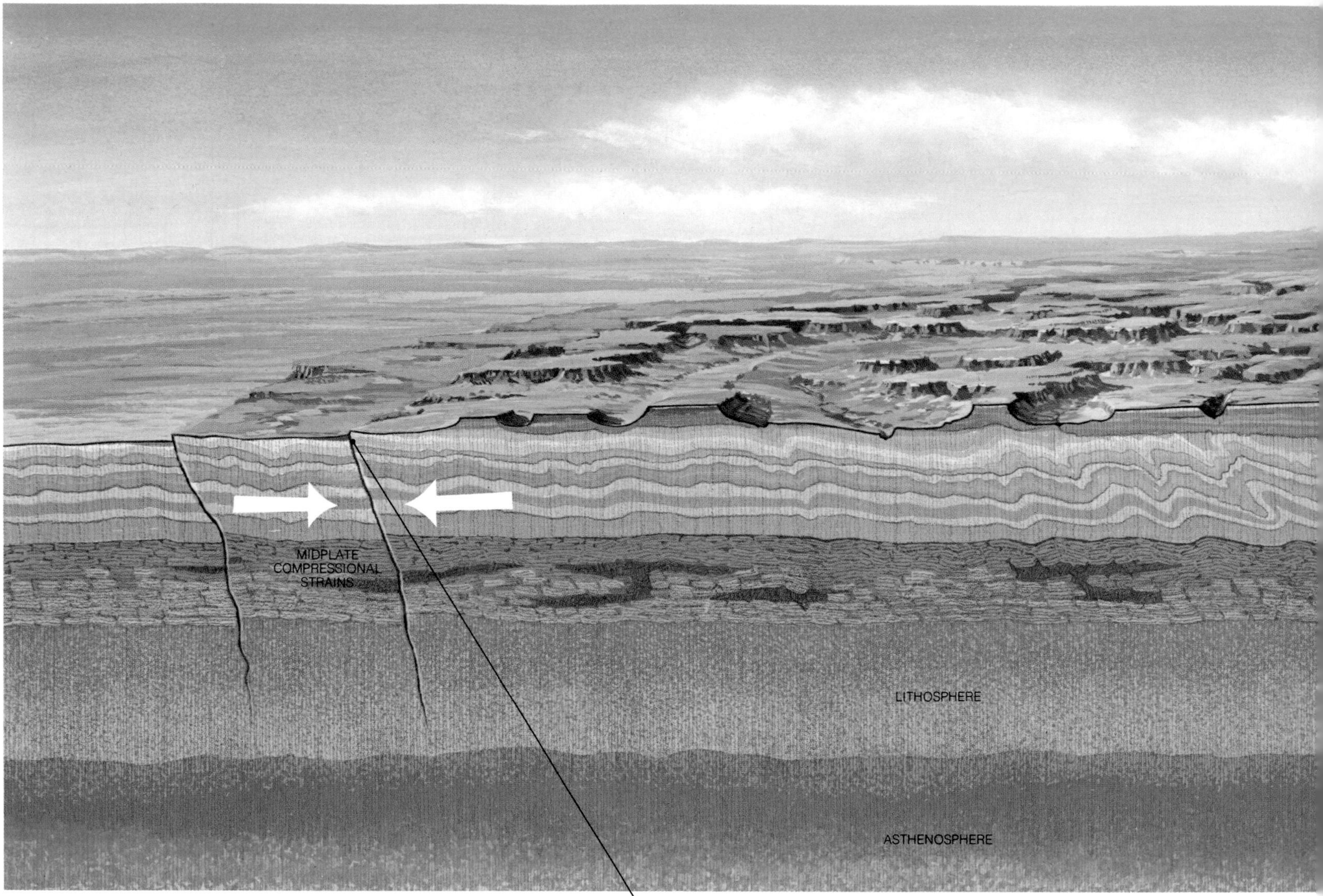

When tectonic plates carrying continents converge, there is no subduction process such as occurs at the ocean trenches. Instead, the plates simply smash together head on—and fold up like an accordion. This dramatic process has created some of the world's mightiest mountain ranges, the Alps and the Himalayas, as well as vast tracts of radically disarranged, seismically active land.

Such areas include Italy, Yugoslavia and Rumania, and parts of Turkey and Iran where the plate bearing Africa plows into the Eurasian Plate. But the most awesome example of collision earthquakes is on the Asian subcontinent, where the Indo-Australian Plate ponderously invades the Eurasian Plate at a speed of two inches a year—a process that has been continuing for 40 million years and that has generated earthquakes throughout Asia.

Collision earthquakes most often occur in the top 16 miles of lithosphere, generally near plate borders. But the enormous compressional effects are far-reaching, and huge faults torture the earth thousands of miles from the plate borders.

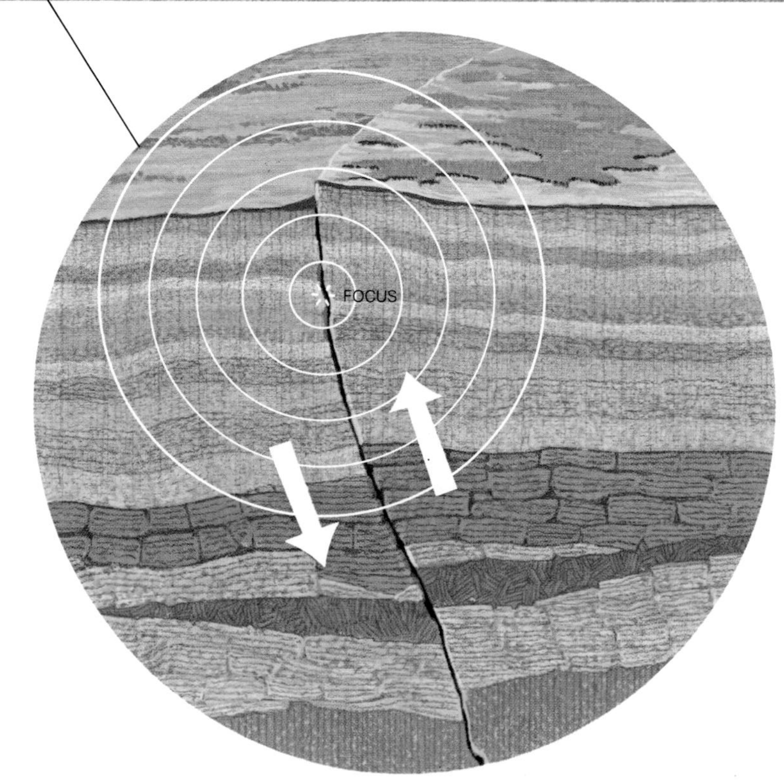

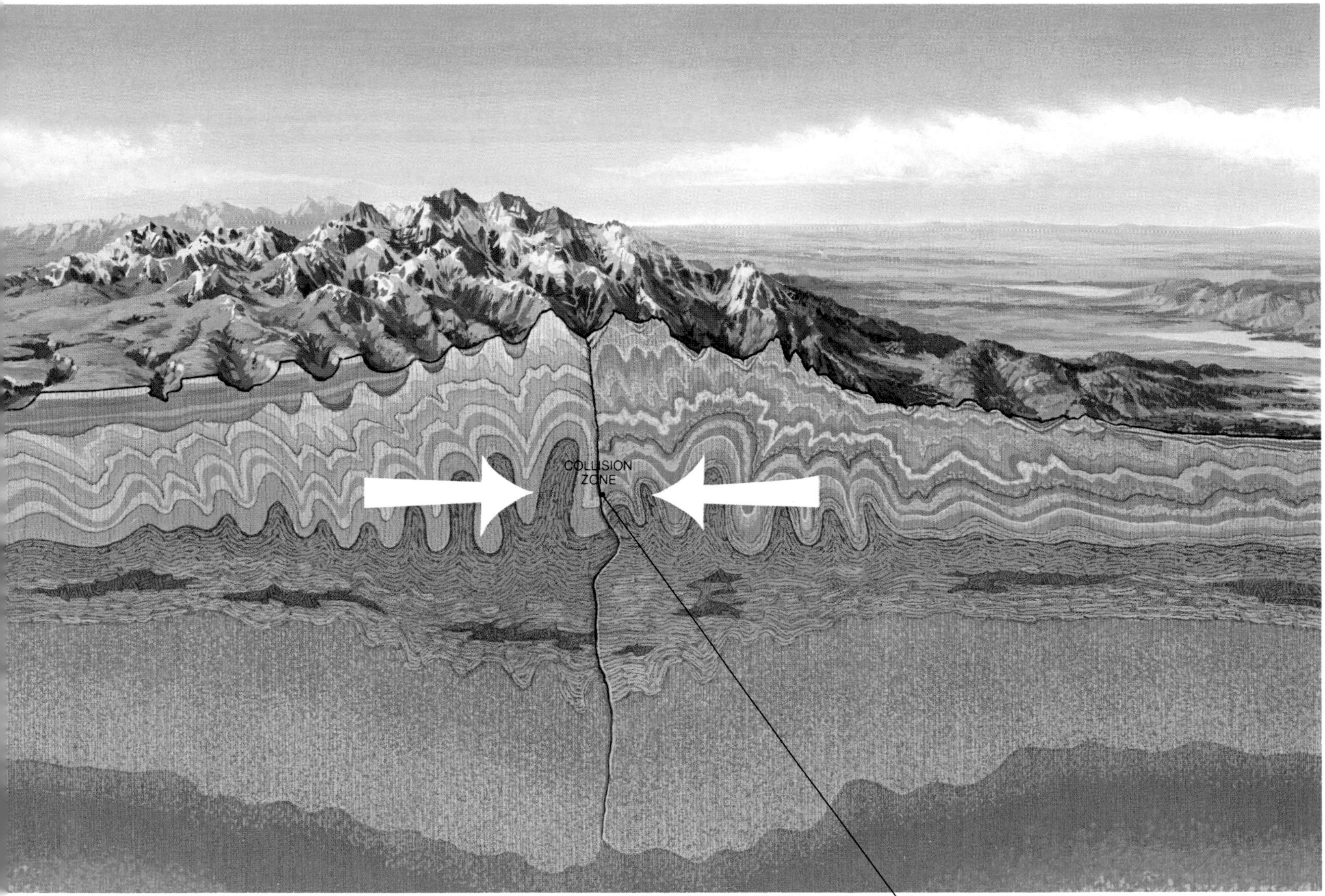

COLLISION ZONE

Continental plates crunching together compress and distort the lithosphere's upper layers, creating mountains and triggering earthquakes near plate borders and beyond. Over eons of time, segments of the plates will suture together because the 20-mile-thick and relatively diffuse continental crust is too buoyant to sink into the earth's mantle.

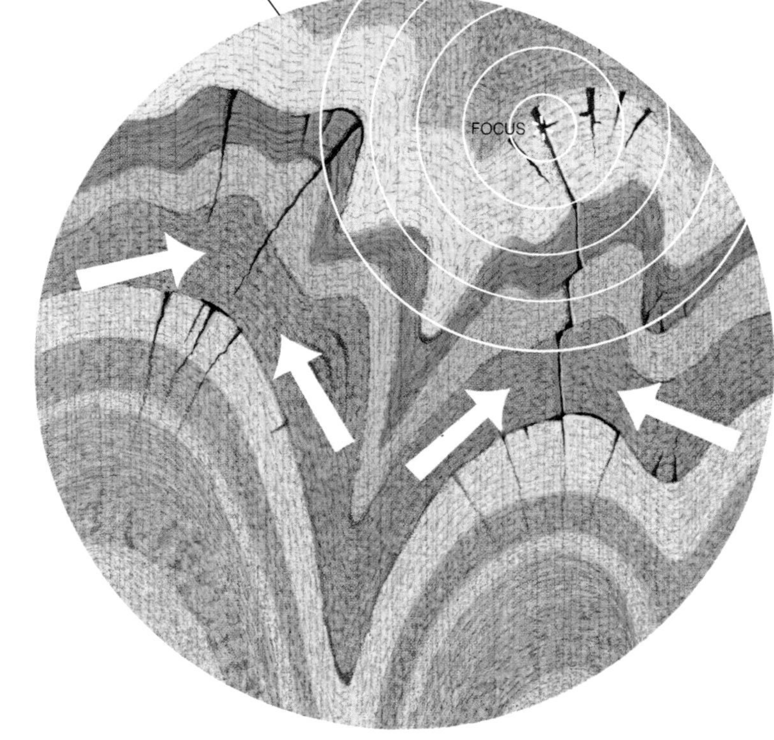

In a weak zone in the middle of a colliding plate, backup pressure snaps rock, causing an earthquake. In these tremors, one side of the fault may drive over the other side *(as shown)* or slide horizontally past, depending upon the direction of the stress.

Tremendous compressional force near the top of the lithosphere ruptures a section of tortured, twisted rock near the front end of colliding tectonic plates. These slips have both vertical and horizontal movement and can cause major earthquakes.

Chapter 4

A VICTORY FOR THE VISIONARIES

"We are like a judge confronted by a defendant who declines to answer, and we must determine the truth from the circumstantial evidence." For the German meteorologist Alfred Wegener, soon to become a prophet of modern earth science, the defendant was the planet itself. And the truth he sought in the first decades of the 20th Century was elemental—the underlying secrets of earth mechanics, what forces shaped the continents and oceans, what made mountains and volcanoes, what caused the earth to rupture and shake.

Gathering circumstantial evidence from several disciplines of science—including biology, climatology, geology and seismology—Wegener in 1915 published a vision of the planet that flew directly in the face of convention. For decades, the firm consensus among earth scientists had been that the surface of the globe was a static skin over a molten, gradually cooling interior. As it cooled, they believed, the globe contracted and the outer surface became contorted, wrinkling into mountains and valleys like a drying apple, occasionally shearing, collapsing and settling in violent earthquakes. It was held as fact that the major features of the earth—the oceans and continents—remained as they had been formed, except for the distortions of the shrinking process.

Now came Wegener with a long list of observations and questions that could not be explained or answered by the accepted theories. If mountains were formed by the contraction of a cooling planet, said Wegener, they would be scattered more or less uniformly over the surface of the earth, but in fact they were concentrated in narrow bands that suggested an altogether different process. Wegener noticed, as others had, the remarkably close fit of the east coast of South America when juxtaposed, on a map, with the west coast of Africa; but, unlike others, he could not accept it as a curious coincidence. Wegener collected evidence of close parallels in the geological and biological history of the two coastal areas, and asked a question unanswerable in terms of then-current geological belief: How did the same life forms come to be living on similar rock formations on two coasts separated by thousands of miles of ocean?

In 1912 Wegener postulated his answer in the form of a theory of "continental drift." The earth's surface was not static, he proclaimed, but dynamic. The continents and oceans were in constant motion relative to one another. Wegener argued that the continents had once been joined in a single great land mass, a mammoth island in a world of water. But then, in eons past, this super-island had somehow split into fragments that wandered the face of the globe like so many icebergs drifting in the sea.

Wegener's striking hypothesis was greeted with hoots of derision from the scientific community. A colleague sneered that Wegener's methodology con-

La Soufrière volcano puffs ominously as a quake shatters the Caribbean island of Guadeloupe in this contemporary engraving of the calamity that took 5,000 lives in 1843. Volcanic activity and earthquakes frequently accompany each other; in this case, the quake may have agitated the volcano's underground magma chambers and opened a path to the surface.

sisted of "an initial idea, a selective search through the literature for corroborative evidence, ignoring most of the facts that are opposed to the idea, and ending in a state of auto-intoxication in which the subjective idea comes to be considered as an objective fact."

There was a certain amount of truth to the charge. Wegener's evidence was, in fact, extremely thin, and not much of a springboard from which to leap to such mind-boggling conclusions. Yet in the decades ahead, earth scientists would come to acknowledge Wegener's prophetic vision, at first grudgingly, then enthusiastically. And they would find that much of the evidence that was transforming their science revolved around the study of earthquakes.

Although German scientist Alfred Wegener is remembered for his theory of continental drift, in his own lifetime this weather-beaten, gimlet-eyed eccentric was equally renowned for other scientific interests. He trained as an astronomer, wrote textbooks on meteorology and geophysics and led three expeditions to explore the Greenland icecap, whose barren wastes eventually claimed his life.

The first seismological data supporting a radical new view of global mechanics came to light in the 1930s, as scientists began taking a close look at earthquakes along the rim of the Pacific Ocean. Immediately seaward of the island chains off the east coast of Asia lies a series of enormous ocean trenches, the deepest depressions in the earth's crust. Earth scientists had been aware of these chasms for many years, though they did not yet have the means to plumb the full extent of their depths—which would later be found to reach an astonishing 36,000 feet near the Marianas Islands. The chasms and their associated island arcs mark the seaward edge of the great circum-Pacific earthquake belt.

One of the first to explore this remarkable convergence of geological detail and seismic activity was a young Japanese seismologist named Kiyoo Wadati. After graduating from the University of Tokyo in 1925 with a degree in physics, Wadati had joined the Central Meteorological Observatory to analyze the data from its seismograph network. He began plotting the exact locations of earthquake foci in the Japanese archipelago, and discovered that the closer to the Asian continent the earthquakes occurred, the deeper their focus. In the seabed near the Japan Trench the earth would rupture only a few miles down. But to the west, the depth of focus progressively and dramatically increased—50 to 150 miles beneath the islands themselves, 300 miles under the Sea of Japan, a remarkable 400 miles beneath the coast of Manchuria, about 600 miles from the Japan Trench. The earthquakes inclined downward from the trench toward the Asian continent at angles of between 35 and 60 degrees.

According to prevailing theories, at the depths and pressures of the deepest earthquakes the substance of the mantle was not supposed to be brittle enough to fracture. If the crust was a thin surface over a molten interior, as was assumed, stress applied to the liquefied material beneath the crust should cause it to flow, not snap. Yet here was evidence to the contrary, with seismic shocks originating deep inside the earth's dense mantle, almost a tenth of the way to the center of the planet.

In the late 1940s, Hugo Benioff—the same man who had refined the design of seismographs at Caltech—began studying tremors along the Pacific coast of South America, where another deep trench creases 2,800 miles of seabed from Ecuador south to Chile. He found the same inclined focal plane as had Wadati, this time slanting eastward, under the South American continent. And when Benioff investigated the earthquake foci of the Tonga Trench, between New Zealand and Samoa, he found the identical pattern—an inclined plane cutting under the Tonga Islands and west toward Fiji at a 60-degree angle. As other ocean trenches came under scrutiny, it became apparent that all along the Pacific rim there were massive zones of earthquake activity, larger than anyone had imagined, angling downward into the mantle of the earth.

In 1954, Benioff presented his findings in a landmark paper in which he suggested that enormous sections of ocean floor were thrusting downward beneath the adjacent land. The force of this "subduction," as it later came to be known, was not only causing earthquakes but was also sparking the volcanoes that dot the Pacific island arcs. Benioff found no evidence of subduction along the coast of California and British Columbia, but he thought it had probably taken place there sometime in the distant past. His findings, he said in a notable understatement, were "at variance with those older concepts" that were based on the idea of a static earth.

While everyone agreed something important was happening to the ocean floor along these so-called Benioff zones, many respected seismologists could not immediately accept Benioff's explanation of what it was. To argue that the seabed was being driven downward into the mantle seemed boldly premature; Benioff's critics pointed out that he had not explained the source of the massive amounts of energy needed to propel it. Moreover, while he had announced that the earth's crust was being gobbled up as it descended into the trenches, he had not suggested what was replacing it—as something surely must be replacing it, since the surface of the planet was still entirely covered by crust.

The answers began to emerge from seismic studies of the seabed itself, commencing in the mid-1950s. Columbia University had just set up its Lamont Geological Observatory, and in 1953 its first director, marine geophysicist Maurice Ewing, had converted an old three-masted sailing schooner, the *Vema,* into a research vessel. He had fitted her out with sounding equipment, seismometers and other gear for examining the ocean bottom. And for the next 20 years, the *Vema* crisscrossed the North and South Atlantic on voyages of discovery that eventually covered nearly half a million miles.

Along the way her crew of researchers bounced man-made seismic waves off the sea floor—first by dropping makeshift TNT bombs over the side and later with a sound-wave generator towed behind the vessel. Analysis of the results revealed not only the contours of the seabed but the nature of its composition to a depth of several miles. As they studied the refractions and changes in velocities of the seismic waves, the scientists slowly accumulated the first detailed picture of the earth's crust beneath the oceans. It was an astonishing view. "You can't imagine how primitive our knowledge was," said Bruce Heezen, then a graduate student on the *Vema* expedition. "Just the problem of what was there on the bottom occupied us completely. We were in a state so primitive that other scientists couldn't even understand how this could be science."

The first surprise concerned the sediment on the ocean floor. It was nowhere near as thick as the Lamont researchers expected it to be. Given the eons during which sea organisms had been depositing their skeletal remains and the continents had been eroding seaward, the sediment was expected to be enormously thick, but it was relatively thin, averaging less than a mile. The sediment was thickest near the continents, and grew progressively thinner toward midocean, where a long, steep ridge rose from the abyssal plain. Portions of this great underwater mountain chain had appeared on nautical charts for many years, but until the voyage of the *Vema,* augmented by similar missions carried out by other research vessels, no one had suspected the ridge's vast extent, its imposing heights—or its central role in the global mechanics of earthquakes.

The mid-Atlantic Ridge, as profiled by the *Vema* scientists, resembled no mountain range on earth. They had found a monumental crest bisecting the Atlantic Ocean from the Arctic nearly to the Antarctic, its path almost exactly midway between the continents on either side. Unlike the Alps and the Rockies, which consisted mostly of limestone, shale and granite, the ridge was composed of basalt—hardened lava. Its escarpments rose in sharp, rugged increments, jutting like a staircase thousands of feet above the ocean floor.

Strangest of all, in the middle of the ridge, instead of a peak there was a huge crevasse—a rift eight to 30 miles wide and deeper than Arizona's Grand Canyon, running the full length of the ridge. In many places the ridge itself was cut at right angles by precipitous chasms. And in a number of places it was sharply offset—coming to an abrupt end at a bisecting chasm, then resuming its course just as suddenly many miles to the left or right.

There was very little sediment on the ocean floor near the ridge, and some of the Lamont researchers took this as evidence that the sea floor was somehow moving away from the ridge. Such movement, they said, would explain why the sediment was so thin near the ridge, where the floor was youngest, and thicker at greater distances. It would also explain why there was generally less sediment on the sea floor than previously believed; much of it had been carried away, as if on a conveyor belt, by the moving floor. The questions of where it was carried and what happened to it remained unanswered for the moment.

While the *Vema* plied the seas, other Lamont researchers were recording and studying seismograms of earthquakes beneath the Atlantic, painstakingly calculating distances and directions in order to pinpoint their epicenters. The researchers found another unexpected pattern—almost every quake was located along a narrow band that coincided exactly with the mid-Atlantic Ridge. The tremors were occurring either in the great central crevasse or in the chasms that crossed the ridge at right angles, which the scientists concluded must be fault lines. When the Lamont team went on to explore midocean ridges of the Pacific and Indian Oceans they discovered the same features—basalt escarpments climbing up from the seabed to a canyon at the top, which was continually shaken by shallow-focus earthquakes.

A picture started to take shape that increasingly meshed with Wadati's and Benioff's studies of trenches and island arcs. The great earthquake belt that fringed the Pacific coincided with the Benioff zones, areas where the ocean bed was thrusting down under the continent. The Lamont researchers, in the course of charting the midocean ridges, had discovered a corresponding belt where it appeared that the seabed was spreading outward toward the subduction zones. The irresistible conclusion was that both were part of the same global movement, in which the earth's crust was continuously regenerating itself, welling up at the center of the midocean ridges, gliding outward, then disappearing into the deep ocean trenches—and in the process generating 95 per cent of the world's earthquakes.

Here was powerful evidence in support of Wegener's theory of drifting continents. If the earth's crust was in motion, then the idea of moving continents no longer seemed ludicrous. The new information did not support Wegener's view that the continents were somehow barging through the crust, but it did suggest that they formed part of a system in motion. However, the evidence was still far too incomplete to win general acceptance from the scientific community. As logical and consistent as the idea might appear when stated in its broad, sweeping terms, the task of proving its scientific validity was a daunting one. Indeed, an early statement of the theory was termed by its author, Harry H. Hess, to be an exercise in "geopoetry"—in wry acknowledgment of the fact that at first there was more intuition in the theory than hard scientific evidence.

But the utility of the new view became increasingly apparent as more evidence accumulated. In the early 1960s, two studies—one theoretical, the other practical—gave the hypothesis a critical nudge across the line separating blue-sky speculation from respectable consensus. Both studies concerned the quakes that occurred in the faults that crossed and offset the midocean ridges.

In 1962 Lynn Sykes, a graduate student working for the Lamont Geological Observatory, was plotting the epicenters of earthquakes along the section of the midocean ridge off Central and South America that is known as the East Pacific Rise. He found that tremors did not occur in all the faults that bisected the oceanic ridge, but were confined to faults where the ridge was broken and offset. What is more, the quakes did not occur along the entire width of these faults; rather they were concentrated in that portion of each fault lying between the offset ridges. The faults themselves extended outward for distances of up to 600 miles from either side of the ridges, but earthquakes rarely struck outside the ridges—only between them.

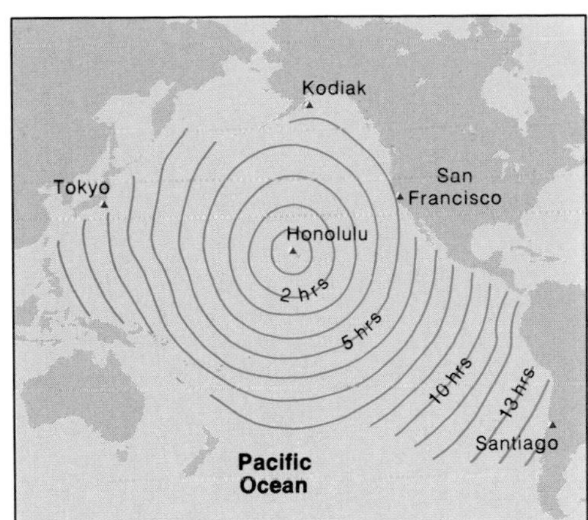

Focusing inward like the strands of a giant spiderweb, the lines on this tsunami warning map show the computer-calculated travel times to Hawaii of seismic sea waves generated at various places around the rim of the Pacific Ocean. A wave originating at Santiago, Chile, for example, would hit Hawaii in 15 hours.

The killer sea waves known as tsunamis are so quiet in their approach from afar, so seemingly harmless, that until recently their history has been one of surprise attack.

Out in the middle of the ocean, the distance between tsunami wave crests can be 100 miles and the height of the waves no more than three feet: Mariners can ride one and suspect nothing. At the shoreline, the first sign is often an ebbing of the waters that leaves fish stranded and slapping on the bottom. But anyone foolish enough to rush forward to garner an easy dinner will not live to enjoy it. For this is not a retreat but rather a gathering of forces. When the great waves finally do strike, the demons within are revealed, and they rear up and batter harbor and coast as if all the ocean were hell-bent on swallowing the land.

These seismic sea waves—or tidal waves, as they are sometimes called—bear no relation to the moon or tides. And the word "tsunami," Japanese for "harbor wave," relates to their destination rather than their origin. The causes are various: undersea or coastal earthquakes, deep ocean avalanches or volcanism. Whatever the cause, the wave motion starts with a sudden jolt like a whack from a giant paddle that displaces the water. And the greater the undersea whack, the greater the tsunami's devastating power.

In 1883, Krakatoa volcano in the East Indies erupted, and the entire island collapsed in 820 feet of water. A tsunami of tremendous force ricocheted around Java and Sumatra, killing 36,000 people with walls of water that reached 115 feet in height. In 1896 on the eastern coast of Japan 82- to 115-foot-high waves smashed more than 100,000 homes and drowned 26,000 people.

In 1946 at Unimak Island, near Alaska, a magnitude 7.2 earthquake set in motion a seismic sea wave great enough to wipe out not only Scotch Cap Lighthouse and five men inside—32 feet above sea level—but also the radio antenna perched at 103 feet. The wave then bounded 2,300 miles to the Hawaiian Islands, where without warning it killed 159 people and inflicted millions of dollars of damage *(overleaf)*.

Today, the Hawaiians and other Pacific peoples can be warned. The 1946 tsunami led to the creation of the Tsunami Warning System, whose nerve center in Honolulu keeps a round-the-clock vigil with the aid of computers, teletypewriters and communications satellites. When there is a tsunami threat, wave arrival times to Honolulu are computed and a tsunami watch is issued. An ocean-wide network of sensitive tide gauges provides additional data.

If seismic sea waves are confirmed by the Honolulu center, warnings are transmitted within a few hours to all threatened Pacific points. While tsunami damage remains unavoidable, lives lost today are more likely to be in the tens than in the thousands. Tsunamis have been deprived of their most deadly sting—surprise.

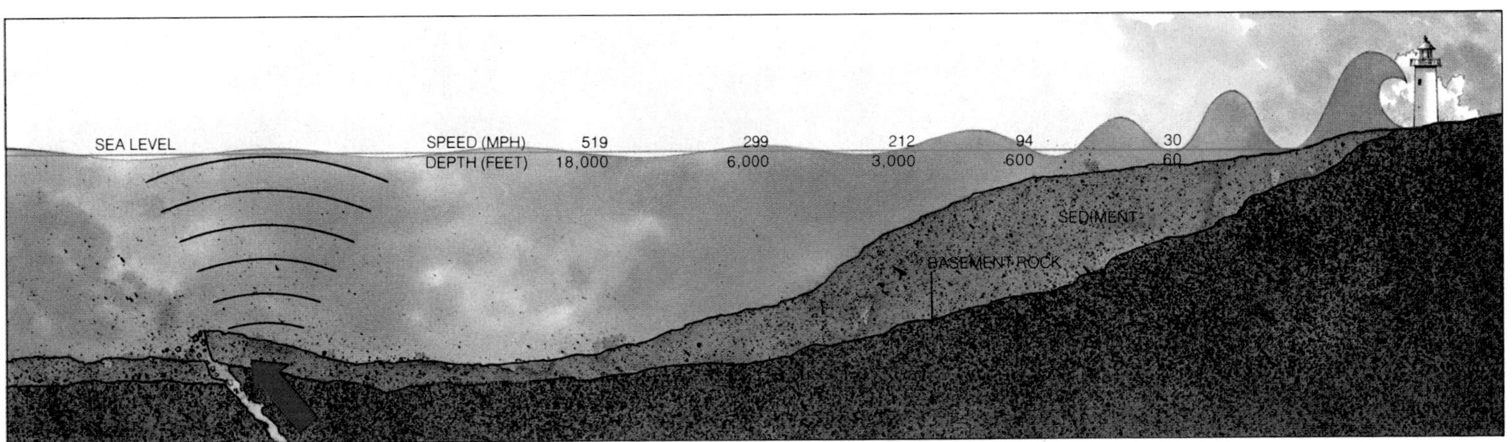

Tsunami prediction uses a principle of hydrodynamics that correlates the speed of a wave column with the square root of the ocean depth at any given point. Thus, as shown in the diagram below, a wave in 18,000 feet of water will travel 519 mph, with speed gradually slowing to 30 mph in 60 feet of water. Decreasing depth has a braking effect on the bottom of the wave column, but the top continues to push forward, bunching higher and higher until it topples with tremendous force on the shore.

Alone with his destiny, a man stands transfixed before a world of water about to engulf him at Hilo, Hawaii, on April 1, 1946. This tsunami, which originated in the Aleutian Islands near Alaska, was still powerful enough when it hit Hawaii to rise 30 to 55 feet, and it continued to hammer at the islands for more than two hours. The S.S. *Brigham Victory,* from which this photograph was taken, managed to survive the onslaught, but 159 people in Hawaii, including the man seen here, were killed.

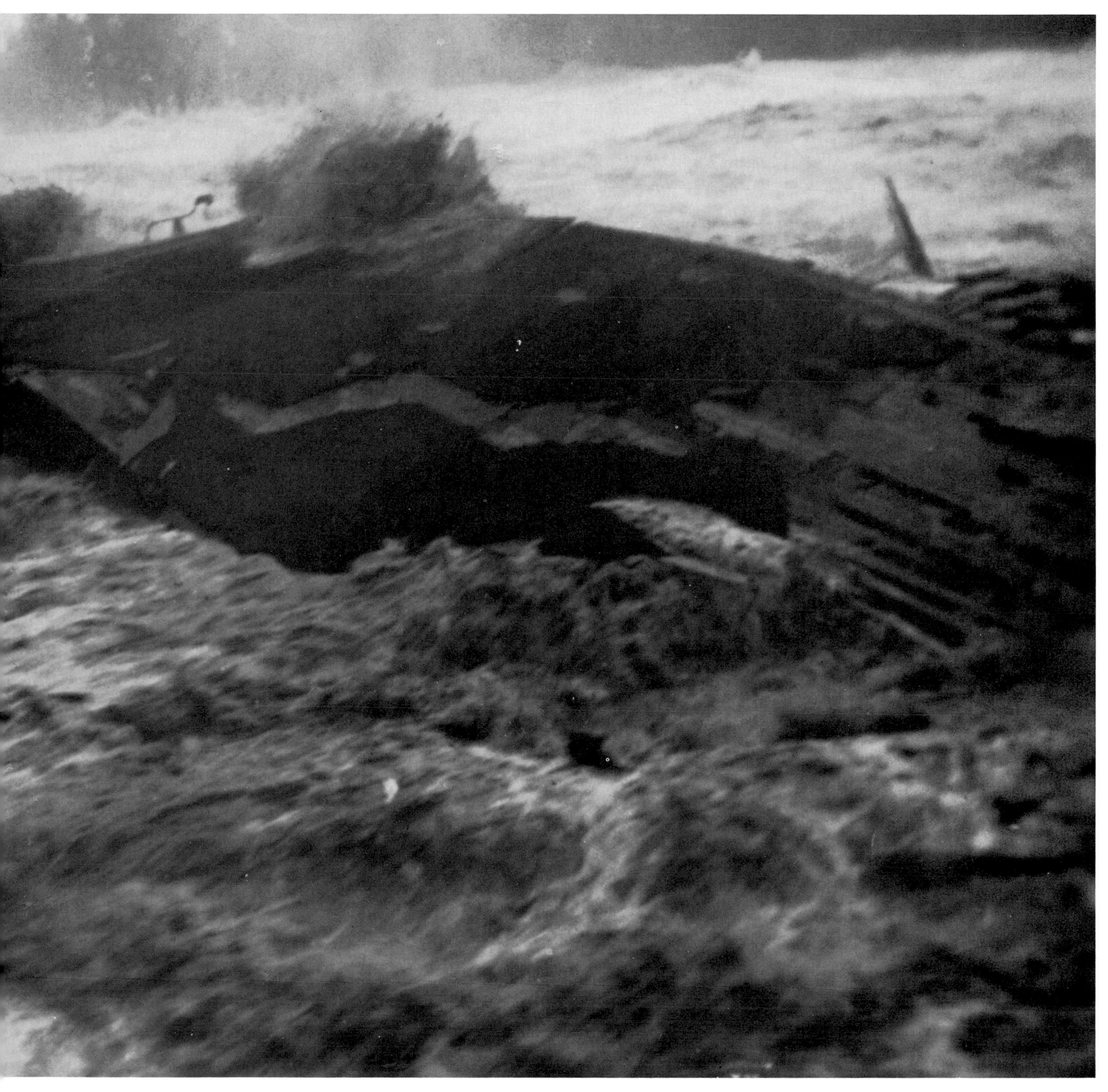

A Canadian geophysicist, Tuzo Wilson, was studying the concept of sea-floor spreading at the time and saw in Sykes's evidence a possible confirmation of the hypothesis. If it was true that the ocean bed was moving outward from the ridges, then along the faults between two sections of offset ridge, Wilson deduced, the basalt would be moving in opposite directions, grinding and straining at the fault line and occasionally fracturing in an earthquake. But outside the offset ridges, he reasoned, the floor on each side of the fault would be moving in the same direction at the same pace, thus producing no strain at the fault line *(pages 98-99)*. Because what he was describing was a transformation of forces and their directions along the fault line, Wilson called these areas transform faults. "Proof of their existence," he concluded, "would go far toward establishing the reality of continental drift and showing the nature of the displacements involved."

For his part, Sykes continued at Lamont, using the newly available facilities of the World Wide Standardized Seismograph Network to gather more detailed seismic records on the East Pacific Rise and on similar ridge formations in the mid-Atlantic and the Gulf of Aden. He analyzed the seismograms for the direction of movement along the fault lines and found that the sea floor was moving exactly as Wilson had suggested. "The deduced mechanisms and the distribution of earthquakes," wrote Sykes, "both seem to demand a process of seafloor growth at or near the crest of the mid-ocean ridge system."

Throughout the earth sciences, similar bits of evidence were pointing to the validity of the emerging theory. Oceanographers took core samples from the ocean floor that confirmed one prediction based on the theory of sea-floor spreading—the crust was younger at the ocean ridges, more ancient toward the subduction zones. Precise measurements of changes in the force of gravity along ocean ridges and trenches yielded figures that were consistent with the concept of dense basalt welling up at the ridges and descending at the trenches. Careful records of the temperature of the crust at subduction zones and midocean ridges showed that hot material was rising from beneath the ocean ridges and colder material was descending at the subduction zones. Detailed evidence of anomalies in the magnetic polarity of broad bands of the ocean floors enabled scientists to construct a precise history of the varying rates of sea-floor spreading. And scores of other findings in many fields were emphasizing the inadequacy of the traditional theories of earth mechanics.

The bastions of the establishment's static-earth position tottered dramatically in 1966 and crumbled utterly in 1967 at a series of scientific meetings in the United States. Although the revolution had been announced by the German meteorologist Wegener, it was fought largely on British and American ground after the Second World War because of the undertakings of such institutions as the Lamont Geological Observatory, the U.S. Geological Survey and Britain's Cambridge University. The critical round of engagements began in November of 1966 with a symposium on the earth's crust held at the Goddard Institute for Space Studies in New York City, and continued in April 1967 with the annual meeting in Washington, D.C., of the American Geophysical Union. Both groups were jolted by the impact of dozens of papers, the results of independent lines of research, that pointed in the same new direction. Among the most exciting was Lynn Sykes's evidence, presented for the first time at the 1967 meeting, supporting the concepts of transform faults and sea-floor spreading.

What caused an even greater furor was a radically different explanation of the transition zone between the earth's crust and the mantle below. One major objection to Wegener's theory of continental drift had been a matter of simple mechanics: In the rigid, compact body that the earth was assumed to be, it simply was not possible for the surface to slide. Everything that was known about earth structure seemed to deny even the possibility of massive, horizontal contortions that would permit the continents to shoulder their way through thousands of miles of solid earth.

But now seismologists theorized that an area of transition within the mantle might not be so solid, indeed might be fluid enough for great plates, or sections of crust, to move about somewhat as Wegener had suggested. They based their idea on a new interpretation of the phenomenon discovered by Beno Gutenberg more than 50 years before. From his studies of seismic wave behavior, Gutenberg had discovered what came to be known as the Gutenberg Discontinuity, beginning about 90 miles beneath the surface, a region where seismic waves lost velocity—indicating that there the rock was less rigid. He had carried the discovery no further.

But now as seismologists worldwide searched for ways to explain subduction zones and sea-floor spreading, they believed that they had found at least a partial answer in Gutenberg's low-velocity layer. The rock in this region may not actually be fluid, they concluded, but the seismic evidence indicated that it did become softer, like a chunk of iron in a blacksmith's forge. Under the right conditions of heat and pressure, it might be soft enough to allow the plates of the earth's crust to edge along very slowly, carrying the continents with them. This was the major departure from Wegener's theory—he had thought that the continents moved through the crust instead of with it.

As few gatherings had been in the annals of science, the 1967 meeting of the Geophysical Union was a turning point in earth studies. Nearly 70 papers were presented on the subject of sea-floor spreading—many of them submitted by skeptics who had been spurred to a review of their data in order to refute the new global mechanics, only to find confirmation instead. Others, like George Plafker, of Alaska repute, were already in the vanguard of the revolution. Indeed, Plafker's analysis of the massive uplift and subsidence in Alaska in 1964 had been instrumental in convincing many scientists at the 1967 meeting that the Pacific ocean bed was indeed being thrust under the coast of Alaska. His observations could not be explained in terms of the earlier theories, which assumed that the forces of contraction acting on the earth's crust would produce faults that were vertical in relation to the surface, and would cause crustal motion that was straight up or down near the fault. The massive deformations of Alaska were in harmony with the concept of one mobile block of crust angling downward beneath another.

One of the meeting's most concise summations of the new situation was contained in a paper by Lynn Sykes and two Lamont colleagues, Jack Oliver and Bryan Isacks. They recounted the global picture of moving plates and demonstrated that the accumulating seismological data supported it. The entire surface of the planet, they wrote, was divided into a half a dozen or so immense plates, which jostle and collide like chunks of river ice in a spring thaw. Where the plates break apart, or rub together, or force their way under one another, there are earthquakes. The movement of the plates is ponderously slow, no more than a few inches a year, but it is continuous and inexorable, and it has shaped and reshaped the face of the earth. The shifting of the plates has widened the oceans and narrowed them again. It has raised mountains, created volcanoes, and then destroyed them as the continents have drifted around throughout geologic time.

The movement of the plates explained the pattern of earthquake epicenters on global seismic maps *(pages 92-93)*. Densely clustered epicenters delineated the plate edges, where they crash together or spread apart. The thin trail of earthquake activity in midocean marked the ridges where the plates had their genesis. The great circum-Pacific earthquake belt defined the outer rim of the main Pacific Plate, which pushed northwest from the East Pacific Rise to smash into the Asian archipelagoes and Alaska, scraping past California en route. All of North America and half of the North Atlantic Ocean were riding westward on a single plate. A garland of epicenters encircled Africa, outlining the African Plate; another ring of epicenters marked the edges of the plate that carried India and Australia.

Thus formulated, the concept of a dynamic earth crust came to be known as the theory of plate tectonics, and after the 1966-1967 meetings it rapidly became the dominant theory of earth sciences. For years the very idea that the earth's crust was mobile had been subject to such contempt within the scientific community that a confessed belief in the concept might have raised questions about a young geologist's academic future. The attitude expressed by Rollin T. Chamberlin in 1928 had held firm for almost 40 years: "If we are to believe Wegener's hypothesis we must forget everything which has been learned in the last 70 years and start all over again." But by 1970, the remaining opponents of plate tectonics had assumed a plaintive tone that illustrated the overwhelming nature of the transformation that had overtaken them. As the Soviet geologist V. V. Beloussov observed, the new ideas "have cast a hypnotic spell and thrown a shadow over much that is old and familiar."

While the theory of plate tectonics accounted satisfactorily for 95 per cent of the earth's seismic energy, it did not explain the other 5 per cent. There remained unanswered questions about major earthquakes that occur far from the nearest plate boundary.

A series of tremors that was among the most fearsome ever experienced in North America had occurred in the winter of 1811-1812 in southeastern Missouri and Arkansas, virtually in the middle of the North American Plate. It was fortunate that there were few settlers in the region in those early days—perhaps 3,000 frontier trappers and farmers in log-cabin villages along the Mississippi River. For when the earth started heaving on December 16, 1811, at around 2 a.m., great tracts of forest crashed to the ground and giant fissures opened up, some so broad that no horse could jump them. At New Madrid, Missouri, the largest settlement, the terrified residents leaped from their beds, their cabins splintering about them, and raced outside. They reported eerie flashes like distant lightning in the sky, and air heavy with sulfurous vapors. Geysers of sand and coal dust spouted from the ground, dotting the landscape for miles.

Two more great earthquakes struck the Midwestern frontier in the next few months and the second of these, on February 7, was the most violent of all. The shocks were so powerful that they rattled windows and agitated chandeliers in Washington, D.C., stopped clock pendulums in Charleston, South Carolina,

Boatmen struggle toward shore as massive tremors transform the Mississippi River into a raging sea in this depiction of an unusual quake that hit Missouri in 1811. Far from any known plate boundary—and the subject of much speculation to this day—the quake rattled most of the eastern United States and devastated a wide area along the Mississippi.

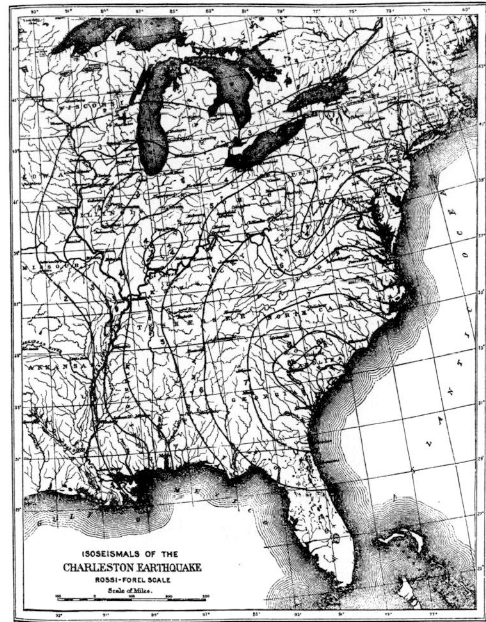

Ribbon-like bands on this seismic intensity map plot the effect of an earthquake that rocked a supposedly trouble-free area around Charleston, South Carolina, in 1886. The tremors caused considerable building damage in zone 9 and were felt in zone 2, almost 1,000 miles away. Near the epicenter *(right)*, scores of craterlets up to 21 feet wide were formed by the sinking of loosely packed sediment.

set church bells tolling in Richmond, Virginia, and wakened residents of Pittsburgh, Pennsylvania. In nearby Kentucky, naturalist John James Audubon reported that "the ground rose and fell in successive furrows like the ruffled waters of a lake. The earth waved like a field of corn before a breeze."

By the time the earth stopped shaking, the landscape had changed beyond recognition. Fields and riverbanks were crisscrossed by a maze of furrows and crevasses. Thousands of acres of prairie had been converted into swamp, a lake bed had been raised to become dry land, and eruptions of sand had deposited wide mounds of white quartz grit across the bottom lands. New Madrid, which was situated near the epicenters of two of the three quakes, had been leveled and the land under it had slumped 15 feet. Islands had disappeared from the Mississippi, and in places the banks had collapsed, temporarily damming the river's flow. Despite all this disruption, casualties had been few—a man buried under his roof at New Madrid, some people drowned when their boats capsized in the Mississippi.

The effort to explain that quake continues today, and with increasing urgency. What was wilderness in 1811 has become the populous industrial heartland of America. An earthquake there of similar force today would endanger some 12 million people from Little Rock, Arkansas, to Evansville, Indiana, with property damage running to $50 billion or more.

In the late 1970s, seismologist William Stauder and his colleagues at St. Louis University uncovered what may be the first real clue to the mechanics of the 1811-1812 earthquakes. The Mississippi River, throughout its millennia of flow, had layered the valley with deposits of sediment many thousands of feet thick. These deposits had disguised any evidence of faults in the area of the earthquakes. But when Stauder's investigative group set up a dense network of seismographs in the vicinity, the instruments detected frequent micro-earthquakes. To everyone's surprise, the region was still seismically active 160 years after the great cataclysm of the 19th Century. Furthermore, the St. Louis team found that the epicenters of the micro-earthquakes were located in distinct regions that probably constituted a shallow fault zone under the sediments. The apparent fault zone ran from Arkansas northeast toward southern Illinois, a distance of more than 120 miles.

Expanding upon the St. Louis team's discovery, seismologist Mark Zoback and others at the U.S. Geological Survey took a deeper look into the New Madrid fault area using several new techniques, including one known as seismic reflection profiling. Artificially created seismic waves were projected deep into the bedrock beneath the Mississippi sediments. The seismic picture that the reflected waves produced suggested that the fault zone was far larger than had previously been supposed—200 miles long and 50 miles wide in places. It was a zone of general weakness, possibly caused by the parting of the continents during the formation of the Atlantic Ocean more than 190 million years ago. As the North American Plate continues its westward drift its bottom drags along the underlying mantle. The Survey scientists suggested that stress on the weakened zone caused by the friction between the plate and the mantle was responsible for the severe earthquakes.

Increased knowledge of the midcontinent seismic zone may provide a key to understanding other intraplate earthquakes in the eastern and central parts of the United States. In August 1886, the eastern third of the country was rocked by an earthquake centered near Charleston, South Carolina, that approached the intensity of the New Madrid quakes. Although tremors in the area remain frequent to this day, no great fault traces similar to those of the Mississippi Valley have been located beneath South Carolina. The answer seems to be in a different phenomenon.

Geophysicists have detected an area of high magnetism and density in the Charleston area, only a few miles below the surface and close to the focal points of recent tremors. Sometime in the distant geologic past, they speculate, molten rock from the upper mantle pushed into the crust above it and solidified. The resulting extremely dense structure is so heavy that it is believed to exert massive stresses on the surrounding rock, possibly enough to trigger earthquakes in ancient fault zones.

Geophysicists have discovered a similar anomaly—called a pluton—in the ocean off Cape Ann, Massachusetts, and believe it may indicate the location of another congealed upwelling of mantle rock. Stresses from this pluton could have brought on the tremors that so alarmed Boston in 1755. Similar plutons have been identified in Maine, New Hampshire and Quebec, all of which experience tremors from time to time. Plutons have also been found in the fault zone under New Madrid.

The difficulty of explaining the intraplate earthquakes constitutes a ragged edge of the theory of plate tectonics. Until the various hypotheses about these diverse seismic events can be tied into a cohesive, systematic theory related to the movement of the crust, they will continue to be a source of encouragement for the few remaining opponents of the new view of earth.

An 8,000-foot plume of smoke *(top)* signals the detonation of 6,700 tons of explosives on the North Sea island of Helgoland in 1947. One of the greatest nonnuclear explosions of the era, the blast was conducted by the British Navy for the purpose of destroying the remains of a German military installation. Besides leveling the installation *(below)*, it gave seismologists an opportunity to monitor a scheduled man-made earthquake.

Another type of earthquake that does not necessarily occur at the edges of the crustal plates—the volcanic earthquake—presents no such problem for the theorists of plate tectonics. It is the easiest kind of earthquake to study and comprehend—and perhaps for that reason volcanoes were once thought to be the only cause of tremors. It is now known that the relationship between volcanoes and earthquakes accounts for only a small fraction of the earth's seismic activity, but the results of the interaction can be spectacular.

On September 29, 1955, the Kamchatka Peninsula, which juts downward from the Siberian land mass to within a few miles of the Kurile Islands, was jolted by a moderate earthquake. During the next week there was a minor earthquake every day and by the end of the third week more than 100 tremors were rocking the peninsula daily. Seismograms located the epicenters of the earthquakes in the immediate vicinity of the Bezymianny volcano, which had been quiescent for so long that it was thought to be extinct. By October 22 the earthquakes had reached a frequency of more than 200 per day and their number mounted to nearly 1,300 all told. On that day Bezymianny began to erupt.

As the volcano spewed out ash, steam and gases, the number of earthquakes increased to 450 a day. For a month a plume of ash five miles high spread outward from Bezymianny, reaching over the Pacific Ocean 75 miles away. At the end of November there was a sudden drop in earthquake activity, and a simultaneous decline in the number of eruptions. For four months the volcano rested and the earth remained comparatively still—until March 30, 1956.

On that day Bezymianny literally blew its top in a stupendous eruption of molten lava—not just ash and steam. The blast pulverized the top 650 feet of the mountain, created a mile-wide crater and blew down trees 15 miles away. Simultaneously, a great earthquake rocked the Kamchatka Peninsula.

After the main blast and accompanying tremors, both seismic activity and eruptions weakened dramatically; by June, the mountain and the earth were again still. During the eight-month period there had been more than 33,000 earthquakes, whose frequency and energy levels had approximately paralleled the ferocity of the volcanic activity.

From detailed studies of such events, scientists have come to understand the mechanics of volcanic earthquakes. As the molten lava, or magma, wells upward from the earth's interior, it applies heat and pressure to the bedrock, seeping into cracks and orifices, swelling the rock through which it passes and eventually the mountain itself. The strain of the magma spreading outward triggers the swarm of earthquakes that precede eruption. And as the magma concentrates nearer the surface, the earthquake foci become more shallow and are grouped closer to the mountain. The force of the eruption itself may trigger a massive earthquake, as seemed to be the case at Bezymianny. After the eruption, as the magma withdraws, the bedrock settles and contracts, applying new stresses that can cause further quakes with increasing focal depths and decreasing magnitude until the process is complete—and the volcano is dormant.

While erupting volcanoes often bring on earthquakes, sometimes the process is reversed, and a strong earthquake sparks a sleeping volcano. This occurred on November 29, 1975, when a fault ruptured beneath the coast of the island of Hawaii, 30 miles south of Hilo. Less than an hour after the main shock Mount Kilauea in the southeast part of the island began to erupt. Deep fissures opened up along the crater, pouring out streams of lava, and incandescent lava fountains spouted into the dawn sky.

The molten rock in Kilauea's magma chambers, superhot and seething with dissolved gases, had reacted to the shaking of the earth like carbonated water in a bottle, ejecting bubbles of superheated steam in an eruption that lasted for 18 hours. Rivers of lava as deep as 10 feet, traveling as fast as 30 miles per hour, cascaded down the sides of the mountain to the sea. Though marvelously spectacular, the eruption caused far less damage than the earthquake, which blocked roads, disrupted electrical service and collapsed a few older buildings.

But sometimes the connection between earthquakes and volcanoes is less easy to trace. One of the more active seismic regions in North America lies within the rugged sweep of the central Rocky Mountains, from Montana in the north to Utah in the south. These mountains were pushed up more than 100 million years ago, which is ancient as mountains go, and the volcanic activity associated with their growth has long since ceased—except in one spot. Yellowstone National Park, in northwestern Wyoming, still simmers with hot springs and geysers, the persistent epilogue of a massive series of volcanic cataclysms. On three occasions in the present era of geologic time, the Yellowstone region has erupted—and the last outburst 600,000 years ago spread great sheets of lava over hundreds of square miles. The entire park, in fact, is the sunken crater of a gigantic prehistoric volcano. Here, on August 17, 1959, the earth was convulsed by the strongest quake ever recorded in the Rockies.

The main shock struck Hebgen Lake, just west of the park boundary, shortly before midnight. A fresh fault scarp tore through the nearby hills, dropping the land on one side by as much as 20 feet. The lake bed tilted, causing the water to surge angrily back and forth for 11 hours. Some of it spilled over Hebgen Dam, where it raced down the riverbed, scouring away the banks and uprooting trees. Downstream, the entire massive face of a mountain broke away and came roaring down on a party of vacationers who were camping below. Of 150 people in the group, 28 died, buried under millions of tons of rock. The avalanche dammed the Madison River to form a new body of water—soon named Earthquake Lake—a mile wide and five miles long. The earthquake was felt across an area of 580,000 square miles, and jolted Yellowstone Park with enough force to start some new geysers spouting.

From their studies of the seismic waves generated by the earthquake, U.S. Geological Survey scientists discovered that an enormous pear-shaped body of magma, some 30 miles in diameter and up to 150 miles deep, lies just under the park. Its distance from the surface is not yet known. Seismic P waves lose velocity there; gravity and magnetism are abnormally low, electrical conductivity is high, and the region gives off heat at 20 times the average rate for the rest of the continent—all indications of an underground body of magma hot enough to be partially melted. The pressures generated by this subterranean hot spot may have contributed to the stresses that split the rock at Hebgen Lake.

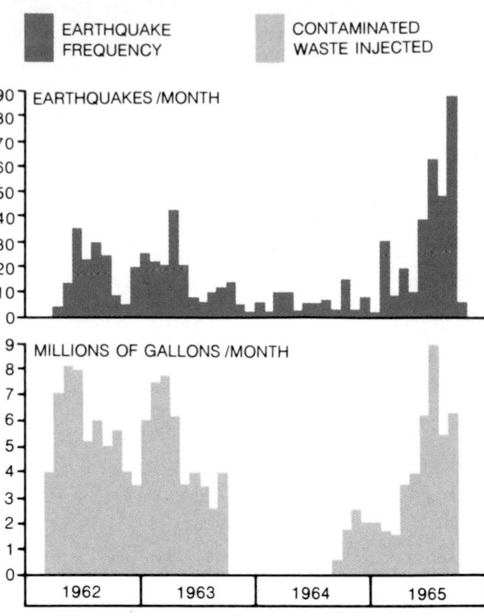

These graphs for the years 1962 through 1965 demonstrate the direct correlation between the sudden occurrence of swarms of small earthquakes and the pumping of waste fluid into a deep well at the Rocky Mountain Arsenal, near Denver, Colorado. The U.S. Army stopped the pumping in 1966 because of the tremendous number of tremors.

Occasionally, mankind will bring an earthquake on itself. These manufactured tremors seldom reach the magnitude of those at Hebgen Lake, but some have been just as destructive, and just as unexpected. A prime example occurred in 1935, with the completion of Hoover Dam on the Colorado River. Most likely there had always been unsuspected low-level tremors in the region, but as water began backing up behind the dam, creating Lake Mead, the earthquakes increased in size and number. In 1940 they reached magnitude 5—enough to cause some minor but annoying shaking in nearby Las Vegas. The tremors continue periodically to this day.

As the technology of building giant dams spread to other countries, the problem recurred. In southern Africa in 1958, Zambia began letting water into Lake Kariba, behind a 420-foot-high earthen dam, and in the five years it took the reservoir to fill, the dam site was shaken by more than 2,000 tremors of magnitudes as high as 5.8. Seismologists started monitoring China's Hsingfengkiang Dam, near Canton, in 1959 when the water started pouring into the reservoir, and over the next dozen years they detected a total of 250,000 shocks. Most were relatively slight, but one, in 1962, reached a magnitude of 6.1 on the Richter scale and severely damaged the concrete dam structure.

The worst dam-induced earthquake occurred at Koyna, India, in 1967. Over the years, there had been no suggestion of seismic activity at Koyna. But as soon as the dam was finished in 1962 and the lake started filling, the earthquakes commenced. They came in veritable swarms each year after the rainy season, building up to a devastating 6.5 jolt on December 11, 1967. The Koyna area is thickly dotted with towns and villages; more than 1,500 people were injured and 177 killed by the tremors.

For many years seismologists did not understand the mechanism behind these convulsions. According to their calculations the weight of water would not by itself be sufficient to fracture the bedrock. They believed that some other force, more subtle and complex, had to be at work. Evidence of its nature emerged by chance in the mid-1960s at the U.S. Army's Rocky Mountain Arsenal near Denver, Colorado.

The arsenal was being used to manufacture chemical weapons in processes that generated large amounts of liquid toxic waste. To dispose of this contaminated water the Army drilled a well, five and a half inches in diameter and more than two miles deep, in an isolated section of the arsenal. In March 1962, the Army started pumping the effluent into this well, under pressure, at the rate of 300 gallons a minute. A month after the pumping started, local seismographs started jumping, although no significant tremor had shaken the Denver area in

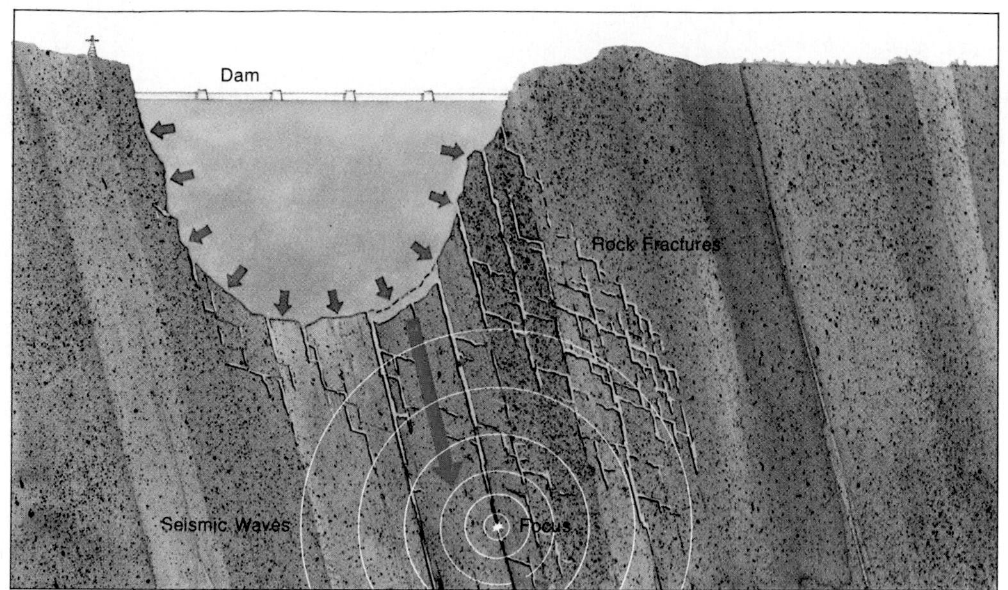

How the filling of a large reservoir can bring on an earthquake is illustrated in this diagram, which shows water behind a dam pressing down on and infiltrating the rock underneath. The weight of the water *(small arrows),* combined with seepage into fractures, reduces the basement rock's frictional strength and induces slippage *(large arrow)* along the fault.

80 years. By 1966, more than 165 million gallons of waste had been injected into the hole and more than 1,000 earthquakes had been recorded, some with Richter magnitudes as high as 4.6. When the pumping stopped, so did the earthquakes; when the pumping resumed, the quakes did, too *(opposite).*

The U.S. Geological Survey moved in with a battery of 64 seismographs with which to monitor the tremors, and after studying the seismograms they thought they understood what was happening. A number of old faults crease the Denver area, most of them long inactive but still under some stress. As liquid was pumped down the hole under pressure, it would seep into these cracks, following the fault lines and lubricating them, eventually allowing the rock to slip, causing an earthquake that otherwise would not have occurred.

The Geological Survey investigators soon had a chance to test their thesis. They went into a depleted oil field at Rangely, in western Colorado, where they knew some tectonic strain existed because of the infrequent, small earthquakes in the area. Over a period of four years, Survey scientists injected water into the substrata via the old oil wells, varying the volume and pressure and monitoring the results with a special array of seismographs. The effects were gratifyingly straightforward. Whenever the water pressure in the pores of the bedrock reached 3,700 pounds per square inch, earthquake activity dramatically increased. When the pressure dropped below that level the quakes stopped. The thesis that was suggested by the accident at Denver had been confirmed by controlled experiment at Rangely.

The same principle explains the genesis of earthquakes beneath large dam sites. As the reservoir fills, water finds its way into the pores and crevices in the underlying rock, lubricating existing fault lines and upsetting the balance of the forces within the rock. When the water pressure reaches the critical point, the faults slip and there are earthquakes *(above).*

By the early 1970s, the science of seismology was well launched in a new direction and its practitioners were heartened by the advances in their understanding of the forces at work in the planet. But for many experts the tests of the new theory had only partly been met. As the 19th Century English philosopher and scientist William Whewell put it, "The hypotheses which we accept ought to explain phenomena which we have observed." The concept of plate tectonics was passing this test admirably. "But they ought to do more than this," Whewell went on. "Our hypotheses ought to *foretell* phenomena which have not yet been observed." Many scientists believed the most important work of seismology still remained undone: the task of developing a reliable way to predict where and when an earthquake will strike. **Ω**

A FORECASTER'S TREASURE CHEST OF TOOLS

Inspecting fresh cracks in the ground at Parkfield, California, in June 1966, a party of visiting seismologists offhandedly predicted that a large earthquake would soon shake the area. Two weeks later, on June 28, 1966, the joke became a jolt, when Parkfield was rocked by a tremor that reached 5.3 on the Richter scale of magnitude.

The prediction, although largely accidental, was taken as something of an omen by the visitors, who were, in fact, winding up a conference on earthquake prediction that was attended by seismologists from Japan and the United States. In laboratories and in the field, they were taking part in burgeoning research programs aimed at assembling data and deducing patterns that would allow science to chart the steps in the slow dance of the continents and the oceans.

The studies continue today with mounting intensity—and some success. Seismologists obtain data about changes in the earth's crust from a wide variety of increasingly sophisticated instruments, arrayed in seismically active areas around the world. They range from giant radio telescopes measuring the drift of continents against signposts at the edge of the universe to suitcase-sized instruments reading the motion of atomic particles in order to discover changes in the magnetic properties of rocks.

Despite their almost incredible accuracy—some measurement errors are reduced to one part in 10 million—most of these instruments operate on simple principles, illustrated with diagrams here and on the following pages. For clarity, strain is depicted as a break in the crust.

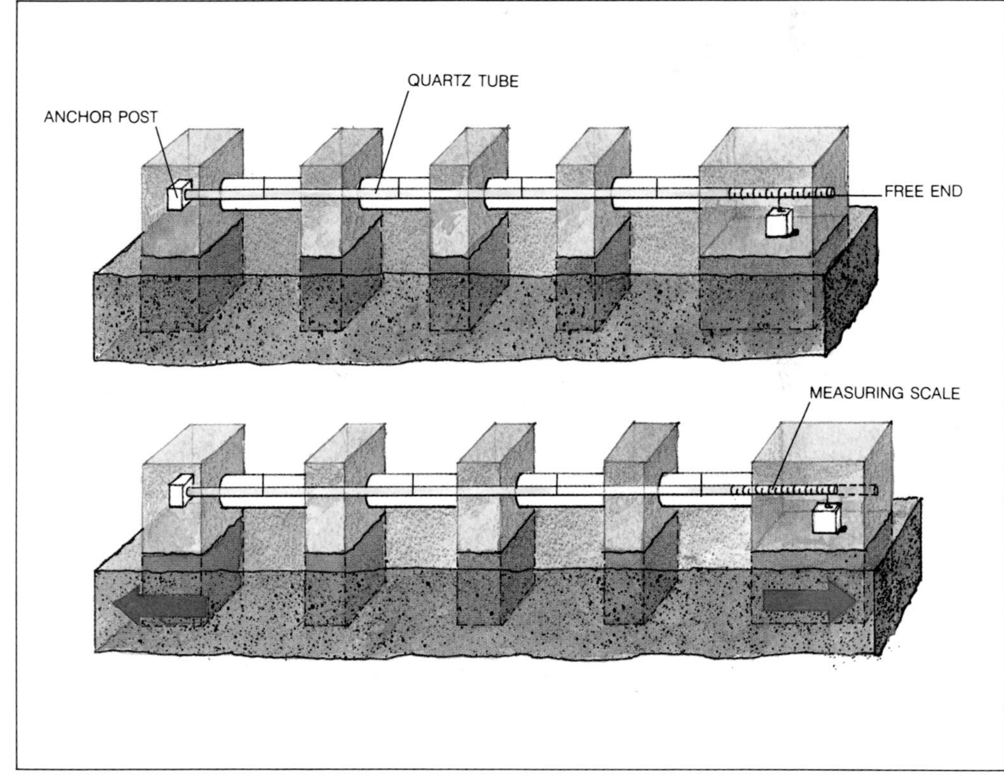

In a tunnel originally built as a refuge for Emperor Hirohito in World War II, a scientist of Japan's Matsushiro Seismological Observatory checks a 330-foot quartz-tube extensometer that senses expansion and contraction of the rock beneath it. The tunnel provides a stable environment for the observatory's instruments, shielding them from error-inducing temperature changes and from man-made vibrations.

This extensometer consists of a long quartz tube firmly attached at one end to an anchor post but moving freely against a post at the other end. As the rock deforms, extending or contracting, the quartz rod maintains its length, and the change in the distance between terminal posts is indicated by the relative movement of the free end of the rod. The measurement may be read optically against a scale or may be measured electronically; exceedingly long extensometers, such as the one at Matsushiro, have intermediate posts as added support for the quartz rod.

A geophysicist takes a reading from a gravimeter, which is used to measure changes in gravitational strength brought on by rising or falling land or variations in the density of underlying rock. The apparatus records the position of a small mass suspended on a spring; fluctuations in gravity change the weight of the mass, which moves up or down accordingly. The most sensitive gravimeters, which read the position of the mass electronically, can register a change in land height of about one-half inch.

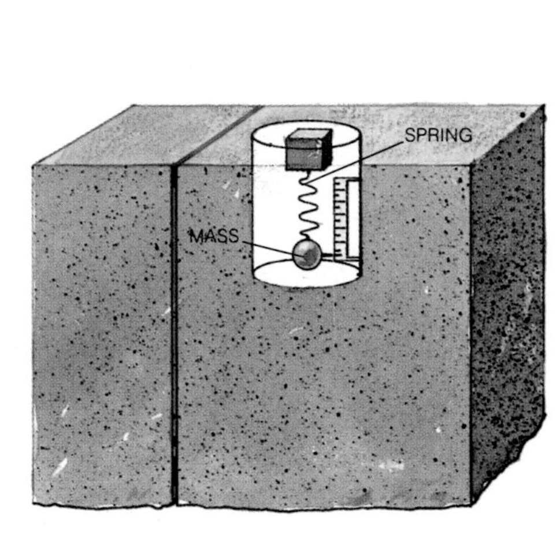

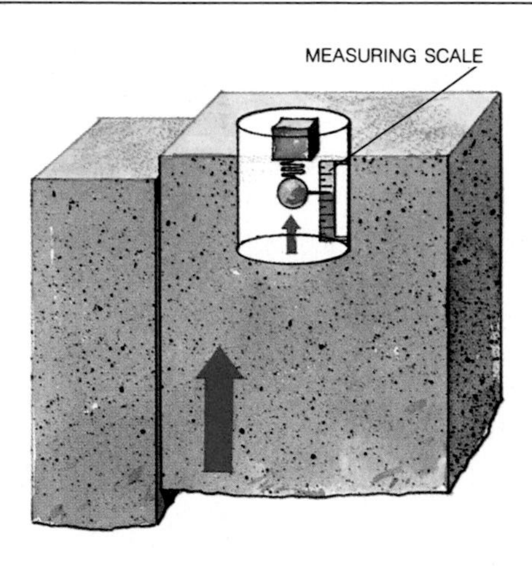

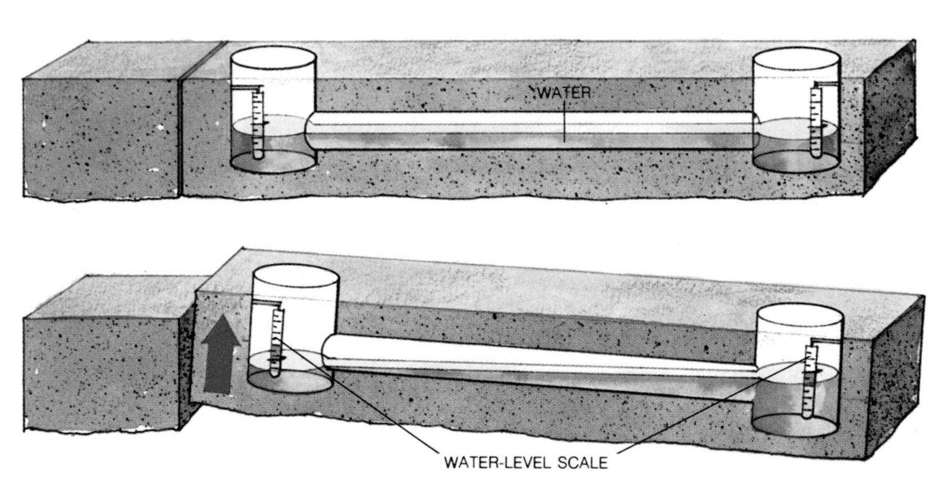

A pit houses the monitoring instruments for a tiltmeter, used to sense changes in the slope of land near a fault. In a water-tube tiltmeter, a tube connects two water-filled containers so that a shift of the ground causes the water level to rise in the lower container and fall in the higher one. The water level may be monitored visually or electronically; a 30-foot tiltmeter of the type used in field installations can detect tilt changes as small as $^1/_{10,000,000}$ degree.

Finding Signs of Strain on the Surface

In fault zones where the edges of moving tectonic plates are locked together, the energy of the plates accumulates as strain until a fracture of the fault releases it suddenly as an earthquake. Geophysicists watching these seismically active regions have identified a number of subtle physical changes in the near-surface rocks that appear to be related to strain accumulation.

The most visible evidence of strain is a phenomenon called creep, a slow, uninterrupted movement along part of a fault that offsets the land and cracks walls and pavements. Tilting of the land around a fault has

Readings from a proton precession magnetometer can identify strain-related changes in the earth's magnetic field. At regular intervals a brief magnetic field aligns the spinning protons of hydrogen atoms; the much weaker force of the earth's magnetic field then exerts a different pull, causing the protons to precess, or wobble like a top. A change of precession from one reading to the next indicates a shift in the local magnetic field. A control instrument detects widespread variations not related to local strain.

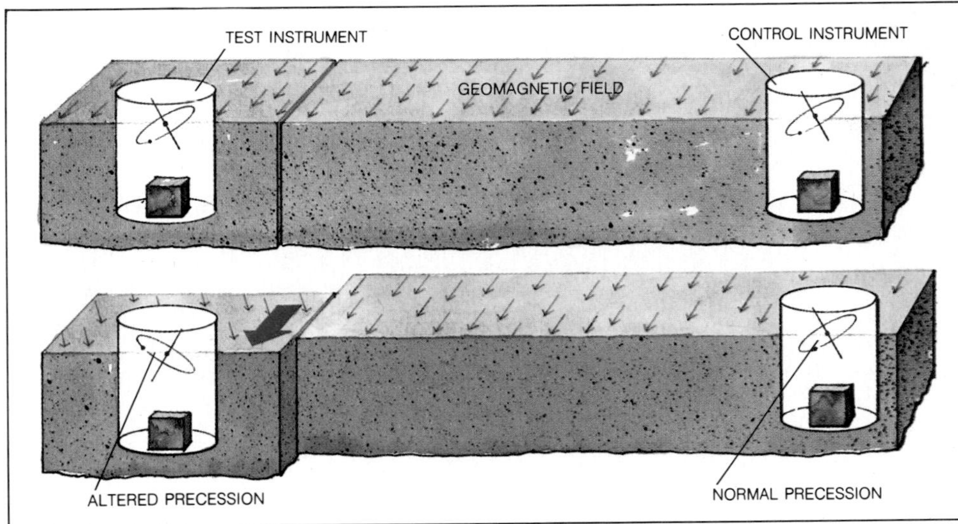

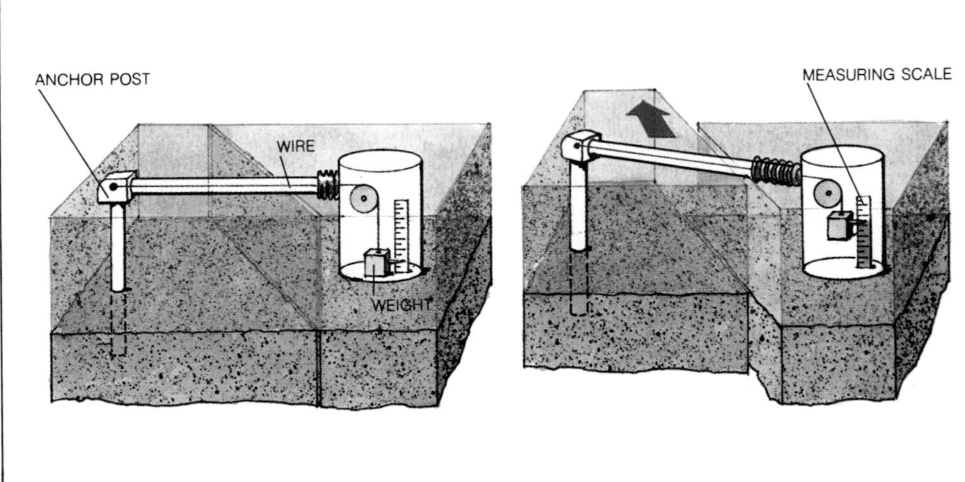

Crawling down to check a creepmeter, a technician inspects one end of a 30-foot wire that runs through a variable-length conduit to another pit across a creeping fault. Clamped at one end to an anchor post, the special wire is free to move relative to the instrument post at the other end. A hanging weight maintains tension on the wire, and rises or falls with respect to the instrument post when movement occurs on the fault and changes the distance between posts.

also been linked to build-ups of strain, as have changes in gravitational strength and fluctuations in the geomagnetic field. By monitoring these variations continuously, researchers can assemble a data base for models of seismic activity.

One of the most intensively studied fault zones in the world is in California, where researchers have surrounded the San Andreas and its subsidiary faults with hundreds of instrument sites. Unlike major seismological observatories, where huge devices are housed in tunnels and vaults, most of these field sites are designed for simplicity and accessibility. Though some instruments are put into holes drilled thousands of feet deep, many are simply installed in relatively shallow pits dug through the overlying soil.

A telescopic sight magnifies distant targets for a very accurate laser ranging apparatus *(right)*. The precisely positioned instrument is used to find ranges to as many as nine points arranged in a radial pattern around a laser site. Outside the field station *(below)*, a time exposure captures the ranging beam as it zeroes in on five different targets.

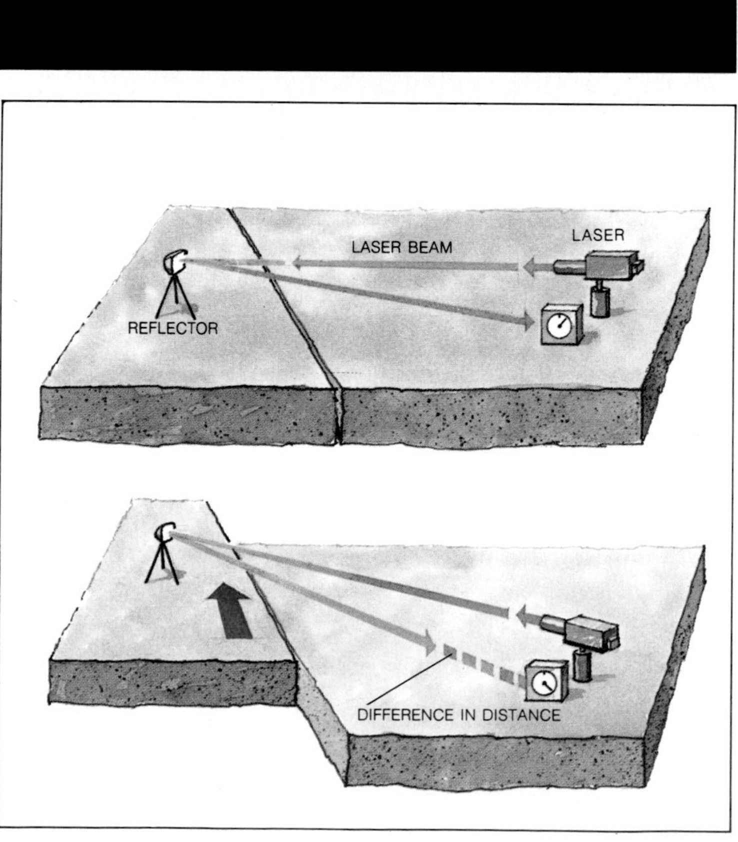

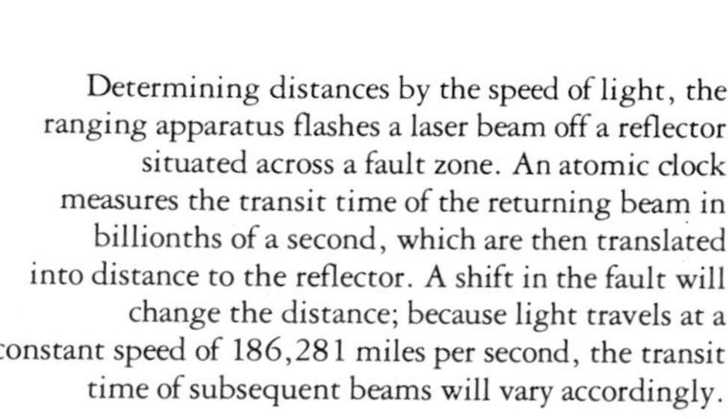

Determining distances by the speed of light, the ranging apparatus flashes a laser beam off a reflector situated across a fault zone. An atomic clock measures the transit time of the returning beam in billionths of a second, which are then translated into distance to the reflector. A shift in the fault will change the distance; because light travels at a constant speed of 186,281 miles per second, the transit time of subsequent beams will vary accordingly.

A jewel sparkling atop an unsteady crown, the laser beam of a ranging instrument flashes above Hollister, California. It has measured surface movements in the area of as much as one-sixth inch in 10 days.

Making Measurements with the Speed of Light

By the middle of the 20th Century, most of the world's topography had been mapped, its points plotted by triangulation using optical instruments and principles of trigonometry. Mapping surveys located each geographical feature by determining its bearing from two other points, at the ends of a base line of known length. Accuracy depended on the length of the base line—and measurements extending over the 10-mile lengths common for geological surveys might vary by as much as six inches.

While this technique was acceptable to mapmakers, it was useless to geophysicists seeking to study tectonic fault movements that amounted to only fractions of inches per year. A breakthrough came in the 1960s, with the development of sophisticated laser ranging devices.

A laser aligns light waves to produce a powerful, narrowly focused beam that maintains much of its intensity over long distances. The devices determine distances by measuring the time it takes a laser beam to reach a reflector target and return to its source. The first laser ranging instruments reduced error dramatically, but required an aircraft to measure variable atmospheric conditions along the measurement path.

In the mid-1970s, advanced laser systems were developed that eliminated the need for atmospheric readings. And these devices permit geophysicists to measure the changing face of the earth to within $^{1}/_{15}$ inch over a distance of 10 miles.

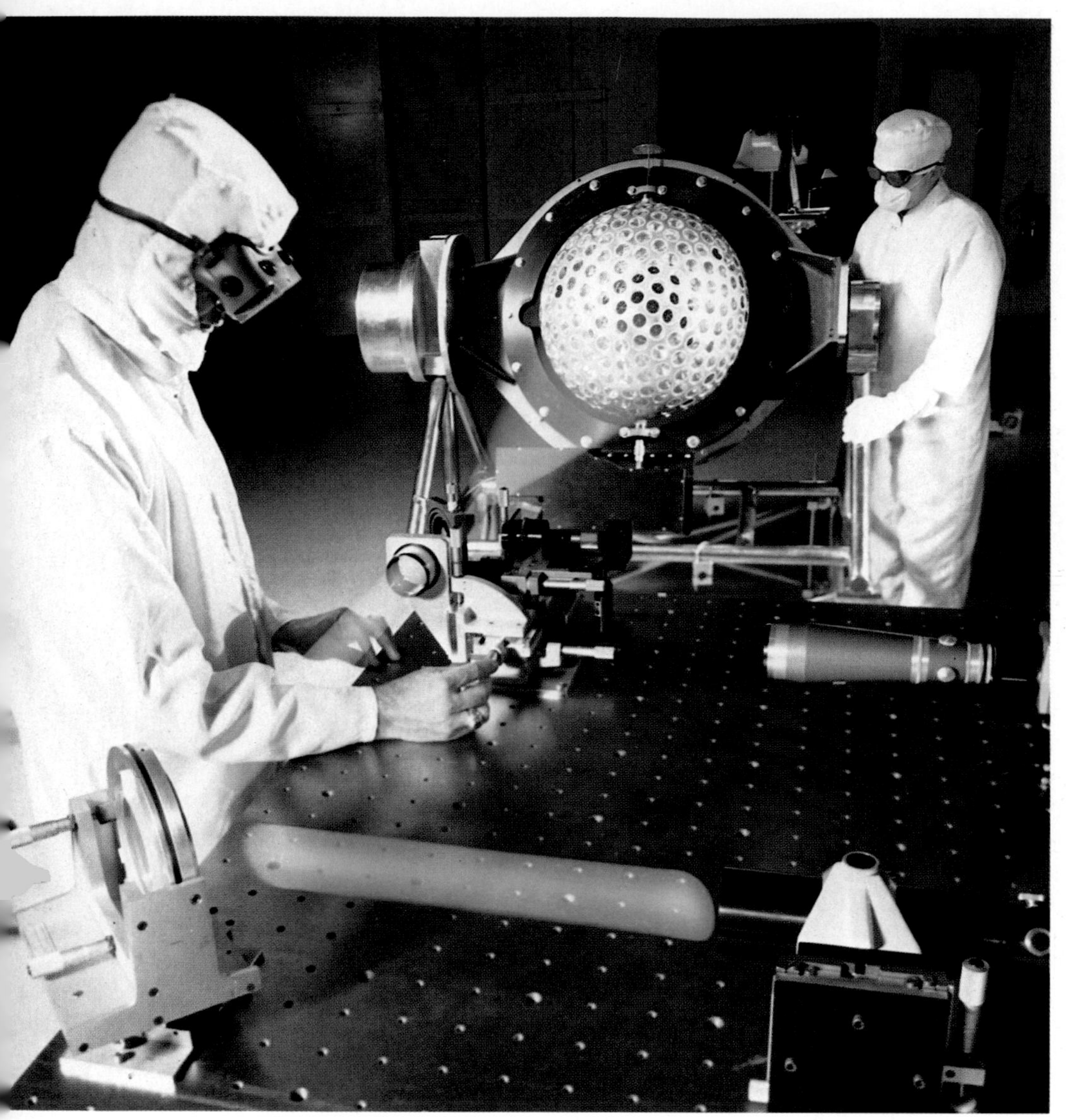

Helping Hands from Explorers in Space

In order to plot broad movements of the great tectonic plates responsible for most earthquakes, geophysicists require precise measurements over distances that are often continental in scale instead of just a few miles. The job is beyond conventional laser devices. But it is tailor-made for the marvelous technology of space exploration.

Two main devices are employed: radio telescopes and orbiting satellites. Both systems operate on essentially the same principle. They are keyed to a reference point in outer space, from which scientists can plot the relative positions of points on a base line on earth hundreds or thousands of miles in length.

The closest approximations of stationary points in the known universe are extragalactic radio sources. These quasars and radio galaxies are so incredibly distant that if one of them were moving away at half the speed of light—93,141 miles per second—in a line perpendicular to the axis of the earth, it would take 400 million years for its angular position to shift by so much as a single degree. Other reference points in space can be provided by satellites lofted into orbits that change little from revolution to revolution.

The measurements conducted with the aid of these two techniques are so accurate that earth scientists may be able to detect a movement of the tectonic plates as slight as one-half inch per year.

Laboratory technicians test the silica laser reflectors on a Lageos (Laser Geodynamic Satellite) orbiter. Laser pulses beamed to the satellite from a pair of ground stations located on opposite sides of a plate boundary start timers that run until the reflected pulses are received back at the stations. A computer combines this elapsed time with the known position of the satellite to determine the exact position of the ground station. Any movement of the ground station is registered as a change in the elapsed time.

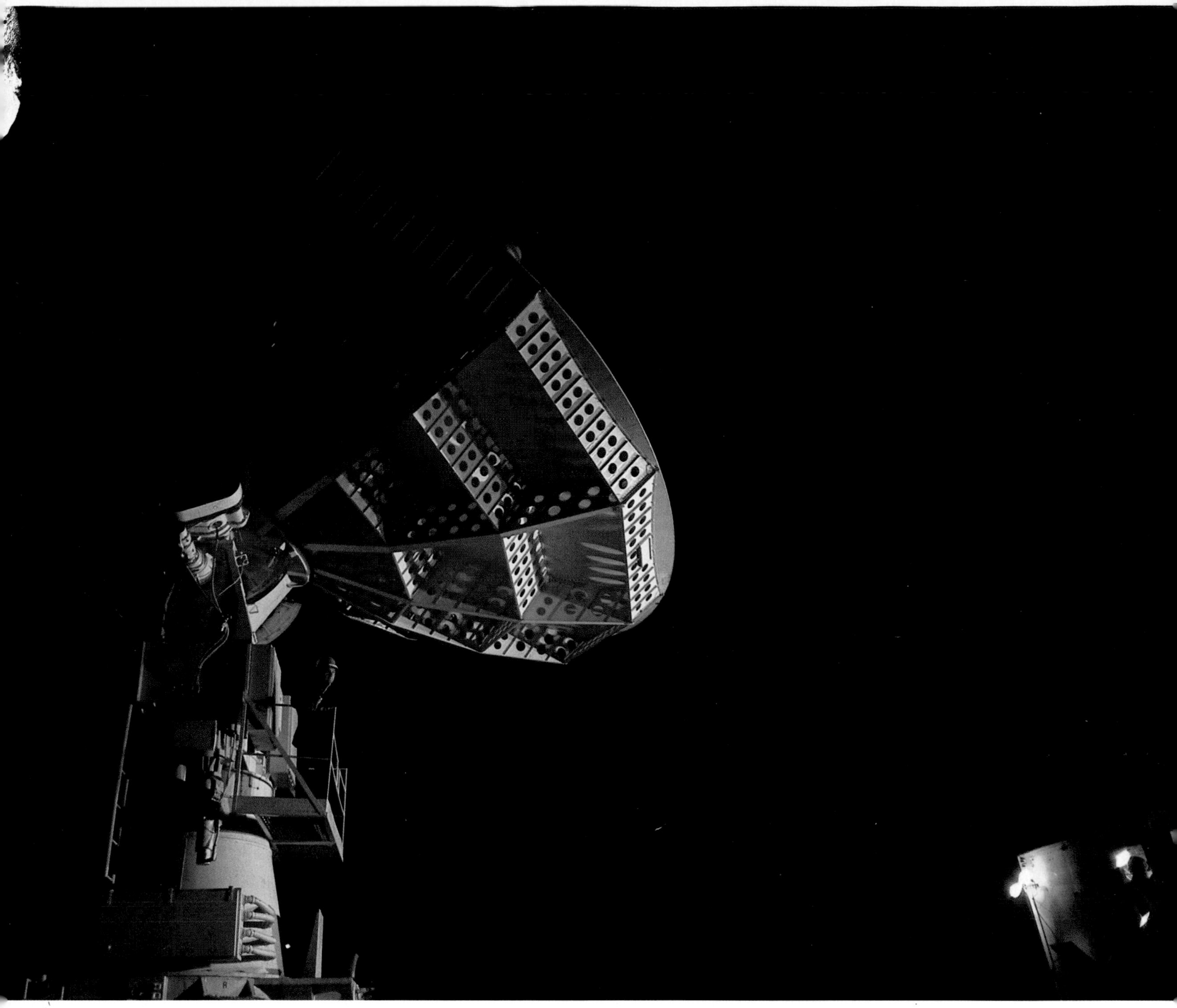

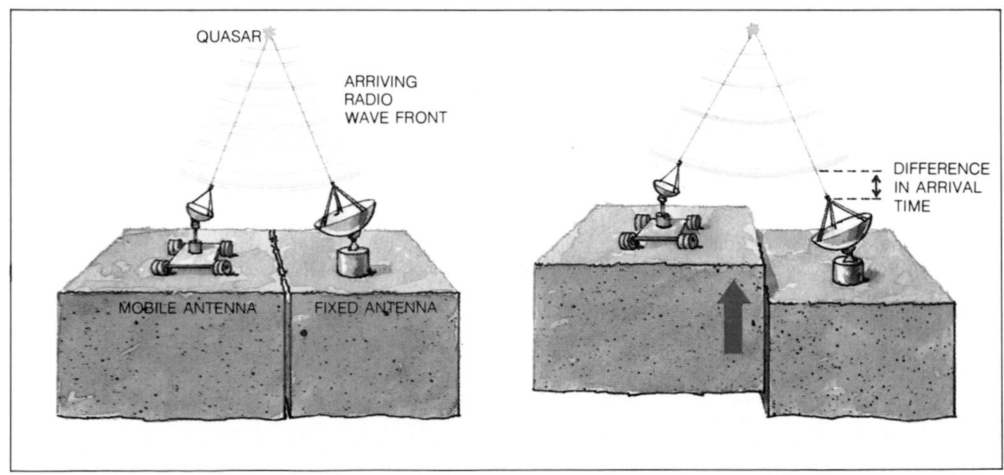

Measuring movements on earth with an interstellar yardstick, a mobile radio telescope homes in on the faint signal generated by a quasar five billion light-years distant. An atomic clock measures the slight difference in the arrival time of the radio wave fronts at the telescope and at a second unit located across a plate boundary. The time delay and antenna aiming angles are used geometrically to compute the distance between the stations; both factors change when crustal deformation shifts the relative positions of the stations.

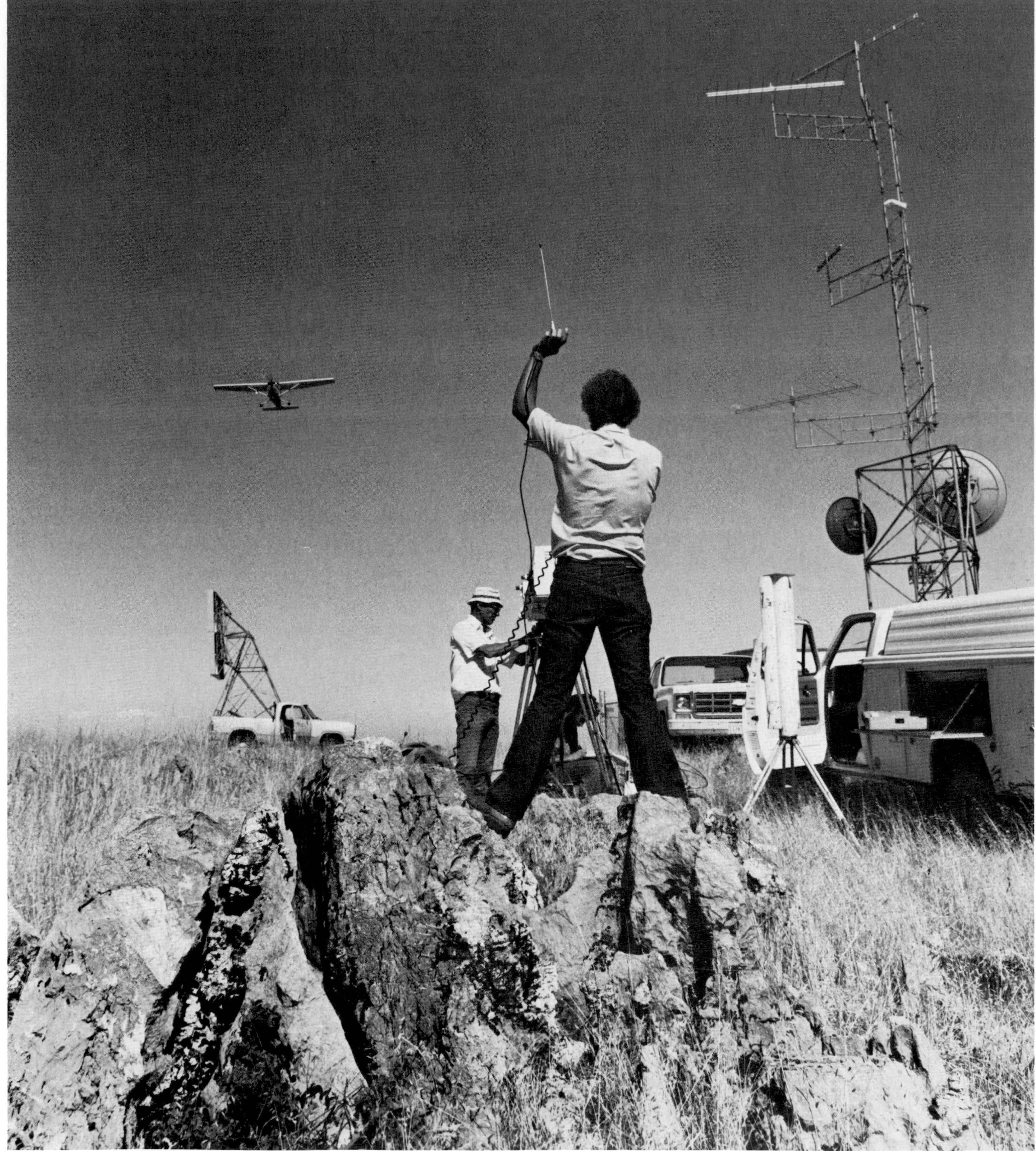

Chapter 5

DREAMS OF KNOWING WHEN AND WHERE

Along the San Andreas Fault in California, seismologists bounce laser light beams off a distant reflector while a plane monitors the atmospheric temperature and humidity, which affect the speed of the beams. By measuring changes in the round-trip travel time of the beams, researchers can detect even the most minute shift of rock along the fault.

"The people of the civilized earth would be glad to know," observed geologist-geographer Grove Karl Gilbert in 1909, "whether or not the time has yet come for a scientific forecast of the impending tremor." The 65-year-old Gilbert was ranging far outside his primary field when he raised the subject of earthquake prediction in a January 1 address to the American Association of Geographers. But he was not in the least apologetic. He was, he said, "an advocate of the principle of scientific trespass." And though he had carved a renowned career for himself as both a geologist and a geographer, he had at the same time pursued a passionate avocation of seismology.

Gilbert had achieved an understanding of the principles of earthquake mechanics that was remarkable for his time, and in his address he applied his knowledge to the subject of prediction. Many decades later a U.S. Geological Survey spokesman would call Gilbert's speech "the most perceptive, encompassing and balanced analysis" to appear until the 1960s.

Gilbert began by discussing the widely held assumption that earthquakes occurred with some discoverable regularity and that when enough was known about the past a pattern would emerge that would permit a reliable prediction of their recurrence. Gilbert thought this rather unlikely. "In view of the complexity of the conditions and the intricacy of the interaction among strains," he wrote, "it is not to be supposed that the status at any one epoch will ever be exactly repeated."

He examined factors believed to act as earthquake triggers, such as tides, winter snow loads and increases in barometric pressure. While recognizing that such phenomena might touch off an earthquake where tectonic strain had accumulated to the point of fracture, Gilbert thought that their varied effects made them almost useless for purposes of long-range forecasting. He also discussed immediate precursors of earthquakes, such as preliminary rumbles and the reported odd behavior of some animals. He found them interesting, but not very useful.

Looking ahead, Gilbert said he thought it more likely that scientists would be able to pinpoint the location of an impending earthquake than to forecast the exact moment of its occurrence. Nevertheless, he held out the hope that at some future date "adaptations of seismographic appliances and methods" would enable the seismologist to serve society in the way that the meteorologist does: "He makes no attempt to control the course of nature; but inspired by science he foretells the coming changes so that his lay client may take warning and be prepared. The crops are harvested before the rain, the herds escape from the lowland before the flood, the ships reach harbor before the gale; and man chants a hymn of praise to science."

Gilbert, who died in 1918 at the age of 74, was known by geologists chiefly for his detailed studies of the San Francisco earthquake of 1906. His prophetic assessment of the prospects for earthquake prediction remained shrouded in obscurity for nearly half a century, while the subject of prediction itself was almost completely ignored as seismologists labored to understand what earthquakes were and why they happened. It remained for a killer quake to shock the scientists of one nation at least into a sudden and vigorous quest for reliable forecasts.

On July 10, 1949, a magnitude 7.5 quake shattered the mountainous Garm region of Tadzhikistan, in the south-central Soviet Union, burying the village of Khait under a massive rockslide and killing 12,000 people. It was one calamity too many for the Soviet government. The previous October, as many as 20,000 people had died in a catastrophic earthquake almost 700 miles to the west, in Ashkhabad. Soviet officials decided that such monstrous disasters must give signs of their approach, and they were determined not to be caught unprepared a third time.

As a start, they mounted a geological study of the afflicted area on a scale never before attempted. Scores of scientists were moved into Tadzhikistan and settled in remote hamlets where they began measuring every earthquake-related aspect of local geology. They made detailed surveys of the land, and measured gravity, magnetism and electrical resistance. Great emphasis was also placed on obtaining seismograms from continuing but relatively mild earthquakes.

Year after year the data accumulated, with a truck arriving at each station once a week to bring supplies and carry out records as the Soviets built up a vast seismic data bank for the region. It was not until 15 years had passed—in the mid-1960s—that the Russians found evidence of what appeared to be a consistent early-warning signal of earthquakes.

For a period of time before each sizable local tremor, seismic records showed a curious fluctuation in the relative speeds of P and S waves reaching the seismographs from micro-earthquakes in the same area. Something seemed to be happening to the rock that affected the progress of seismic waves. Normally, P waves traveled roughly 1.75 times faster than S waves; but every so often the ratio would drop to about 1.6. Because they had so many seismographs in the area, the Soviet scientists were able to compare the seismic records and determine where the change in velocity was taking place. The new ratio might last for a few days, a few months, or for years. Then it would return to normal—and shortly afterward there would be a relatively large tremor. Furthermore, the longer the ratio stayed below normal, the greater the magnitude of the ensuing tremor.

The Soviets presented their stunning findings at an international scientific meeting in Moscow in 1971, and there was a sudden surge of confidence among seismologists that here might be the key to consistent earthquake prediction. Lynn Sykes—whose seismic research along the midocean ranges had contributed to the theory of sea-floor spreading—was in the Moscow audience. And while he was greatly encouraged, he was nonetheless concerned that the Soviets might have simply stumbled onto a phenomenon peculiar to the geology of Tadzhikistan. As soon as he returned to the Lamont Geological Observatory (its name had changed to Lamont-Doherty shortly before), where he was head of the seismology department, he urged one of his students, Yash Aggarwal, to pursue the Soviet line of research in New York's Adirondack Mountains.

Aggarwal, a 31-year-old doctoral candidate, began an intensive review of the seismic records from Lamont-Doherty's seismograph station near Blue Mountain Lake in upper New York State. He had plenty of raw material from a swarm of micro-earthquakes that had occurred there in 1971, and he soon reported that there had, in fact, been changes in seismic wave properties before the quakes. He further noted, as had the Soviets, that the duration and scale of the changes seemed to have a direct relationship to the magnitude of the eventual tremor. Aggarwal and Sykes suspected that P waves were more affected than S waves, and their suspicion was soon confirmed.

Three geophysicists at Caltech had been spurred by the Moscow conference to review their seismic records of the years prior to the 1971 San Fernando earthquake, a magnitude 6.6 tremor that had killed 64 people and destroyed $500 million worth of property. They found that there had been a change in the relative velocities of seismic waves passing through the region for almost three years before the earthquake. And they discovered something the Soviets had missed: It was only the P waves that changed speed, slowing by 10 to 15 per cent while the S-wave velocity remained virtually undiminished.

The evidence was accumulating rapidly, but before scientists could put any faith in the phenomenon, they had to test it extensively. And they needed to understand why it was happening.

The first suggestions had come in the mid-1960s from an American scientist making laboratory studies of the properties of rock. Geologist William Brace of the Massachusetts Institute of Technology had been squeezing rocks in powerful viselike compressors to see what happened to them under stress. Just before a rock fractured, he found, it tended to swell, or dilate—the result of hairline cracks that opened just before the main break occurred. Along with this swelling, various changes took place in the rock's physical properties; it became more porous and conducted electricity more easily, but it slowed the passage of high-frequency waves—compressive pulses identical to seismic P waves. Unaware of the evidence collected by the Soviets, Brace speculated that the effects of dilatancy—the rocks' swelling—might provide warning of an earthquake, but he did not pursue the matter.

It remained for two of his former students, geophysicists Amos Nur of Stanford University and Christopher Scholz of Lamont-Doherty, to connect the theory of dilatancy with the P-wave velocity shifts. Nur was the first to theorize that there was a direct relationship between dilatancy and changes in wave velocity. As the stress on bedrock approached the point of fracture, it first riddled the rock with a multitude of minute fissures, causing dilatancy. One effect of the opening of the cracks, he reasoned, would be to provide more space for existing groundwater. Nur explained that P-wave speed is unaffected by a crack filled with water but is slowed by air space. Thus, when dilatancy opened the myriad cracks in the fracture zone, air was introduced where there had been solid rock and pressurized water before, and P waves dropped in velocity.

When the cracking reached its maximum and paused, just before the ultimate fracture, fresh groundwater from the surrounding region seeped into the cracks, eventually restoring the water pressure and permitting the P waves to return to normal velocity. The greater the dilated region, the longer it would take for the water pressure to be restored—the entire process could take years. Later research indicated that P-wave velocity changed a few months before a magnitude 6 earthquake, a year before one of magnitude 7 and as much as 10 years before one of magnitude 8.

Working from Nur's hypothesis, Christopher Scholz suggested that the principle of dilatancy might be directly related to several of the phenomena observed before earthquakes in the Soviet Union and elsewhere. The increase in the volume of the rock caused by the cracking accounted for the crustal uplift and tilting observed before many earthquakes. The presence of more water in the rock increased its electrical conductivity. The fissures increased the area of contact between rock surfaces and water, and thus the quantity of radioactive elements carried into well water. The Russians had measured increased amounts of one radioactive element—radon—before earthquakes.

Armed with promising new techniques and a comprehensive theory, seismologists in 1973 began making cautious predictions. The first came from Yash Aggarwal, who had acted on the evidence he found in the seismic history of the Blue Mountain Lake area. Early in July he had augmented the existing Lamont-Doherty seismological station at Blue Mountain Lake with seven portable seismographs capable of detecting micro-earthquakes and of determining the location of any changes in wave velocity. For two weeks he had driven 100 miles daily to check the records of each seismograph, and toward the end of July he detected the telltale signs of reduced P-wave velocity in the area.

On August 1, Aggarwal found that the P-wave velocity had apparently returned to normal. It seemed to him a classic example of the pattern that Soviet scientists had found in Tadzhikistan and that he had observed in local seismic records. Putting his conviction on the line, he called Lynn Sykes at Lamont-Doherty with a flat prediction. A magnitude 2.5 earthquake could be expected,

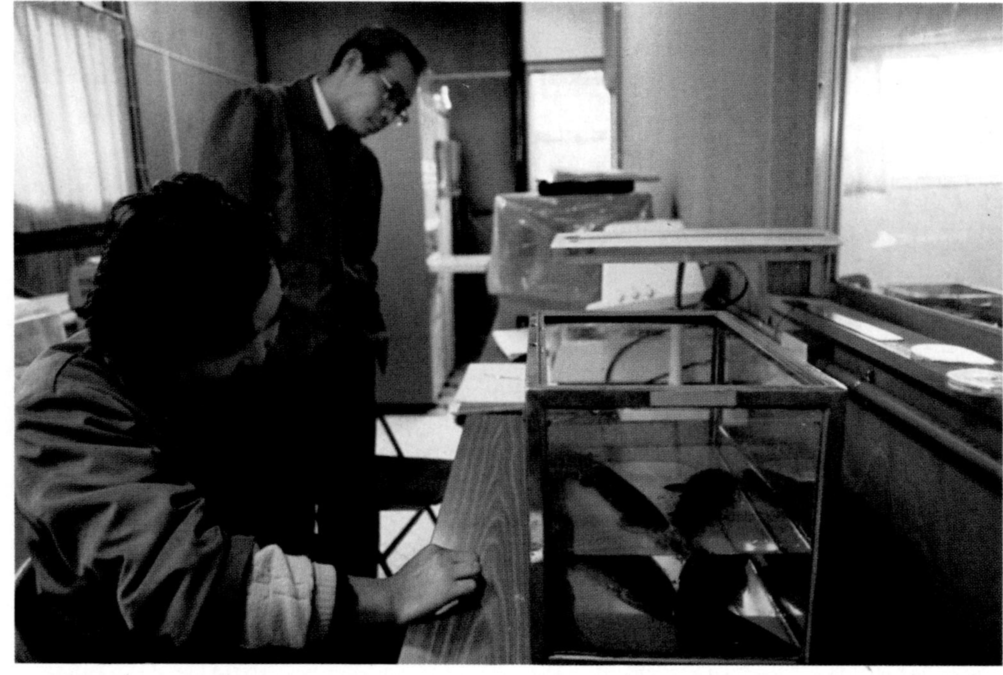

Watching for behavioral patterns that might signal an impending earthquake, Japanese zoologists study catfish at a Tokyo laboratory. The normally sluggish fish have at times become agitated shortly before large upheavals, possibly because of their extreme sensitivity to vibrations and electrical impulses.

he said, "in a couple of days." He based his estimate of magnitude on the size of the area in which the P waves had slowed down, and his prediction of the day of the quake on the length of time before the velocity returned to normal.

Two days later, precisely on schedule, a tremor of the predicted magnitude rumbled through Blue Mountain Lake. Said Aggarwal: "I was so excited I nearly drove into a tree." A visitor from the Geological Survey was greatly impressed but knew that victory was not yet won. "You will be famous," he told Aggarwal, "if you can do this three times."

Four months later another prediction was attempted by James H. Whitcomb of Caltech, who observed that P-wave velocity had dropped near Riverside, California, in 1972 and had stayed below normal through most of 1973. When the velocity began to increase again in November, he predicted that a magnitude 5.5 quake would occur within three months. When the tremor hit, on January 30, its magnitude was only 4.1, but the forecast was accurate enough to constitute yet another triumph.

These successful applications of the dilatancy theory seemed to many to be the perfect "adaptations of seismographic appliances and methods" that G. K. Gilbert had foreseen in 1909, and the belief was spreading that a reliable augury of earthquakes had at last been found. The chairman of the National Academy of Sciences' Panel on Earthquake Prediction, Clarence Allen, was highly enthusiastic: "The general opinion is that we are onto something very

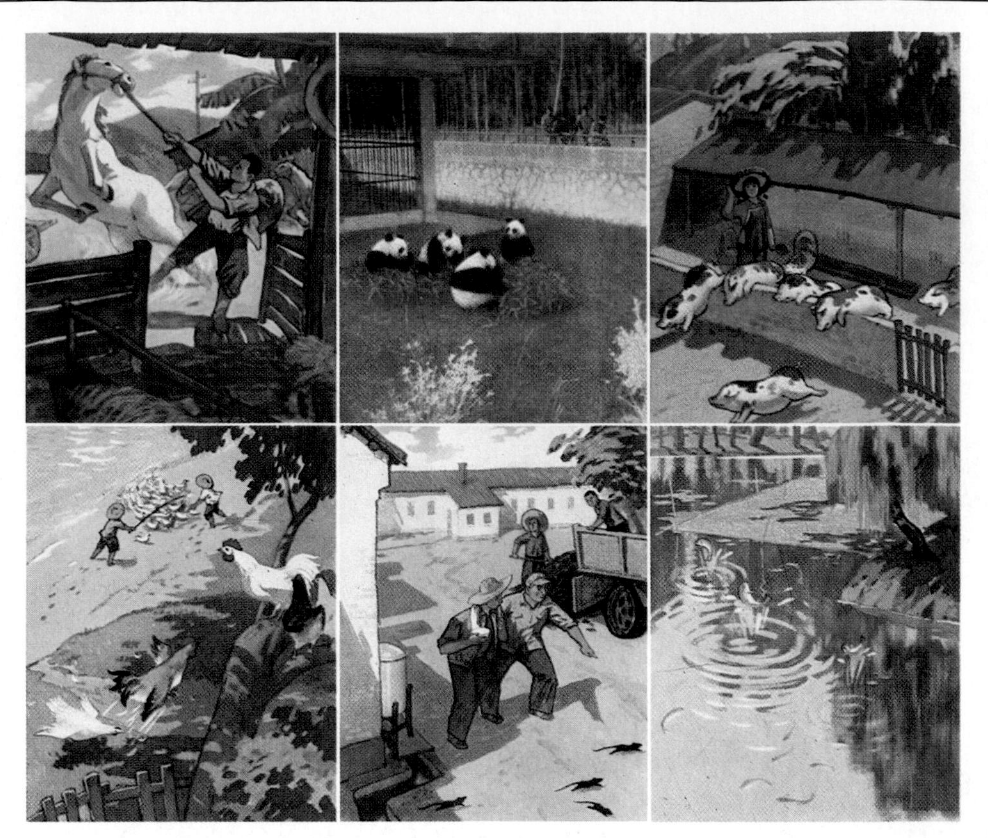

Horses rearing, pandas moaning, mice fleeing houses, these and other illustrations of odd animal behavior, taken from a widely distributed poster in the People's Republic of China, demonstrate the belief that animals can sense the coming of an earthquake. By combining sophisticated seismological data with reports of strange happenings from rural communes, Chinese scientists have been successful in predicting several earthquakes, including a major one that struck Liaoning Province in February 1975.

exciting and very promising." The following year these preliminary successes were overshadowed by the most dramatic prediction, with the most widespread effects, yet seen. It came from the Peoples' Republic of China.

Despite thousands of years of terrible punishment from earthquakes, most of China's 800 million people continue to live in mud-brick, tile-roofed houses that are virtually certain to collapse when shaken. Other construction materials are scarce, and the Chinese must make do with what they have. In March of 1966, two large shocks destroyed the Hsingtai region, some 200 miles southwest of Peking, causing incredible destruction. Premier Chou En-lai was so moved by the suffering and damage that he declared a "People's War on Earthquakes." As the Soviets had done in 1949, he threw the country's resources into an intensive prediction campaign. By 1974 the Chinese had set up 17 major observatories and 250 regional seismic stations, and had trained 10,000 full-time observers to man 5,000 local monitoring posts. An army of amateur earthquake watchers was also enlisted—farmers, workers, students, telephone operators, radio broadcasters, some 100,000 in all—and began making regular observations of ground tremors, water levels and the like.

The Chinese looked for all the warning signs identified in the Soviet Union, the United States and elsewhere: the velocity changes of P and S waves, preliminary swelling of the ground, changes in electrical conductivity and geomagnetic variations. And they discovered other possible precursors. They noticed, for example, that ponds and irrigation canals sometimes became muddy and roiled in advance of an earthquake, and often gave off unusual odors—possibly because of an increase in underground gases. Immediately before large upheavals, the sky sometimes glowed with eerie, neon-like flashes, similar to heat lightning, and balls of fire floated up from the ground. These rare pyrotechnics have not yet been satisfactorily explained: They may be jets of methane gas shaken from the ground by the first tremors and somehow ignited, or they may be the result of electric charges accumulating in certain rock crystals under stress.

Unlike most Western observers, the Chinese were much impressed by the weird behavior of certain animals just before a quake. They documented instances of dogs howling, chickens fleeing their roosts, horses, mice and rabbits becoming panicky, and fish suddenly thrashing about in ponds and aquariums.

As part of their massive earthquake watch, the Chinese paid particular attention to Liaoning Province in Manchuria. Ever since the catastrophe at Hsingtai, there had been a series of moderate earthquakes, each one closer to the heavily settled, highly industrial Liaoning. Few tremors were being recorded in Liaoning itself—in fact, since a large earthquake near the port of Dairen in 1856, the province had been unusually quiet. This in itself seemed threatening.

By 1974, a large force of specialists was in the area, running surveys, mapping fault lines, making seismograms and installing geomagnetic monitors and tiltmeters. The scientists discovered that much of the region had been uplifted and tilted toward the northwest. In addition, they found that the strength of the area's magnetic field was increasing. But there is no indication that they ever detected any changes in the relative velocities of P and S waves.

During the first five months of 1974, there was an ominous increase in the number of minor tremors, to five times the normal frequency. The State Seismological Bureau in Peking issued a tentative forecast: A moderate to strong earthquake would occur within two years. On December 22, another burst of tremors began, the strongest registering 4.8 on the Richter scale. Local party committees started briefing families on what to do in case of a major quake, and the Seismological Bureau refined its prediction: There would be an earthquake of a magnitude of 5.5 to 6 somewhere in the vicinity of the major industrial port of Yingkow during the first six months of 1975.

As February began, the portents became more frequent and more worrisome by the day. Wells started bubbling, rats and mice were observed leaving their holes and weaving about like drunks, snakes crept out of winter hibernation and lay frozen on the icy roads. A swarm of minor tremors began, with more than 500 spasms recorded in 72 hours, culminating in a 4.8 jolt on the morning of February 4. Then there was an eerie quiet.

The Seismological Bureau told the local party committees to prepare for a cataclysm. At 2 p.m., as the temperature dropped to a frigid −4° F., a military commander in a commune near Yingkow went on the radio with an urgent broadcast to the area's residents: "There probably will be a strong earthquake tonight. We require all people to leave their homes." A similar announcement was made at Haicheng, a city of 90,000 some 30 miles inland, and was telephoned to other towns and communes in the threatened area. All told, three million people were affected.

Without panic, the citizens of southern Liaoning Province closed their shops, extinguished their fires, and moved outdoors to parks and fields, where straw shelters and tents were being set up in anticipation of the earthquake. Patients were evacuated from hospitals and livestock was led out of barns. Then, bundled against the cold, the people of Liaoning sat quietly and waited.

The earthquake roared in at 7:36 p.m. Great sheets of light flashed across the sky, and the earth heaved in sickening undulations. Roads buckled, bridges twisted and crashed, 15-foot jets of water and sand shot into the air. Rural communes were tumbled into utter ruin. Almost 90 per cent of Haicheng's buildings were severely damaged or destroyed. Yingkow looked as though it had been battered by a wrecker's ball.

But when the dust settled, casualties were amazingly light. In one Yingkow commune, not a single person had been hurt among the 3,470 residents. More than 3,000 people lived in Haicheng's badly mauled Dingjiagou Brigade, yet only one child was reported injured. So it was throughout the province. In an area of three million people, where a quake of this violence might be expected to bring death to tens of thousands, the estimated toll was only about 300.

A Chinese family inspects well water at a commune in this poster distributed as part of a campaign by the People's Republic of China to involve the general populace in earthquake prediction. At bottom are shown five things to look for as possible signs of an impending quake: increased cloudiness of the water, turbulence, changes in level, bubbling, bitterness.

The advance warning had averted a catastrophe, and seismologists everywhere hailed it as a milestone. "Nowhere else in the world had this size earthquake been predicted with this kind of precision," marveled Massachusetts Institute of Technology geophysicist Frank Press. And the Chinese triumph seemed to certify that reliable earthquake prediction was just around the corner.

Buoyed by their success and the worldwide acclaim it brought, the Chinese pressed their prediction campaign onward. In the summer of 1976 they thought they had spotted sure signs of an approaching tremor in Kwangtung Province and issued a warning; inhabitants spent two months living in tents before the authorities had to conclude that their forecast was mistaken.

In the months that followed the 1975 Yingkow-Haicheng tremor, China's earthquake watchers had been perplexed by a series of possible precursors observed in northern China around Tangshan, an industrial and coal-mining city of a million people. Some medium-sized tremors had jostled the area in 1975, but no one could tell whether these were aftershocks from Haicheng or the foreshocks of a major upheaval to come. Chinese seismologists stepped up their surveillance, found some long-term changes in gravity and electrical resistance, and in January 1976 recorded a sharp change in magnetism. An open-ended, long-term alert was issued. Late in July, sudden variations in groundwater level and strange animal behavior were reported. But they were too scattered and ambiguous to support an amended and more urgent forecast.

Shortly before 4 a.m. on July 28, the inhabitants of Tangshan and its environs were awakened by what they thought was daylight—incredible sheets of white and red lights blazed in the sky, lights that were visible from a distance of 200 miles. A moment later the ground shook with such savagery that many people were hurled against the ceilings of their homes. Countless thousands of houses collapsed instantaneously as if, a survivor said, they were made of cards. Twenty square miles of cityscape fell into utter ruin.

A visiting French group was in one of the hotels that crumbled into a heap of rubble. Astonishingly, 22 of 23 members survived and picked their way through the wreckage barefoot. "It was horrible," one of them recalled. "We were lost. It was like an ocean, an ocean, everything moving." When European survivors flying out that afternoon looked over the ravaged city from the air, all they could see standing upright was a single smokestack.

Many of the residents of Peking, 100 miles to the west, were showered with falling plaster and flying window glass. Some older buildings collapsed, and wide cracks appeared in the city's main department store. A large proportion of the 7.6 million people living in the Chinese capital fled their homes to set up housekeeping in the streets and parks until the threat of aftershocks passed.

Seismographs around the world lurched with the arrival of the monstrous seismic waves. Scientists located the epicenter at Tangshan itself and calculated the Richter magnitude to be 8, the largest recorded anywhere since the 1964 Alaska quake. The area of north China affected was seismically active and riddled with fault zones, one of which ran directly under Tangshan in a northeast-southwest direction. But it had been inactive for so long that some seismologists thought it harmless. The fracture produced visible surface faulting for five miles through the city's center, shearing off walls, buildings, roads and canals with a lateral movement that in places measured more than four feet.

Great as the original tremor was, it did not entirely relieve the tectonic strain. Just 16 hours later an aftershock with a Richter magnitude of 7.4 punished the area again, and more than 125 tremors with magnitudes of at least 4 struck within 48 hours.

Seismologists later agreed that the upheaval was one of a series of related major earthquakes that occurred in 1976 along an arc from Italy through Uzbekistan in the Soviet Union to the New Hebrides islands north of Australia. Seismologists ascribed the unusually heavy seismic activity to a northward

The night sky over Matsushiro, Japan, glows a ruddy orange in this rare 1966 photograph of "earthquake lights," an electrical phenomenon of unknown origin that sometimes accompanies tremors. Some scientists believe the lights might give a clue to impending earthquakes and have proposed monitoring ground electrical levels where the lights have occurred.

surge of the African and Indo-Australian Plates. But none of this was known in time to be of assistance to the hapless people of Tangshan.

Deeply embarrassed by the failure of its vaunted forecasting efforts, the Chinese government suppressed all news from the disaster area. Visitors were hustled out of the stricken cities, and the area was closed to foreigners. All the government news agency would say was that Tangshan had suffered "great losses to the people, life and property."

Almost a year went by without any further official mention of the tragedy. Seismologists visiting Peking on other matters found their questions about Tangshan turned aside. Finally, in May 1977 the Chinese reluctantly began sharing geological aspects of the disaster with other scientists. Details of the social impact remained secret. But Western experts have estimated that as many as three quarters of a million people died—a death toll that would make Tangshan's earthquake the world's most murderous in more than 400 years.

The Tangshan quake brought an abrupt and brutal end to the growing belief that reliable earthquake forecasting was at hand. It was obvious that many events identified by the Chinese and others as sure signs of an impending tremor were not sure at all—they appeared before some earthquakes but not before others. Wells might bubble, animals might behave strangely, radon gas might appear in groundwater, foreshocks might occur—or, apparently, they might not. Even dilatancy, which had been so rapidly gaining credibility as a key precursor, failed the test of universality—and not only at Tangshan. At Coyote Lake, south of San Francisco, for instance, a magnitude 5.9 earthquake struck in 1979 without an iota of prior evidence of dilatancy, either in seismic wave velocities or in changes of ground level. The cause and effect relationship, the clear evidence that if a certain thing or combination of things occurred then an earthquake was certain to follow, still eluded the world's seismologists.

If there is one characteristic typical of a scientist—other than curiosity—it is tenaciousness. While seismologists were halted short of their goal in a number of areas of inquiry, there were other paths to travel and other exciting ideas to pursue. In the late 1960s, the tectonic plate model of earthquake mechanics breathed new life into the old idea that the rhythm of past earthquakes might yield foreknowledge of the next tremors. According to the theory of plate tectonics, major fractures along the great earthquake belts can be expected to occur with approximate regularity, because the crustal plates are crunching together or scraping past each other at a fairly constant rate. Thus, where a fault had slipped recently, it would probably remain quiescent for a number of years. But the longer the time period since a fracture had taken place, the greater the likelihood of a fracture occurring soon. The area of a seismically active fault that had been unusually quiet was called a seismic gap.

Unlike the time-consuming field work of identifying possible precursors, locating the seismic gaps was an academic exercise. On a map of the world's seismic belts, researchers marked the sectors where there had been recent fault movement. The unmarked areas were seismic gaps. By focusing on these areas of probable seismic activity and relating the physical length of the gap to the probable magnitude of the eventual earthquake, scientists made some remarkable forecasts. Lynn Sykes contributed to a paper calling attention to several gaps along the Alaska coast in 1971, and a year later one of them, at Sitka in the Alaskan panhandle, suffered a magnitude 7.6 shock. Another at Yakataga, southeast of Valdez, is expected to be the scene of a major quake by the year 2000.

While seismic gaps give a long-range view of the earthquake potential in a large area, they have not yet supported the specific predictions of time and place that scientists so ardently yearn for. In some places, the plates may slip quietly past each other for long periods of time. Even where the fault is locked into

The seismic gap theory of earthquake prediction is illustrated on this plot of activity along the Mexican and Central American coasts, where the Cocos, Caribbean and North American tectonic plates collide. In the areas marked by gray shading, strain-relieving tremors have occurred within the last 30 years, but in the red-shaded areas no large quake has been observed and strain is still mounting. By zeroing in on these seismic gaps, scientists can sometimes detect the subtle warning signals of an imminent rupture.

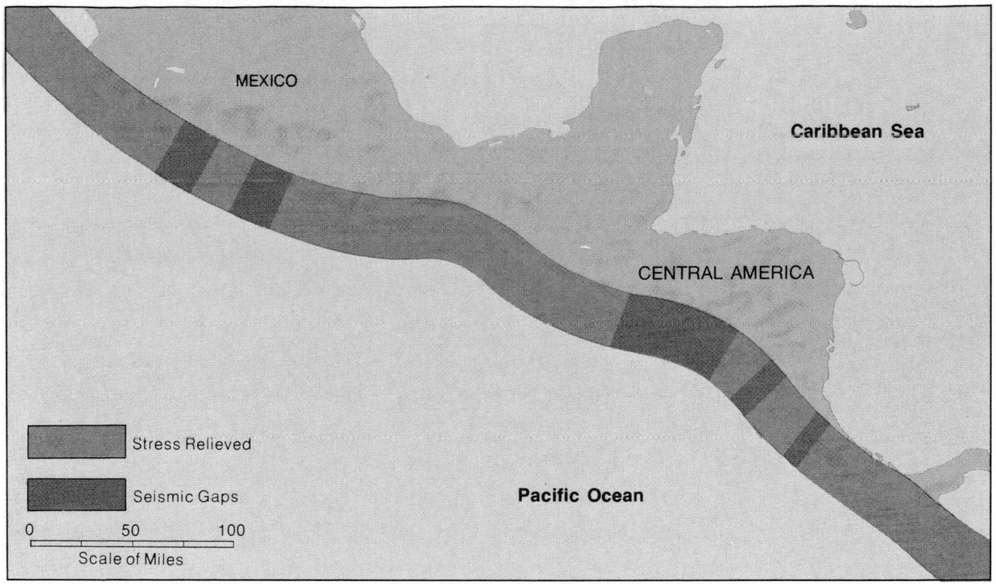

immobility and the forces are known to be accumulating for a major upheaval, the exact time when the quake can be expected remains uncomfortably vague.

But in recent years a brilliant refinement of the seismic gap concept has nourished new hopes for prediction. The theory postulates two phases to the prelude: an alpha phase, during which there is no seismic activity whatsoever, and a beta phase for a few days or a few weeks before the earthquake, during which there are frequent small foreshocks—the ominous preliminary cracklings of the crust just before the main fracture.

The possibilities of the idea were dramatically demonstrated in the Mexican state of Oaxaca in 1978. Along the southern coast of Mexico, a portion of the Pacific ocean bed is being subducted beneath the North American Plate. In 1977, scientists at the Geophysics Laboratory of the University of Texas at Galveston concluded that a 185-mile stretch of plate boundary along the coast of Oaxaca exhibited all the signs of a seismic gap in the alpha phase. Reading the seismic record, they found that moderate earthquake activity along that section of the subduction zone had stopped altogether in the middle of 1973. After further study, the Texas geophysicists published a paper identifying the phenomenon as a "probable precursor to a large earthquake." They thought it would strike in the center of the gap, along the coast, and they forecast a beta phase of modest foreshocks preceding the large earthquake. The length of the dormant section of the fault indicated to them that the main quake would reach a magnitude of between 7.25 and 7.75. But they could make no prediction of when the earthquake would strike.

As it happened, a senior research fellow from Caltech was at Mexico City's Institute of Geophysics in August 1978, when alarm bells started jangling in the institute's basement seismograph room. Karen McNally followed her Mexican hosts to the revolving drums. A moderate tremor was shaking Oaxaca, and the seismologists told her that it was the second quake to hit the region in five weeks. The Oaxaca seismic gap appeared to be coming alive.

The American researcher sensed a perfect opportunity to study the beta phase of the seismic gap thesis—the preliminary grumblings of a major earthquake. But she would have to hurry. "We didn't have the luxury of time," she recalled. "We can always go back and rework, reargue the data," she told the Mexican scientists, "but we might never have another opportunity to go out with the instruments."

What Karen McNally proposed was a network of portable seismographs arrayed near the possible fracture; she intended nothing less than recording the complete patterns of small foreshocks leading to a major quake. By November 8 a seven-station network was in place and recording in the Oaxaca wilderness.

For a week the seismographs were quiet. Then came a series of small tremors, measuring up to 3.2 on the Richter scale. They petered out after November 15, and for another 13 days nothing happened. On November 28 the lull was broken by a second series of tremors. Measuring up to magnitude 3.7, these shocks started at one end of the Oaxaca gap and swept inward, toward its center. There was another quiet period, lasting 18 hours. And then, just as forecast by the Texas seismologists, a major earthquake, magnitude 7.8, rocked a large, sparsely settled area of Mexico. No one was killed, but minor damage was done as far away as Mexico City, 290 miles to the northwest.

For the first time, scientists had in effect trapped a great earthquake within a network of sensitive instruments. "It was right in the middle of our array—exactly!" exulted Karen McNally. The data she recorded provided seismologists with a complete seismic picture of the foreshocks that precede a major earthquake. The foreshock activity, much of it in the form of micro-earthquakes, does not show up on ordinary seismographs unless they are in the immediate vicinity. It was Karen McNally's hope—much encouraged by the triumph at Oaxaca—that by using the seismic gap theory to select areas for intensive instrumentation, scientists could record more foreshock patterns and eventually use them to support accurate predictions of threatening earthquakes.

No region of North America stands in greater need of reliable earthquake forecasts than the area along California's San Andreas Fault. There the great tectonic impulse of the Pacific Plate, welling up at the East Pacific Rise and spreading northwestward until it slides under the south coast of Alaska, carries a 700-mile sliver of California northward at up to an inch and a half a year, scraping and jostling the continent's edge as it goes.

The movement is obvious to the residents of Hollister, midway along the fault, where it causes curbstones and house foundations slowly to crumble and swerve. The Hollister area is shaken by occasional moderate earthquakes, but it has never suffered a really big one. Along these middle reaches the San Andreas inches along in a generally benign manner known as fault creep.

What worries seismologists most are two sections where the fault is not moving. Near its northern end, at San Francisco, the San Andreas has remained fixed for many decades. Moderate tremors occur there with some frequency, but they are the result of fractures along lesser nearby fault zones. The San Andreas itself has not budged near San Francisco since the cataclysm of 1906. The strain has been steadily building, and the main fault will inevitably give way again.

Near Los Angeles, 350 miles to the south, the situation is the same. There have been some notable earthquakes in the area, but these, too, resulted from movement along various side faults. The last time the San Andreas ruptured near its southern end was in 1857—and the next time it goes the effects are expected to be similar.

The 1857 earthquake—Southern California's strongest in historic times and an equal to the 1906 San Francisco quake—struck on January 9 at 8:33 in the morning. The ground shook for as long as three minutes as the San Andreas fractured for 217 miles through south-central California. Trees whipped so violently that their branches swept the ground, and cattle fell bellowing to their knees. Sixty miles north of Los Angeles at Fort Tejon, a military base near the fault, the post commander rushed outside in time to see the entire outpost tumble into ruin. Few people had settled in Southern California in 1857; apparently only two died in the quake, and there were few works of man to damage. But the earthquake scarred the landscape indelibly, opening fissures and offsetting stream beds by as much as 30 feet. The southern San Andreas has remained relatively stable ever since, but the strain along it continues to build.

A repeat of either the 1857 Los Angeles or the 1906 San Francisco quake,

The Little Lab at the Bottom of the Sea

The origins of most of the great earthquakes that afflict Japan lie near the deep ocean trenches off the Pacific coastline where the Philippine Plate and the Pacific Plate descend under the plate that carries Eurasia. Yet until recently, all of the monitoring stations in Japan's extensive earthquake prediction network were installed on land far from the ocean bottom, where minute stresses and strains in the underlying bedrock may provide warnings of the next big rupture.

To gain access to undersea rumblings, Japanese scientists have developed several types of innovative instrument packages that can function at great depths beneath the sea. The most practical and economical for short-term observation is a capsule *(right),* two and a half feet in diameter, that is constructed of high-tensile-strength aluminum alloy and is designed to hold sensitive detection devices: seismographs, tiltmeters, geomagnetometers and gravimeters. So durable and efficient is the capsule that it can operate at depths of 19,000 feet and remain unattended for as long as 40 days.

Deployed singly or in multiple units, the 265-pound capsule is launched from a ship and lowered to the seabed. Weighted down with 176 pounds of ballast, it descends slowly and lands gently on its braced legs, like a spaceship on the surface of the moon. Seismic observation begins with an ultrasonic command from the mother ship.

After completing its mission of recording seismic waves, crustal slippage and changes in water temperature, magnetic fields and seabed angles of inclination, the capsule receives a release command from the ship, a land station or its own built-in timer. The ballast is then discarded and the pressurized capsule pops to the water's surface like a cork. With its radio beacon and flasher light, the capsule signals the mother ship, and after being picked up and reequipped, it is sent down again for another mission.

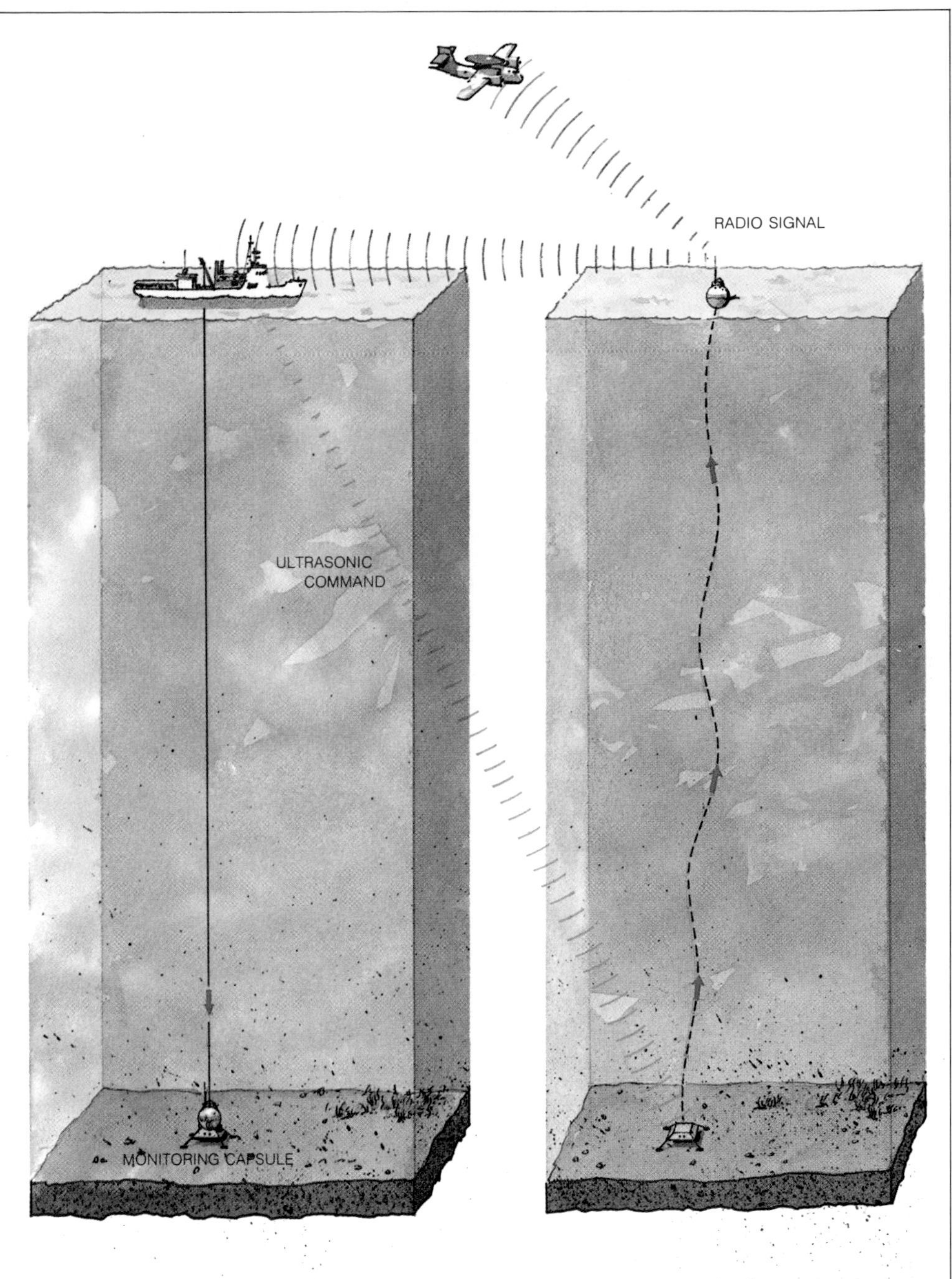

A triumph of remote control, the Japanese seismograph capsule above performs its earthquake-monitoring functions automatically on the floor of the ocean. Upon a command from the mother ship, from land or from its built-in timer, the capsule rises to the surface. Its radio signal and flasher light guide the ship to its location. A spotter plane can also be used to locate the bobbing capsule.

Employing a trenching technique, geologist Kerry Sieh seeks to predict the future behavior of California's San Andreas Fault from its actions in the past. In the 16-foot-deep excavation at top, Sieh uncovered evidence of nine major earthquakes that took place between the 6th Century and 1857, at intervals averaging 160 years. In the bottom photograph Sieh points to one of several layers of peat that were displaced on or about the dates indicated.

given today's urban sprawl, could be the worst natural calamity ever to strike the United States; it has been estimated that as many as 23,000 people might be killed and as much as $70 billion worth of property destroyed. There is little doubt that the San Andreas will rupture again. The question is, when?

Seeking a useful answer to that question, earth scientists have made the San Andreas Fault one of the most thoroughly instrumented geological features in the world. With strain meters, creepmeters, seismographs, galvanometers, gravimeters, tiltmeters and laser beams they are monitoring, measuring and studying every possible avenue along which a reliable precursor of impending cataclysm might appear. The scientists have found a number of ominous signs, but cannot yet be certain what they portend.

To the north of Los Angeles, in the Palmdale area, instruments have revealed a worrisome change in the earth. Between 1959 and 1975 a 32,000-square-mile area of the surface around Palmdale rose like a soufflé in the oven, bulging upward as much as 18 inches. Then (like a cooling soufflé) parts of it began to sink. "That bulge has been collapsing like crazy," said one U.S. Geological Survey scientist in 1980, and the collapse was continuing.

Other measurements showed that from 1972 to 1979, the land on either side of the San Andreas east of Los Angeles had been squeezing together, tightening as if in a massive vise across the fault. Then the vise seemed to relax its grip and the land on either side began to expand as the prevailing stresses suddenly changed direction to run parallel to the fault line. Sophisticated measurements made by space-age laser-beam instruments, satellites and giant radio telescopes focused on a distant quasar are producing data of unprecedented detail and accuracy on plate movement near the fault, but it will be years before scientists have enough of a record to permit conclusions about what is happening, let alone predictions of what will happen.

In 1975 a young graduate student at California's Stanford University named Kerry Sieh decided to dig—literally—into the San Andreas Fault's history. If all the sophisticated instruments were giving confusing or inadequate signals, perhaps it was time for some good old-fashioned pick-and-shovel work. The area had been settled so recently that the 100-year record of the fault's activities was geologically insignificant. "We had always suspected that the San Andreas underwent periodic, dramatic quakes," he said, "but there was nothing tangible to back it up." Sieh hoped to find how frequently the San Andreas had moved in the distant past and thus estimate a time for the next rupture.

Sieh began his investigations by driving along the fault, looking for stream beds offset by prior fractures and showing evidence of centuries of sedimentation in which a geological record would have been preserved. At Wallace Creek, about 200 miles northeast of Los Angeles, he found a gully that had been shifted almost a quarter of a mile, a displacement that he thought might represent as many as 42 earthquakes. In an ancient peat bog that straddles the fault at Pallett Creek, 34 miles northeast of Los Angeles, he cut a trench 15 feet down through accumulated layers of silt, gravel and carbonized organic matter. In the process he uncovered scars of eight separate fault movements, and with radiocarbon dating techniques determined when they had occurred. Sieh found that the earthquakes exposed by his trench had taken place anywhere from 55 to 275 years apart, beginning in 565 A.D., with an average repeat time of 160 years. He confirmed his figures at another site along the fault where he peeled back the layers of geologic time to uncover 6,000 years of seismic history.

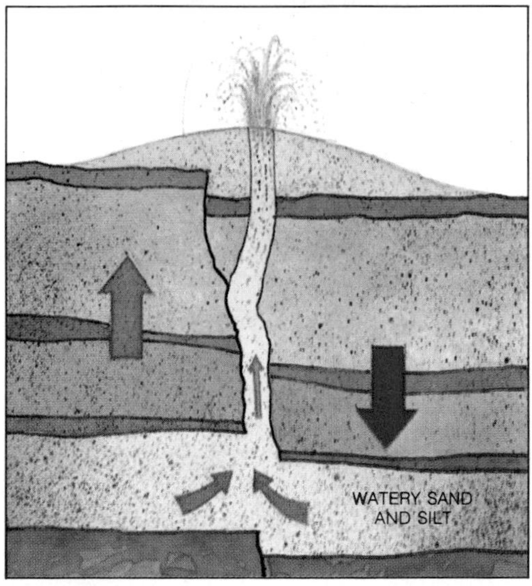

Remnants of a sandblow—a spouting of sand and water caused by moderate to severe earthquakes—can be seen in the photograph of a cross section of an old California stream bed that was rocked by a quake around 1700. Sandblows occur, as illustrated in the drawing at bottom, when a layer of subsoil takes on liquid characteristics during tremors. Pressure drives the watery sand and silt up through a fissure, leaving a mound of sediment on the surface that geologists can use to identify and date the earthquake.

If Sieh's research discovered an average time period between great earthquakes at these locations, it also showed that seismic events pay little attention to the timetable and can vary their occurrence by as much as 50 per cent from the average. Thus when Sieh turned from his research to look into the future, his language was highly circumscribed. "The next great earthquake in Southern California," he said in 1981, "would not break millennial tradition if it occurred within the next decade. Neither would the prehistoric record be contradicted if that event failed to occur within our lifetime." Although Sieh did not consider the advent of the earthquake overdue, he believed that "we are clearly well along in the process—too far along in fact to neglect serious preparations for the eventuality."

The closest Sieh allowed himself to come to a specific prediction was this: "I think the chances of a great earthquake in Southern California within the next 40 years are at least greater than 50 per cent." That is not the kind of forecast in which civil-defense officials can take much comfort. It calls to mind the 1909 reservations of G. K. Gilbert about whether the complexities of earthquake mechanics would ever permit predictions on the basis of earthquake regularity. "The hypothesis of rhythmic recurrence," he said then, "has no sure support from observation, and is not in working order." And his general assessment of the prospects for earthquake prediction applies as well to the final years of the 20th Century as it did to the first: "The determination of times of danger belongs to the indefinite future. It still lingers in the domain of endeavor and hope." Ω

In most earthquake-prone regions of the world, the dangers are largely invisible. The great fault lines and fracture zones lie deep within bedrock, where only sophisticated seismological instruments can pinpoint their location. But in California, along the San Andreas Fault, the earthquake is a palpable presence, its scar in many places clearly visible.

Here, the fracture zone rises to the surface, running 700 miles from Mexico to Cape Mendocino, north of San Francisco, where it dives into the Pacific Ocean. The San Andreas slashes across deserts and farmland, passes under dams and reservoirs, and bisects the towns and cities of one of the most populous areas of the United States.

More than 18 million people live along the San Andreas Fault and associated smaller fractures. The fault intrudes on their lives constantly as it responds to the irresistible tectonic forces at work along its edges. At thousands of spots along its length, the slow, inexorable movement of the fault can be seen in offset stream beds and orchards, and in bridges and buildings gradually being torn apart. Earth scientists anticipate that a major quake will occur somewhere along the San Andreas by the year 2000.

Yet while they can see it and feel it, most Californians regard the San Andreas with a strong sense of fatalism—and a profound belief in the odds. They continue to crisscross the fault with ribbons of highways, aqueducts, power lines and pipelines. Each year, 50 or so new housing developments go up within the fault system. Major industries and universities lie close to the fault. An adviser to the State Commission on Seismic Safety says, "The way many hospitals and schools were built around here, you'd think they used the fault line as a guide."

Indeed, for all the dread potential, many Californians who live close to the fault look upon earthquakes as an acceptable risk in return for the Pacific Coast's salubrious climate and economic opportunity. "Every part of the country has its problems," says one resident. Adds a woman whose house rests only a few yards from the fault: "There are other things I have to worry about day to day. If I let it get to me, I couldn't get anything done."

A scarp thrust up by the San Andreas Fault stands in high relief in the Carrizo Plain in central California. While traces of the fault can be followed for hundreds of miles, it is in this desolate plain that the giant scar is most evident, a clear record of violent upheaval.

Exposed by a California highway cut, a section of the San Andreas Fault near Palmdale reveals the dramatic buckling of rock formations caused by tectonic compression. Two gigantic tectonic plates, the Pacific and the North American, are grinding against each other with such force that they have caused a network of fractures across the state. The map below shows the San Andreas *(red)* and associated faults *(yellow)*.

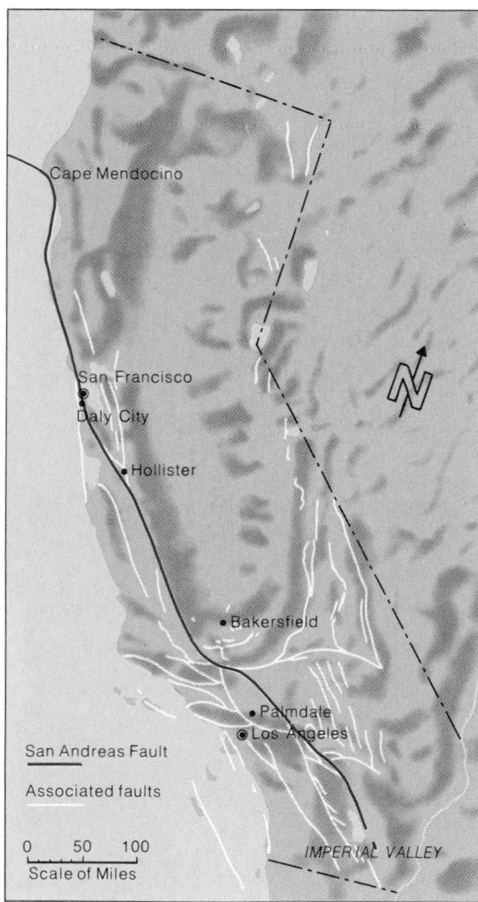

In a classic example of lateral movement along a branch of the San Andreas system in the Imperial Valley, offset rows of trees in an orange grove sliced by the fault show a displacement of approximately 10 feet. The slippage took place in 1940 when a sharp tremor jolted the area.

Ground movement along a branch of the San Andreas near Hollister wrenches this vineyard drainage ditch half an inch out of line every year. A warehouse at the same vineyard is gradually being torn apart, with cracks opening in the concrete floor and gaps appearing in the walls.

Upthrust land along the fault creates a slope that is too steep for cultivation on this farm near Bakersfield. The depression in the center of the ridge is known as a sag pond; it was formed when surface movement along the fault cut off drainage.

Ocean-front homes in Daly City, built on unstable cliffs undercut by the San Andreas Fault, stand in peril of tumbling into the Pacific Ocean in a major earthquake. As it is, landslides, some caused by minor tremors, have closed the seaside highway below.

Slides have already eroded as much as 85 feet of land in front of these Daly City homes. Says one woman, whose house now stands on the brink of the cliff: "I hope it has stabilized, but there is no way to know. I can't afford to go anywhere else."

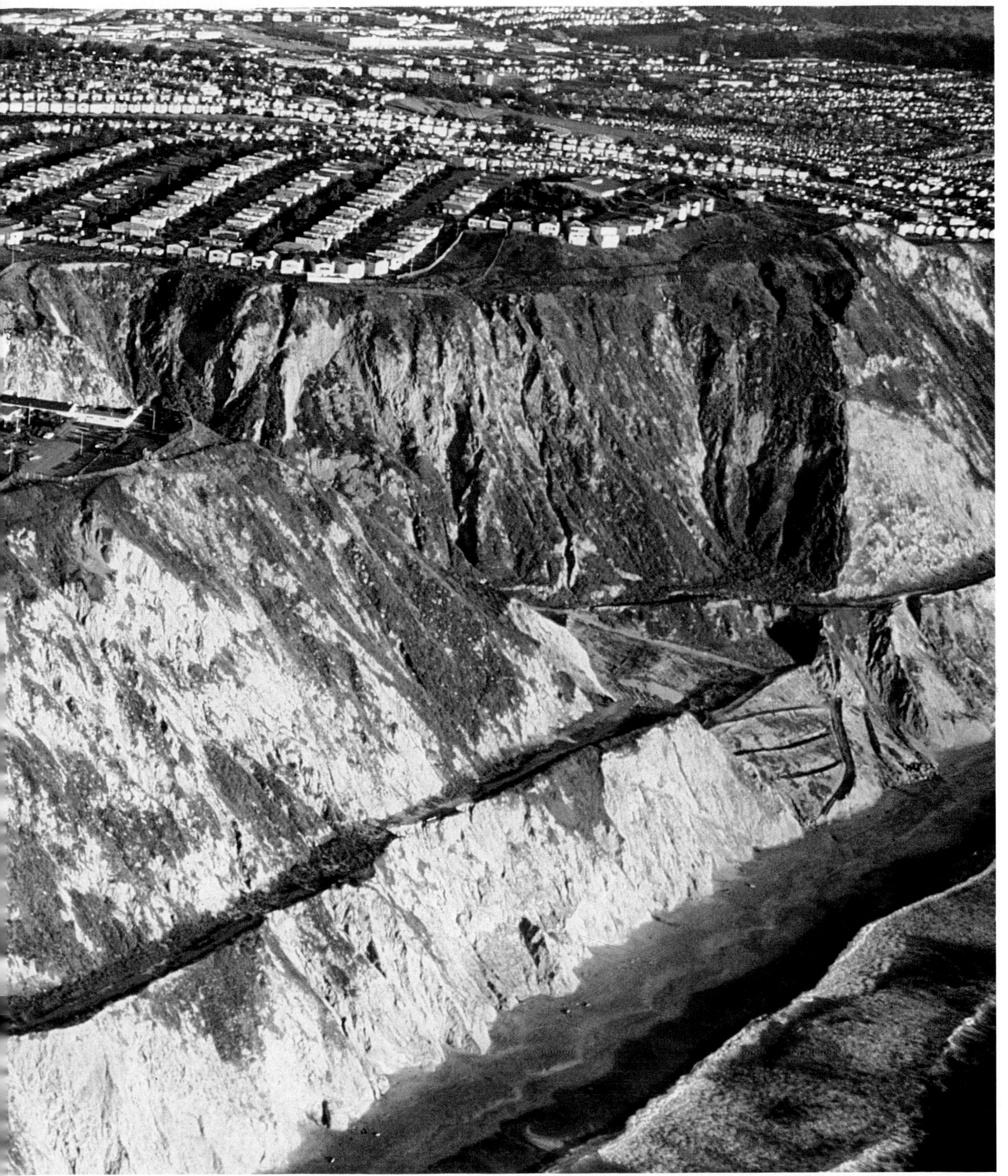

Chapter 6

LESSONS IN FRUSTRATION AND HOPE

Schoolchildren crouch beneath desks, their heads protected by seat cushions, during an earthquake drill in Matsushiro, Japan. Living in one of the most seismically dangerous areas in the world, the Japanese have established both a sophisticated prediction network and a nationwide disaster plan in order to minimize the loss of life and property.

Few threats to the life and property of man are more ominous, more clearly imminent or more colossal than that posed by the floor of the Pacific Ocean. From its genesis along the midocean trench west of Central and South America, the great Pacific Plate edges northwestward past the United States, jostling and endangering California on its way to thrust under the south coast of Alaska. There, at the Aleutian Trench, it unleashes such cataclysms as the Good Friday earthquake of 1964 with its awesome land deformation and huge tsunami. But it is across the Pacific Ocean, 8,000 miles west of its birthplace, that the Pacific Plate offers its greatest threat. There, where the gigantic plate crunches into the Asian continent along the Japan Trench, it places in immediate and mortal peril one of the densest concentrations of humanity on earth.

The islands of Japan contain about the same land area as the state of California, yet are populated by five times as many people—116 million, almost 20 million of them in the Tokyo area. And Japan's susceptibility to earthquakes makes California seem a haven by comparison. For the craggy, crowded islands are battered by 15 per cent of all the seismic energy released in the world.

Each year the Japanese archipelago is rocked by more than 1,000 perceptible seismic tremors. Most of these pass with little or no serious damage. But every few years, somewhere in Japan, earthquakes bring calamity. In the half century since 1930, nine major quakes have killed more than 12,000 people and have destroyed some 80,000 buildings. None of the quakes has occurred near the densely populated areas of Tokyo, and while this has been cause for much thankfulness in the past, it is also the basis for great concern in the present.

A review of the seismic history of Tokyo since 818 A.D. led one researcher to conclude in 1970 that the city has suffered an earthquake of magnitude 8 or more once every 69 years, give or take 13 years. Since no such cataclysm has rocked Tokyo since 1923, the city would seem to be in increasing danger of a recurrence. The probable source of that danger is a fault zone that runs through Sagami Bay and passes within 50 miles of the city to the southwest. Seismologists have kept the area under intense scrutiny, especially since 1964, when the Japanese government took on the prediction of damaging earthquakes as a national project. But while scientists have recorded plenty of microtremors and have measured varying amounts of crustal strain near the fault, they have yet to find anything they consider alarming.

Farther south along the coast, however, in the densely populated, heavily industrialized Tokai region, the seismologists have found evidence that worries them very much. Although it is thoroughly shaken from time to time, Tokai has not experienced a great quake since December 24, 1854, when the then placid area of rice paddies, orchards and fishing villages was devastated by a tremor whose Richter magnitude has been estimated at 8.4. Scores of villages were destroyed and the wreckage was swept out to sea by the subsequent tsunami. In all, 3,000 people were killed and 25,000 homes were destroyed.

The fracture occurred in a large fault zone that runs along the edge of the Pacific Plate to the south of Tokai. Recent analyses show that ever since the 1854 quake, tectonic forces have been accumulating steadily and the strains have been inexorably deforming the adjacent land; one section of coastline has settled at least a foot. In 1977, a committee was set up by the government to consider the danger to Tokai, and in 1979 the area was designated for intensive civil-defense measures. Seismologists could not make a specific prediction, but they increasingly believed that the breaking point for Tokai would come soon.

The previous Tokai quake in 1854 may provide the Japanese with a model for the mechanics and magnitude of the expected earthquake, but contributes little to an appreciation of the human dimensions of the looming disaster. When it comes, it will strike an area that was then sparsely settled and rural but is now populated by almost six million people living in 170 cities and towns and working in hundreds of major factories, chemical plants and oil refineries. If the quake hits without warning, experts predict more than 10,000 deaths and perhaps half a million structures destroyed by tremors, tsunami and fire. The only thing remotely comparable, say the authorities, was an event the Japanese remember with an enduring sense of national mourning: the great Kanto earthquake that smashed into Yokohama and Tokyo on September 1, 1923.

It was Saturday, and in both Tokyo and the seaport of Yokohama 17 miles to the south shops and offices were closing for the weekend as the morning ended. Tokyo's new Imperial Hotel, specially designed by Frank Lloyd Wright to resist earthquakes *(pages 153-155)*, was about to open officially with a gala luncheon celebration. Weekend crowds were gathering in the city's entertainment district and at seashore resorts.

Just before noon, 50 miles south of Tokyo, the earth ruptured along the Sagami Bay fault and savaged a broad sweep of the Kanto Plain, including Tokyo and Yokohama, with almost a full five minutes of shaking. Shortly thereafter a murderous tsunami, reaching 36 feet in height, lashed the coast.

A passenger aboard a ship anchored inside the breakwater at Yokohama saw "a yellow cloud—very thin at first but growing in size every second—rising from the city." He wrote that it "formed a continuous strip all around the bay, growing in size and deepening in color, traveling at great speed toward the north." It was the dust raised by the collapse of thousands of buildings.

Wood was the principal construction material in Yokohama, as it was throughout Japan, and while wood buildings withstand most earthquakes reasonably well, the September 1 convulsion splintered more than 12,000 of the city's 100,000 houses. American Henry W. Kinney, editor of *The Trans-Pacific* magazine of Tokyo, described the destruction: "The houses, most of them two-storied, frail wooden structures with paper windows, crowned with heavy roof tiles, had not only been smashed, but had been torn apart, rended into splintered beams and raveled and torn fragments of boards jumbled together, as if they had been battered by a giant flail. They had been thrown in every direction, backwards, against each other, into the streets. I came to the sickening realization that there could be safety nowhere."

The wooden wreckage soon posed a new threat to the survivors of the quake. The red-hot coals from overturned stoves and charcoal braziers were scattered through the wooden dwellings, landing against paper walls or on straw tatami matting. Scores of homes burst into flame. The fires spread and mingled, eventually joining to envelop the city in a single roaring conflagration.

Tokyo survived the earthquake's convulsions better than Yokohama. The

Skyscrapers topple and flames light up the Tokyo sky in this lurid promotion poster for a Japanese earthquake disaster film. Metropolitan government officials turned popular interest in the movie to civic ends by adding a safety message at bottom ("Put out a fire when you feel an earthquake tremor"), and helped distribute the poster throughout the city.

フィクションのままでありたい地震列島
9月1日は
防災の日
グラッときたら火の始末
地震列島
東宝映画作品

newer residential sections, built on high, rocky ground to the west, were scarcely touched. Most of the damage occurred in Tokyo's older wards downtown, in the sedimented areas abutting the Sumida River, where swampy soil amplified the effect of the seismic waves. Perhaps 5,000 buildings came down, about 1 per cent of those in the city. In the downtown amusement district, Tokyo's tallest building, the 12-story brick Ryōunkaku, or "Rising-over-the-Clouds Tower," swayed to and fro and then, said an observer, "seemed to make a polite bow," and broke apart at the eighth floor. The Imperial Hotel at least partially fulfilled the expectations raised by its earthquake-resistant design and came through with only incidental damage—as did a number of other modern downtown buildings.

In Tokyo, as in Yokohama, it was not the shaking that contributed most to the city's destruction, but the profusion of small fires that blazed up in the ruined houses. As the flames blossomed through the downtown wards, feeding on the timbers of the congested houses, they merged, created their own updrafts and filled the sky with their chrysanthemum reds and oranges. They soon formed two massive fronts, each driving inward toward the Sumida River. Two great crowds of refugees gathered in the narrow streets, their pushcarts laden with food, bedding and valuables. Converging on the river in search of safety, the masses of people started across its wooden bridges only to meet head-on in midspan. There was general chaos as the two high walls of fire raged toward the river from either bank. More than 250 bridges were ignited by falling cinders, and thousands of people were consumed by the flames.

The fire storm burned on through the night, its light so intense that the very air seemed to glow like an incandescent bulb, casting light strong enough to read by 10 miles from the city. By Sunday morning more than 300,000 buildings had burned to the ground and 4,500 acres of the Japanese capital—two thirds of the city—lay in smoldering black ash. The ground still trembled with the earthquake's aftershocks—237 Saturday afternoon and evening, and 92 more on Sunday. As Monday dawned, a dazed and mournful populace began sifting through the rubble for the charred remains of missing relatives.

In a section of Tokyo that was incinerated on that day there is now a small park in which has been erected an earthquake museum and a memorial temple. On every anniversary of the disaster the park is the scene of a solemn rite commemorating the 140,000 people who were lost in the cataclysm.

With the horror of Kanto and the scenario for Tokai as incentives, Japan has become the world leader in learning how to live with earthquakes and mitigate their effects. To be sure, large, heavily populated areas of California along the San Andreas Fault stand in grave seismic peril. But the threat to Japan is stronger and more immediate. For one thing, earthquakes in massive subduction zones, such as the one off Japan, are almost always more severe than those along transform faults such as the San Andreas. And time seems to be working more quickly against the Japanese. While Californians might expect a quake within 50 years, as one expert puts it, "Japan's time scale of hazard is different; it's here and now for them."

Following the 1923 catastrophe, Japanese leaders saw a tremendous opportunity for avoiding, in a rebuilt Tokyo, the conditions that had contributed to its destruction. Viscount Shimpei Goto, the former mayor of Tokyo who was just joining the Cabinet as home minister, assembled the best minds available to draft a master plan for a safe new city. The jumbles of flimsy and flammable wooden structures would be replaced with clusters of squat concrete apartment and office buildings, strongly built and limited in height to withstand shaking. The narrow, twisting streets would give way to broad avenues that could not be blocked by rubble and would act as firebreaks.

But events ran roughshod over the vision. While the planners were drawing

Architect Frank Lloyd Wright

Furnished with terraces, gardens and hand-carved stonework, the ceremonial entrance of Tokyo's Imperial Hotel melds Occidental architecture with Japanese motifs. Many of the design features also served as earthquake safeguards: The reflecting pool, for example, doubled as a fire-fighting reservoir, an expedient that protected the Imperial from the fires that followed the 1923 Kanto earthquake.

When Tokyo's 250-room Imperial Hotel was commissioned in 1915, it was conceived as the Emperor's showplace for foreigners. The ornate edifice designed by American Frank Lloyd Wright is still remembered, one Japanese architect says, "as a sort of sorcerer's palace." Yet the hotel eventually won renown not so much for its architecture as for its novel earthquake engineering.

The seismic hazard at the hotel site was severe: Eight feet of topsoil overlay about 60 feet of treacherous alluvial mud. But Wright, although a novice at seismic design, held unorthodox views. "Deep foundations," he theorized, "would oscillate and rock the structure. That mud seemed a merciful provision—a good cushion to relieve the terrible shocks." He conceived the hotel as "a super-dreadnought, floating on the mud as a battleship floats on salt-water."

This theory was tested with a vengeance on September 1, 1923, just as 200 guests gathered for the hotel's opening. At 11:58 a.m., Tokyo was battered by a quake that registered 8.3 on the Richter scale. Five thousand buildings were shattered and hundreds of thousands more were incinerated.

In the United States, Wright anxiously sifted through fragmented news reports. Nearly two weeks after the quake, he finally got a cable from his Japanese patron, Baron Kihachiro Okura: HOTEL STANDS UNDAMAGED AS MONUMENT OF YOUR GENIUS CONGRATULATIONS. Wright released the telegram to journalists, and a myth was born: Amid Tokyo's ruins, the Imperial alone stood after the Kanto quake.

History's verdict is more equivocal. The Imperial in fact suffered damage. The experimental foundation was a failure: The hotel's central section settled about two feet in the quake, a few floors bulged, and in later years the building continued to sink into the mud until it was demolished in 1968.

But Wright's other seismic innovations *(overleaf)* performed well during the quake. Most important, the hotel passed the one vital test of earthquake design: It survived.

"The terror of the temblor never left me while I planned the building," wrote Frank Lloyd Wright, who resided in Tokyo while his Imperial Hotel was under construction. "Nor is anyone allowed to forget it—sometimes awakened at night by strange sensations as at sea, unearthly and yet rumbling earth-noises."

Wright's main answer to the seismic threat, an unconventional shallow foundation, relied on broad footings supported by stubby concrete pilings eight feet long, grouped every two feet along the foundation wall. Wright theorized that this "pincushion" would supplement the footings, yet let the hotel float on the underlying mud.

Alas, modern engineers have concluded that he was wrong on both counts. The pilings were too short to support the building adequately, so it slowly sank into the mud. And soft earth like that beneath the Imperial actually tends to amplify seismic shocks; such soils move back and forth much more than bedrock, creating rolling ground motions. For both reasons, solidly constructed Tokyo buildings with deep pilings withstood the 1923 quake better than the hotel.

The joints between the Imperial's floors and walls embodied another Wright theory. Floors and walls are normally bonded together with steel and poured concrete, but Wright worried that a temblor might move the walls and drop the floors. Consequently, many of the hotel's floors extended through the walls, forming outdoor balconies and terraces; along a central corridor, the floors were supported by concrete columns.

To engineers, however, the mechanical principle underlying this common-sense design is the same one used in conventional designs. "The hotel had many cantilevers free at one end, making the construction apparent to the layman," wrote Wright's structural engineer, Julius Floto, "but in no other respect does it differ" from conventional buildings.

Nevertheless, other Wright innovations have turned out to be remarkably farsighted. In an era when walls were usually built of unreinforced brick, the Imperial used double-shell walls, with outer layers of brick bonded with a core of steel reinforcing bars and poured concrete. The first-floor walls, which receive the greatest stress in a quake, were especially rigid: They were thicker (the hotel's walls tapered upward) and they had fewer windows than the upper walls.

To prevent a temblor from cracking the Imperial's two 500-foot wings, Wright pioneered the use of seismic separation joints. Every 60 feet along each wing, lead sleeves through the walls, floors and footings divided the building into small sections, creating what Wright called a "jointed monolith." The sleeves enabled each section to move independently, sliding against its neighbors rather than cracking away.

The Imperial's design also anticipated the hazard of loosely connected, nonstructural appendages, such as overhanging parapets and decorative stonework, which during a quake tend to rain down on hapless pedestrians. "Roof tiles of Japanese buildings have murdered countless thousands of Japanese in upheavals," Wright said, "so a light, hand-worked green copper roof was planned." In addition, each of the hotel's myriad pieces of stonework was hollowed, fitted with copper reinforcement and bonded to the building with poured concrete.

Wright was among the first to appreciate that damage to a building's mechanical components—the heating, plumbing and wiring systems—was just as dangerous as structural failure. "Earthquakes had always torn piping and wiring apart where laid in the structure," he observed. So, rather than being embedded in concrete slabs, the hotel's pipes and wires ran through trenches or were hung free of the structure and fitted with sweeping curves rather than conventional right-angle joints. "A look into a pipe shaft at the Imperial is like looking into an animal abdomen—a smooth mass of winding intestines," wrote the architect. "Thus any disturbance might flex and rattle but not break the pipes or wiring."

This concatenation of shrewd seismic precautions more than counterbalanced the weakness of the hotel's foundation. Only four pieces of carved stonework fell from the walls, and the mechanical systems performed flawlessly. Most of Wright's principles have stood the test of time as well: Strong first-story walls, separation joints, sturdy mechanical components and well-anchored appendages all are basic elements of modern seismic engineering.

COPPER ROOF
HOLLOW STONEWORK
COFFERED CONCRETE SLAB
PIPE SHAFT
VENTILATING DUCTS
CANTILEVERED FLOOR
SUSPENDED CEILING
SEISMIC SEPARATION JOINT
STEEL REINFORCING RODS
CANTILEVERED BALCONY
LEAD SEPARATION SLEEVE
CONCRETE CORE
EXPOSED PLUMBING PIPES
CENTRAL CORRIDOR
DOUBLE-SHELL BRICK WALL
CENTRAL CONCRETE COLUMNS
BASEMENT
FOOTING
PIPE TRENCH
FOOTING
GRAVEL
CONCRETE PILINGS
TOPSOIL
ALLUVIAL MUD

In an awesome climax to the devastating earthquake of 1923, Tokyo residents flee in terror as a cyclone of fire ignited by the quake sweeps through the streets of the capital. The phenomenon, shown at left in a contemporary lithograph, is known as a fire storm and occurs when many fires join into a single holocaust so intense that it literally sucks everything combustible into a towering funnel of flame.

their maps, writing their codes and debating appropriations, 1.5 million Tokyo residents were responding to a far more urgent imperative—the need for shelter. Those who were able went immediately to work repairing or rebuilding their homes with packing cases, pine boards and tin roofing; those who had nothing to save, or who were disabled by injuries or grief, left the city by the hundreds of thousands to live with relatives in the countryside. As a result, not only did the congested and flammable neighborhoods reappear almost overnight, but the departure of so many refugees created a massive shortage of labor that made reconstruction projects almost impossible to get under way. All that endured of Goto's vision was a new law limiting the height of buildings in Tokyo to six stories.

Even if the planners had somehow found the time and money to implement their ideas, the result would have been far short of an earthquake-proof city. They simply did not know what elements were required to withstand shaking, as was demonstrated by their focusing on two major damage preventives after the 1923 quake—the use of reinforced concrete and the limitation of building heights. A Tokyo Imperial University report on the damage done by the 1906 San Francisco earthquake had made much of the fact that several California buildings constructed of reinforced concrete had survived the tremors, and thereafter earthquake-conscious builders in Japan had adopted that building technique with increasing regularity. But many such buildings erected between 1906 and the early '20s collapsed in the 1923 Tokyo quake. And many of the buildings constructed after 1924—under the new height limitation—fell in the earthquakes of the late 1920s and 1930s.

The breakthrough that put the emerging discipline of earthquake engineering on a more scientific basis came in 1940. Scientists at Caltech, including a Japanese seismologist, had developed an improved instrument for measuring destructive ground motions. Called a strong-motion accelerograph, or SMA, it was designed to record only those vibrations powerful enough to drive an ordinary seismograph off scale. By 1932 the Caltech scientists had installed six SMAs at locations in Southern California they thought likely to be the sites of strong earthquakes. And one of them was deployed near the small California town of El Centro when a magnitude 7.1 earthquake hit on May 18, 1940.

Despite its intensity, the earthquake left few casualties and light damage, and was soon forgotten by the general public; but it gained enduring fame among earthquake engineers because it provided one of the first detailed pictures ever recorded of the violent horizontal and vertical ground motions that bring down buildings. The new data made it possible for engineers to calculate with precision the forces exerted on a structure by a major earthquake, and to design buildings capable of withstanding them. The El Centro SMA records remained for decades as standard reference for earthquake engineers.

The precise picture of ground movements also made it possible to test a building's stability without waiting for an earthquake. Now that they knew how the ground moved, engineers could reproduce the motions mechanically with a device called a shaking table, on which they could subject scale models of their designs to simulated quakes. A primitive, steam-powered shaking table built by the Japanese in the 1920s to imitate earthquake-induced shaking was replaced after 1940 with models that reproduced the El Centro earthquake motion, and those of later quakes for which SMA graphs were recorded.

The new instruments demonstrated the staggering complexity of the forces that assault any building in a major earthquake. Vertical movement can more than double the effect of gravity, causing failure in any part of a building's supporting structure not capable of bearing twice its normal weight. But this is the least of the problems, because vertical strength is the easiest characteristic to design into a building. What gives structural engineers nightmares is the whiplash effect of an earthquake's horizontal movements, shifting and rotating the building's foundation in virtually all directions at once.

Combined with simultaneous vertical motions, the effect of horizontal movement can be fantastically destructive. Early estimates indicated that the horizontal forces on a building in a large earthquake could approach 40 per cent of its weight, and later research showed that they sometimes reached 100 per cent of its weight—which meant that the building was being subjected to the equivalent of the force of gravity acting sideways. The destructive effects of horizontal motion can be magnified by resonance. If a tall building vibrates at the same frequency as that of the earthquake waves, the resulting resonance can multiply the amount of shaking and the stresses on the building.

The scientists were learning that many modern trends in architecture were exceedingly dangerous to residents of earthquake country. Sheathing high-rise

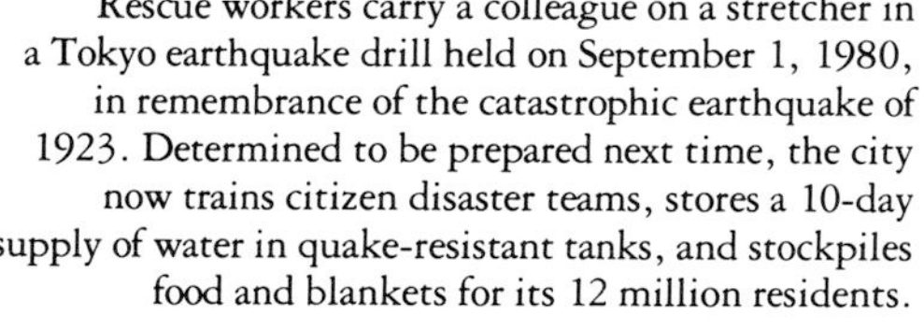

Rescue workers carry a colleague on a stretcher in a Tokyo earthquake drill held on September 1, 1980, in remembrance of the catastrophic earthquake of 1923. Determined to be prepared next time, the city now trains citizen disaster teams, stores a 10-day supply of water in quake-resistant tanks, and stockpiles food and blankets for its 12 million residents.

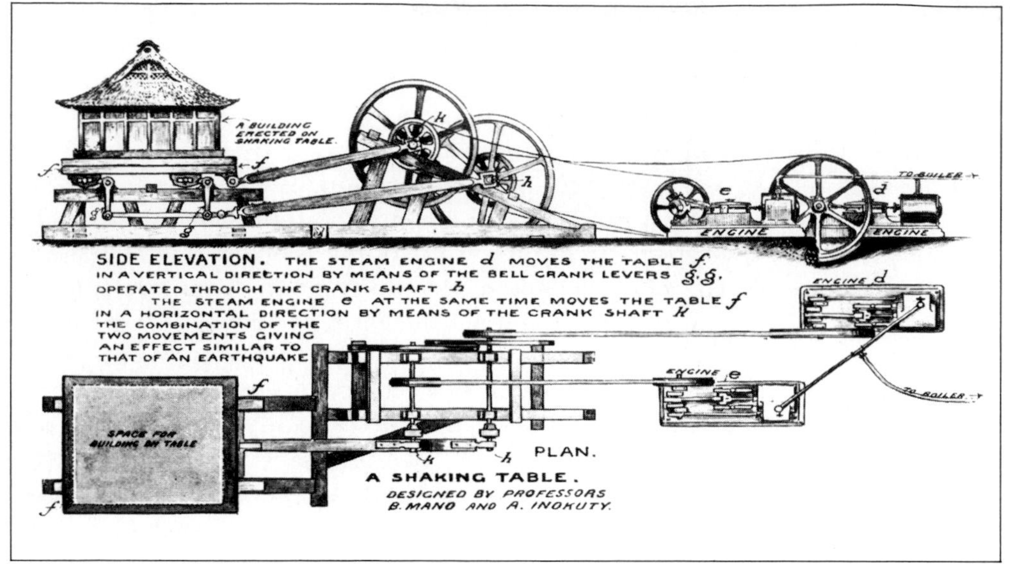

An architectural design tool much favored in Japan is the shaking table, which gauges the resistance of a structure to earthquake-like vibrations. Early versions, like the one above illustrated in a 1923 London newspaper, could test only small-scale models of buildings, but the huge rigs in use today can handle components weighing up to 1,000 tons.

buildings with glass produced a stunning visual effect but interfered with adequate bracing and added the danger of shattered windows to the effects of an earthquake. Raising office buildings on columns to give an airy, graceful appearance also meant that the bottom of the building, when subjected to the churning of seismic waves, would quickly fail. Baroque masonry façades were among the first parts of a building to fall when the shaking started—with terrible consequences for passersby in the street below, as was tragically demonstrated at the J. C. Penney building in Anchorage in 1964 *(page 23)*.

As valuable as these lessons were, researchers soon ran into limitations imposed by the scarcity, and the special nature, of the strong-motion accelerograms. The records were difficult to obtain because they required the presence of the specialized instruments in the immediate vicinity of a major earthquake. Furthermore, an accelerogram detailed the ground movements of a specific earthquake at a certain location. Since any combination of seismic waves is the product of a multitude of variable tectonic forces and geological conditions, an accelerogram is as unique and as distinctive as a human fingerprint. A building designed to withstand the effects of one earthquake at one location might not be at all safe in another.

In 1974, the Universities of Tokyo and California pooled their resources, exchanged experts and went to work on the problem. Within a year they had designed a computer program that could take into account known tectonic forces, local seismic records and geological conditions in vast detail, and create a strong-motion accelerogram of the effects of a hypothetical earthquake on a particular construction site. With these accelerograms, engineers and architects could design their buildings to meet a specific probable threat.

At the same time, increasingly sophisticated shaking tables were being designed to improve testing. In 1971 the University of California at Berkeley developed a model that could reproduce horizontal and vertical movements simultaneously. And in 1981 the Japanese completed a $125-million monster that could reproduce the largest earthquake motions, either of recorded or hypothetical events, and could apply them to model buildings, or actual construction components, weighing 1,000 tons.

As knowledge of what happens to a building in a quake increased, engineers came up with some ingenious countermeasures. They designed a building-sized shock absorber called a shear wall—in one variation a thick wall of triangular steel or concrete components packed into a rectangular frame. When subjected to strong horizontal forces, such a wall does not crack but is bent into a parallelogram as the components shift sideways in the frame. The friction between components absorbs huge quantities of energy that would otherwise contribute to the swaying of the building. An advanced shear-wall design from Japan was used in a 16-story construction-company headquarters built in Los Angeles; it was shaken but not damaged in the 1971 quake. Construction engineers are working on computer-controlled cable-tensioning systems for certain buildings, in which cables running throughout the structure are instantly adjusted by computer to withstand ground motions detected by on-site sensors.

Earthquakes threaten not only buildings, but the transportation, utility and communications networks on which an urban population depends. The protection of these civic life lines has been a subject of increasing attention since the 1960s. Damage to life lines may be "less directly related to the loss of human lives than damage to other structures," wrote Keizaburo Kubo of Tokyo University in 1977, "but it will lead to extreme disorder in a city, which in turn increases the potential for various secondary disasters." Broken water mains make fire fighting impossible; disrupted telephone communications prevent the coordination of rescue and relief efforts; and when bridges and highways are destroyed or blocked, help cannot get into a devastated area and endangered people cannot get out of it.

Some early attention to the life-line problem yielded significant rewards in the 1964 Alaska earthquake. Because the state's main electric generators were equipped with earthquake-activated shutdown switches, and the major gas mains were automatically shut off by sudden pressure changes in damaged pipe, the number of post-earthquake fires was drastically reduced. California has done a great deal to protect its water systems, to make them accessible to repair crews and to provide alternate sources of water for emergencies, but the system's major aqueduct remains in jeopardy because it crosses the San Andreas Fault four times. In Tokyo, the Japanese have stored 400,000 tons of drinking water—a 10-day supply—in underground cisterns and quakeproof warehouses to provide for the probability of broken water mains after a quake. And they have made every effort to get their utility lines underground where the destructive effects of shaking are much reduced.

Japan's government also takes a direct role in defending its people, at home or at work, against earthquakes. In Tokyo, for instance, thousands of wooden houses are replaced by concrete apartment buildings every year; and since 1963, although the limit on the height of buildings in the city was repealed, every blueprint for a structure more than 147 feet high has required the approval of a special committee of earthquake experts.

In 1978 the Japanese Diet approved the Large-Scale Earthquake Countermeasures Act, the most thorough, detailed, sweepingly ambitious and expensive piece of earthquake legislation ever enacted. It provides for the spending of more than three billion dollars a year to prepare for the onslaught of future earthquakes—especially the one that threatens to shatter Tokai. Much of the money is being used to expand and reinforce evacuation routes and to shore up bridges, harbor facilities and public buildings. In Tokyo, the municipal government has lavished an additional $6.6 billion on a five-year refurbishment campaign for similar preparations in the city.

One mandate of the legislation is to teach people how to prepare for a quake, and what to do when it comes. Earthquake exercises are as common as fire drills in schools and offices in endangered areas. Bells clang, sirens wail, and thousands of schoolchildren swiftly put on protective head pads and crouch under their desks, or march to designated evacuation areas. Each of the region's cities and villages has a municipal disaster plan, and many people have enrolled in civil-defense groups. Fire departments stage surprise earthquake drills for their members. Every September 1—National Disaster Prevention Day, in memory of the 1923 quake—the entire region takes part in a unified drill.

As a result of such exercises and a constant stream of pamphlets, posters, broadcasts and lectures, the level of public preparedness in Japan is high. Many

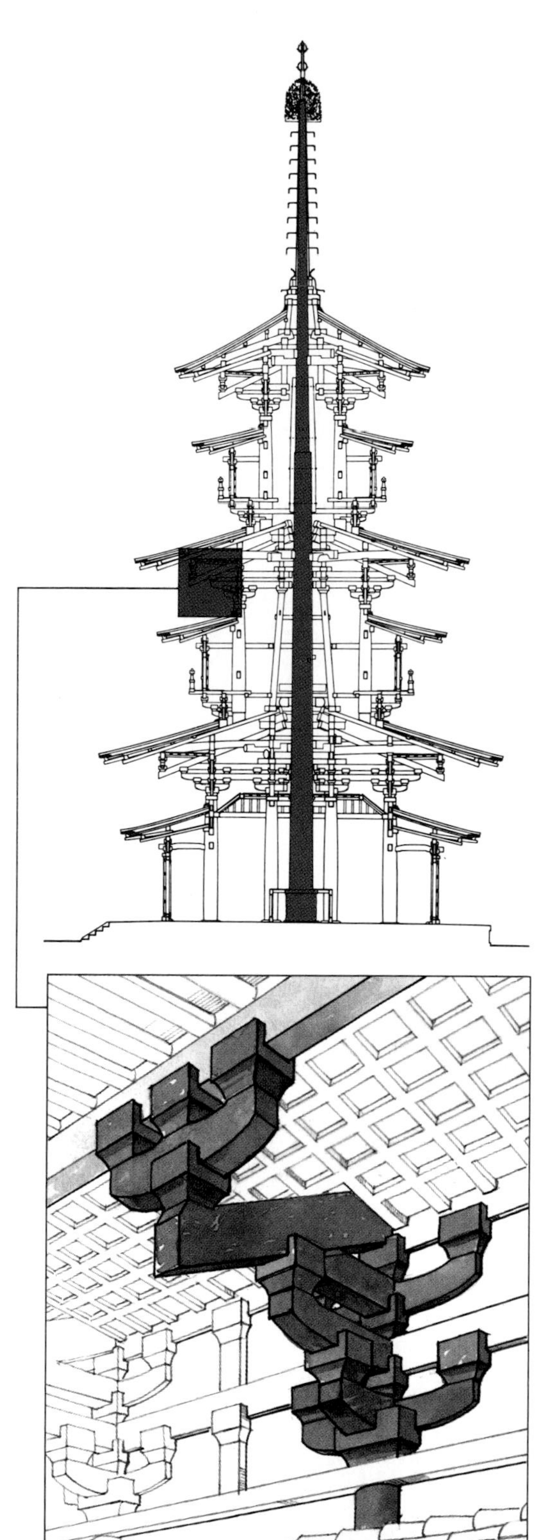

Delicate but enduring, the ancient Buddhist pagodas of Japan were designed with sound principles of earthquake resistance in mind. As shown in this schematic drawing, the heart of the pagoda is its strong central column, which is usually sunk into high, firm ground; the roofs of the various levels hang from this column on joints *(detail)* that are flexible enough to absorb severe vibrations.

householders have learned first aid and have stored extra food and bottled water in their homes. They have assembled earthquake survival kits, containing such things as a fire extinguisher, a flashlight, medicine, bandages and a transistor radio. Commercial organizations have also made preparations—the vast Matsushita Electric Industrial Company, Ltd., holds annual drills for all its employees, and the Toyota Motor Company keeps rice and bottled water on hand for 20,000 workers. One Tokyo structure has an array of 40 water cannon mounted on the roof, with which to battle approaching flames. Food, blankets and baby bottles have been stockpiled throughout the city. One hundred twenty-one parks and open spaces have been designated as evacuation areas, with the roads leading to them clearly marked as such. Most of Tokyo's 28,000 taxicabs carry fire extinguishers, and the city keeps others in sidewalk cases.

The effectiveness of these preparations will depend on whether residents are given enough warning of an impending quake. Despite the inconclusive record of worldwide earthquake prediction efforts, the Japanese are confident that there will be enough preliminary signs of a big rupture to give them some warning. They have deployed one of the world's most extensive earthquake prediction systems to win a few precious hours or days of notice. Along with periodic measurements of crustal deformation, groundwater levels and other possible precursors, the readings from a network of 70 seismographs, especially concentrated in the Tokai region, are constantly monitored at the Japan Meteorological Agency in Tokyo. A technician is on duty around the clock, and if he should see any suspicious readings on the recording drums, he will activate a detailed plan for assessing the danger and, if necessary, sounding the alarm.

The technician will radio the seismologist in charge of the prediction council, who always carries a pocket beeper. The seismologist will gather the council's five other members, and together they will evaluate the evidence. If they decide that a major quake is imminent, they will alert the Prime Minister. The Cabinet will be summoned, the news media informed, and an official warning will be issued. The entire process is designed to take just over two hours.

The warning will be communicated to the public by radio and television broadcasts, patrol-car loudspeakers, and with sirens and alarm bells in every threatened community. Police, fire fighters, military units and Red Cross officials are scheduled to move immediately to predetermined posts to execute their parts in the disaster plan. Factory workers will shut down machinery, and office employees will secure furniture and file cabinets, before taking up safe positions within their quake-resistant buildings. According to the plan, homeowners will switch off gas and electric lines, take up their earthquake kits and calmly march off to predetermined refuge areas.

An experience with an actual earthquake warning in 1978, just before the passage of the Countermeasures Act, caused planners to look again at their provisions for preventing confusion and panic. A moderately strong magnitude 7 quake struck the Izu-Oshima-Kinkai area, in the heart of the threatened Tokai region, on January 14, leaving 25 people dead, more than 200 injured and almost 5,000 buildings damaged or destroyed. Three days later, after several aftershocks, Japan's national headquarters for disaster control predicted continuing and potentially damaging aftershock activity.

On the afternoon of January 18, the Governor of the affected prefecture decided to issue the warning to the public. To the consternation of relief officials, the result was widespread confusion and panic.

Later analysis showed that, despite the elaborate plans for disseminating the warning, a large number of people had been baffled by an overly long announcement phrased in bureaucratic jargon that failed to specify what to expect, and when. The confusion had been compounded by the spreading of misinformation through something called the "propane route." The wholesale and retail propane gas dealers in the area had their own system of communica-

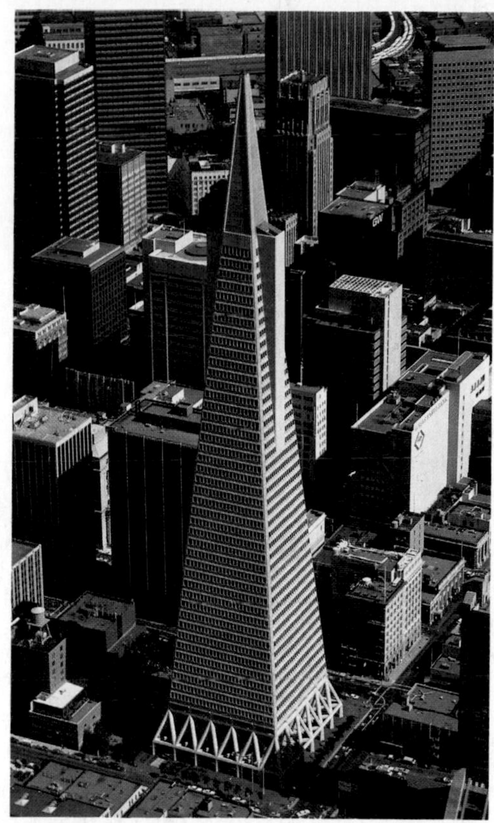

The striking pyramid shape of San Francisco's Transamerica Building makes it a memorable example of modern earthquake-resistant architecture. The triangular trusses and precast concrete-clad steel columns at the base of the 853-foot structure are designed to withstand more than twice the quake-induced stress anticipated by the city's building code. In a major quake the building is expected to sway only 24 inches, compared with the normal sway of a building of similar height of as much as 36 inches.

tions for learning about and preparing for an imminent earthquake, and a propane dealer happened to be present when the aftershock warning came in to the Propane Gas Wholesalers' Association office. His unauthorized calls to friends and customers spread a progressively less recognizable and more alarming version of the warning throughout the area. Many residents thought they were being warned of an imminent major earthquake and began foraging for emergency supplies or desperately fleeing the prefecture.

As a result of the misfire of the aftershock warning, Japanese planners have prewritten and simplified their earthquake warning announcements and have included in their lectures and pamphlets careful explanations of what announcements may be expected and precisely what they mean. By thus clarifying the official warning, they hope to eliminate the credibility of rumors such as those spread by the propane route.

Around the world, the peoples and the governments of earthquake country are learning to fear earthquakes less—and the frailty and flammability of their buildings more. As the senior statesman of seismology, Charles Richter, campaigns for safer construction in seismically dangerous areas, he sounds one theme over and over: "Most loss of life and property has been due to the collapse of antiquated and unsafe structures. In every area of the world where there is earthquake risk, there are still many buildings of this type; it is very frustrating to try to get rid of them." In the race for safety from earthquakes, Richter's home state of California treads most closely on Japan's heels. It has not been easy in the state's multilayered political structure, but since 1971 many jurisdictions have been insisting on geological surveys of earthquake hazards as a prerequisite for development; they also call for an advanced level of earthquake-resistant construction, and increased attention to preparedness. But inconsistency in the laws and their enforcement, niggardly appropriations for disaster-relief planning and public apathy leave California with a long way to go.

Many other seismically active countries are struggling toward earthquake safety, with even further to go. In Iran, reinforced brick construction is slowly gaining favor over the traditional flat-roofed adobe houses that crumble in the mildest quake. In Rumania, the emphasis placed on earthquake-resistant architecture during Bucharest's building boom of the 1950s and 1960s paid off when a 7.2 magnitude earthquake on March 4, 1977, felled 35 older brick-and-masonry buildings in the capital but only three of more recent design. In earthquake-ravaged Tashkent the Soviets have used the latest seismic engineering techniques to replace with modern apartments the mud-brick dwellings smashed in a 1966 earthquake, and have built a new subway with flexible, earthquake-proof connectors between its tunnel sections. Both buildings and subway survived an earthquake in 1977 with virtually no damage.

Such remedies, affecting a building here and a facility there, protecting a few thousand people among the millions endangered, may seem entirely inadequate in the face of so vast a threat. And yet each year they save a few more buildings and a few more people from earthquakes, and science inches its way in the general direction of another victory over a scourge of mankind. "Let's paint a scenario for the future," says Bruce Bolt, head of the seismology department at the University of California at Berkeley, with an optimism that seems at first glance hardly credible. He imagines a futuristic city, "sensibly planned and solidly built," that is shaken by a great earthquake, of magnitude 8 or above on the Richter scale—about the size of the 1923 Kanto quake. "Everyone stays indoors, perfectly safe," says Bolt. "Then, when the shaking stops, we all go outside and look around. There will be a few deaths and injuries, but not many, and a minimum of destruction. This is not science fiction. It could happen."

Perhaps. Not anytime soon, but such prospects are what makes it possible for scientists to strive on in the face of great odds. The battle to understand, to predict and to withstand the killer earthquake has just been fully joined. Ω

THE DAY FUKUI DIED AGAIN

On June 28, 1948, *Life* photographer Carl Mydans arrived in Fukui, Japan, to photograph the textile city's amazing rise from the ashes of war. In 1945, fire bombs had incinerated 97 per cent of the town. Yet now, scarcely three years later, Fukui was largely rebuilt, once again a leading silk producer and home to 85,000 people.

But the story Mydans actually photographed was far different from the one he had anticipated. Shortly after he reached Fukui, a great earthquake roared through the city. And Mydans was in a unique position to capture all the drama and horror of the quake as it happened.

The first tremors hit at 5:14 p.m. as Mydans was eating dinner in the headquarters of the American military government. "The concrete floor just exploded," he recalled. "Tables and dishes flew into our faces and we were all hurled into a mad dance, bouncing about like popping corn. When at last I got near the doorway, I hurled myself at it. But the floor shifted, and I smashed into the crumbling wall a yard farther along."

Mydans finally made it out the door, then remembered his cameras and rushed back to find them. As the tremors continued, he worked his way through the city, recording the desperate scenes shown here and on the following pages.

Mydans stayed in Fukui photographing for 15 hours before he returned to Tokyo. He later learned that the quake had measured 7.3 on the Richter scale, which made it one of the worst to hit Japan in a decade. The town was demolished, and more than 3,500 people died, most of them, Mydans believed, in fires that swept the wreckage. "They were pinned in their homes by fallen roofs and timber while rescuers worked with bare hands to free them," said Mydans. "Their friends and families ran screaming, begging for a saw, an ax—just anything to cut them free—until the fires grew and spread and finally caught them."

In Tokyo, Mydans initiated a campaign to promote individual earthquake kits, containing an ax, a crowbar and wire cutters, to be kept outside homes throughout Japan. And, for the remainder of his assignment, a rescue kit hung outside his front door.

A woman frantically rolls a basket while another leaps across cracks in the street as residents of Fukui, Japan, flee the 1948 earthquake. "Chasms four feet wide opened in the streets," recalled photographer Carl Mydans, who shot this remarkable essay.

宝くじ

The seven-story Daiwa department store in the heart of Fukui tilts ominously as massive tremors wrench its foundation. "It was moving as I took the picture, and made a great crumbling noise, but stopped short of collapse," recalled Mydans.

An American GI garrisoned in Fukui administers first aid to a victim of the quake as buildings crumple nearby. In the hours after the quake, American personnel treated more than 1,000 injured survivors.

A U.S. Army fuel dump goes up in flames after the earthquake, hurling gasoline drums into the air; the drums set off new fires wherever they landed. From a vantage point on high ground, Mydans could see other fires engulfing villages on the horizon, his first knowledge of the extent of the earthquake.

Frightened survivors salvage a few belongings and hurry away as a wall of fire spawned by the quake moves closer. "Some crawled timidly into their collapsed homes to save things, often trivial things," said Mydans. "No one was fighting the flames. There was no water, and it was all so hopeless."

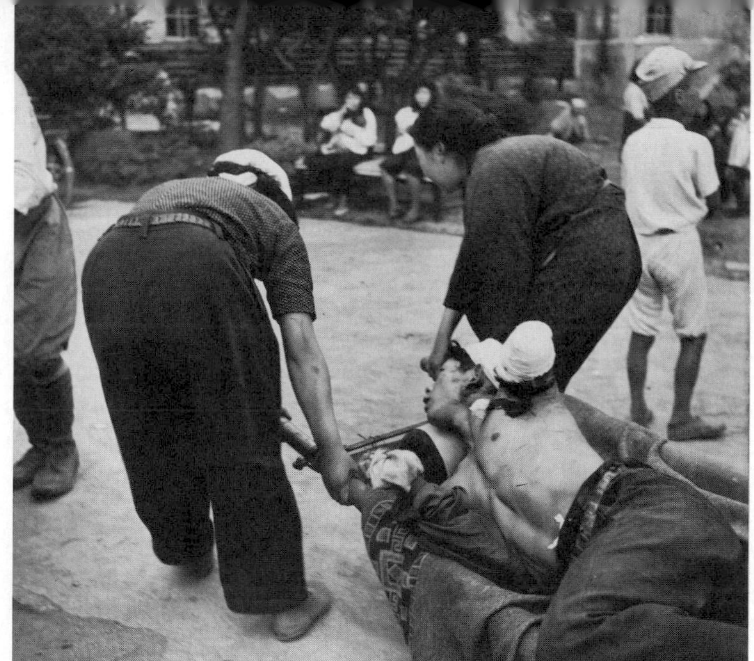

Grasping a makeshift litter, two survivors drag away a man who had been pinned by the arm inside a burning building. "There was no choice, no hesitation and no talk," said Mydans. "The rescuers without a word sawed off the arm."

A husband carries his fatally injured wife on his back, his young son clutching the blanket that is draped over her body. "I asked how the woman was," recalled Mydans. "'Too late,' the man replied, whispering so that the little boy wouldn't know."

Bystanders stare in horror at a severely burned man on a stretcher improvised from a sign. As Mydans took his picture, the man said with traditional Japanese courtesy, "Thank you." He died soon after.

On the morning following the earthquake, a few survivors return to poke through the debris where their houses had once stood. "The city was still smoking," Mydans recalled. "The ground was very hot as they searched for what might be saved."

A jumble of clay roof tiles, one of the few things to withstand the flames, is about all that remains of this Fukui neighborhood. Mydans later concluded that the charcoal-filled stoves burning in each home as suppertime approached had kindled the inferno.

PICTURE CREDITS

Credits from left to right are separated by semicolons, from top to bottom by dashes.

Cover: Fotograf, Padua, Italy. 6, 7: Vittoriano Rastelli, Rome. 8, 9: Mauro Galligani, Milan. 10, 11: Asahi Shimbun Photo Service, Tokyo. 12, 13: J. Eyerman from Black Star. 14, 15: Fotograf, Padua, Italy. 16, 17: Elt Davis © National Geographic Society 1959. 18: Stan Wayman for *Life.* 20: Map by Walter Roberts. 23: Wide World. 24: UPI. 25: Earthquake Engineering Research Library, California Institute of Technology. 27: Richard Schlecht—Steve McCutcheon. 28: U.S. Army Corps of Engineers Photo. 29: Stan Wayman for *Life.* 31: Museum of the American Indian, Heye Foundation. 32: Map by Walter Roberts. 33, 34: U.S. Geological Survey. 36-41: The Earthquake Research Institute of the University of Tokyo. 42: Jean-Loup Charmet, courtesy Collections Historiques, I.N.R.P., Paris. 44: Wilco C. Poortman, Zeist, the Netherlands. 46: Los Angeles County Museum of Art: Gift of Mrs. Louisa S. Janvier. 47: Scala, Florence. 49: Universitätsbibliothek Erlangen-Nürnberg. 50: Aus dem Bildarchiv d. Ost. Nationalbibliothek, Vienna. 51: Courtesy of the British Library, London. 52: Estudio M. Novais, courtesy Museu da Cidade, Lisbon. 53: Photo Bulloz, courtesy Musée Carnavalet, Paris. 54: National Museum of the History of Science and Medicine, Leiden. 55: Rare Books and Manuscripts Division, The New York Public Library, Astor, Lenox and Tilden Foundations. 56, 57: Courtesy of the Trustees of the British Museum, London. 58, 59: U.S. Geological Survey. 60: Library of Congress—Syndication International, London. 61: Map by Walter Roberts. 62, 63: © J. Richard Monaco, San Francisco. 64: Permission of the Fine Arts Museums of San Francisco. 65: California Historical Society, San Francisco. 66: Courtesy The Bancroft Library. 67: © J. Richard Monaco, San Francisco—California Historical Society, San Francisco. 68, 69: California Historical Society, San Francisco. 70: Courtesy The Bancroft Library—Department of Special Collections, Stanford University Libraries. 71: California Historical Society, San Francisco. 72, 73: National Maritime Museum, San Francisco. 74: Chuck O'Rear. 76: Ben Benschneider, courtesy the National Earthquake Information Service. 77: Drawing by Richard Schlecht. 78: Courtesy Jim Mori, Lamont-Doherty Geological Observatory of Columbia University. 79: Drawing by Richard Schlecht. 81: Paulus Leeser, courtesy Peking Arts and Handicrafts Corporation. 82, 83: Background illustration, Ullstein Bilderdienst, Berlin (West); Joseph Natanson, courtesy Osservatorio Sismico Andrea Bina, Perugia, Italy—Joseph Natanson, courtesy Ufficio Centrale di Ecologia Agraria, Rome; Derek Bayes, courtesy Science Museum, London (5). 84: Rizzoli, Milan. 86: Chuck O'Rear—after Bruce Bolt. 89: The Bettmann Archive. 90, 91: Drawings by Richard Schlecht. 92, 93: Map by Walter Roberts, courtesy National Geographical and Solar Terrestrial Data Center of NOAA. 94-101: Drawings by Ken Townsend. 102: Lauros-Giraudon, courtesy Bibliothèque Nationale, Paris. 104: Historical Picture Service, Chicago. 107: Map by Walter Roberts—drawing by Richard Schlecht. 108, 109: Water Resources Engineering Library, University of California, Berkeley. 112: Courtesy of the State Historical Society of Missouri, Columbia. 113: U.S. Geological Survey; J. K. Hillers, No. 11a, U.S. Geological Survey. 114: N. R. Farbman for *Life.* 117: Drawing by Richard Schlecht. 118, 119: Osamu Murai, Tokyo; drawing by Richard Schlecht. 120: Brian Lanker—Chuck O'Rear; drawings by Richard Schlecht (2). 121: Drawings by Richard Schlecht (2); U.S. Geological Survey (2). 122, 123: Chuck O'Rear, except bottom left, drawing by Richard Schlecht. 124: NASA—drawing by Richard Schlecht. 125: Brian Lanker—drawing by Richard Schlecht. 126: U.S. Geological Survey. 130: Kaku Kurita, Funabashi, Japan. 131: Tom Tracy, courtesy U.S. Geological Survey. 132, 133: Tom Tracy, courtesy U.S. Geological Survey—courtesy John Derr, U.S. Geological Survey. 135: Map by Walter Roberts. 137: Drawing by Richard Schlecht. 138: Courtesy Kerry Sieh, California Institute of Technology—Brian Lanker. 139: Courtesy Kerry Sieh, California Institute of Technology—drawing by Richard Schlecht. 140, 141: U.S. Geological Survey. 142, 143: Van Bucher for Photo Researchers; map by Walter Roberts. 144: Clarence R. Allen—Rob Lewine from Transworld Feature Syndicate, Inc. 145: William Garnett for *Life.* 146, 147: Brian Lanker; William Garnett. 148: Osamu Murai, Tokyo. 151: Courtesy Toho Co., Ltd., Tokyo Fire Department and the Fire Chiefs Association of Japan, Tokyo. 153: Courtesy of the Frank Lloyd Wright Memorial Foundation; Yukio Futagawa, Tokyo. 154, 155: Drawing by Victor Lazarro. 156: Library of Congress. 157: The *Yomiuri Shimbun,* Tokyo. 158: *Illustrated London News.* 159: Henry Beville, courtesy Freer Gallery of Art, from *Yakushi-ji,* Iwanami Shoten, Tokyo—drawing by Richard Schlecht. 161: Chuck O'Rear. 162-171: Carl Mydans for *Life.*

ACKNOWLEDGMENTS

For their help in the preparation of this book the editors wish to thank: **In Belgium:** Brussels—Professor François Lechat, Centre for Research on the Epidemiology of Disasters; Jean-Marie Van Gils, Observatoire Royal de Bruxelles. **In France:** Chantilly—Margarethe Mayeux, Les Fontaines; Orléans—Pierre Cheron, B.R.G.M.; Paris—Gérard Baschet, Éditions de l'Illustration; Marie Montambault, Musée du Louvre; Haroun Tazieff; Villebon-sur-Yvette—François Le Guern. **In Great Britain:** Cambridge—Dr. Geoffrey King, Department of Earth Sciences, University of Cambridge; Dublin—Dr. Ronnie Cox, Trinity College; London—Marjorie Willis, BBC Hulton Picture Library; R. T. Williams, Department of Prints and Drawings, British Museum; Elisabeth Moore, *Illustrated London News;* Professor Nicholas Ambraseys, Imperial College of Science and Technology; B. W. Robinson; Major Peter Verney; Newbury, Bershire—Dr. Robin Adams, International Seismological Centre; Newport, Isle of Wight—Leslie Herbert-Gustar; Patrick Nott. **In Italy:** Florence—Fr. Filippo Parenti, Collegio "Alla Querce"; Fr. Dino Bravieri, Osservatorio Ximeniano; Naples—Antonio Nazzaro, Osservatorio Vesuviano; Fr. Ermanno Giardino and Fr. Gerardo Passio, Santuario Madonna Dell'Arco; Perugia—Fr. Martino Siciliani, Osservatorio Sismico Andrea Bina; Pesaro—Brunello Bedosti, Osservatorio Meteorologico Sismico Valerio; Rome—Vittorio Cagnetti, Comitato Nazionale Energia Nucleare; Professor Franco Barberi, Director, Geodynamics Project, Consiglio Nazionale Ricerche; Calvino Gasparini, Istituto Nazionale Geofisica. **In Japan:** Himeji—Manpei Hashimoto; Ibareki Prefecture—Makoto Watabe, Building Research Institute, Ministry of Construction; Hitoshi Haruyama and Koichi Tsukahara, Geographical Survey Institute; Ichiro Takeyama, Kakioka Magnetic Observatory, Japan Meteorological Agency; Tatsuto Iimura, Japan Meteorological Research Institute; Yukio Fujinawa, Dr. Kazuo Hamada and Keiichi Otani, National Research Center for Disaster Prevention; Kiritappu, Hokkaido—Teruo Imada, Hamanakacho Public Office; Shizuoka Prefecture—Nobumasa Kawabata, Shizuoka Broadcasting System; Tokyo—Keiji Oshida, Center for Academic Publications, Japan; Dr. Toshi Asada, Chairman, Coordinating Committee for Earthquake Prediction; Yuji Wada, Institute for Future Technology; Dr. Kiyoo Wadati, President, The Japan Academy; Michimasa Numata, Japan International Cooperation Agency; Shinichi Nihei and Dr. Shigeji Suyehiro, Japan Meteorological Agency; Teruo Nirei, The Mainichi Newspapers; Takeshi Hashimoto and Masakazu Nakagawa, Earthquake Countermeasures Department, National Land Agency; Omori Toshiji, Nuclear Power Engineering Test Center; Toshiji Kitamura, Research Coordination Bureau, Science and Technology Agency; Kay Tateishi; Mitsuo Sakamoto, Tokyo Fire Department; Masao Matsuda, Disaster Countermeasures Department, Tokyo Metropolitan Government; Dr. Hisashi Miyoshi, Tokyo University of Fisheries; Ryoichi Kazama, Tokyo University of Foreign Studies; Sozai Koyano, The Center for the Compilation of the Centennial History of the University of Tokyo; Takayuki Iwata and Dr. Toshikatsu Yoshii, Earthquake Research Institute, University of Tokyo; Dr. Takahiro Hagiwara, Dr. Yorihiko Ohsaki, Dr. Keizo Okabe, Dr. Tsuneji Rikitake and Dr. Yasuo Suyehiro, University of Tokyo; Toyonaka—Osamu Asai, Asai Collection. **In Mexico:** Margarita Armendariz de Lares, The Anthropology Museum; Professor Leonardo Manriquez; Ruben Javier Zamora. **In the Netherlands:** De Bilt—Dr. A. R. Ritsema, Royal Netherlands Meteorological Institute; Leiden—Dr. H. J. W. G. Schalke, Leiden University; Utrecht—Dr. J. I. S. Zonneveld; Zeist—Wilco C. Poortman. **In the People's Republic of China:** Peking—Zhao Fang, New China Picture Co.; Liusheung Shing. **In Switzerland:** Basel—Peter Jung, John B. Saunders, Felix Weidenmayer, Basel Science Museum. **In the United States:** Alaska—(Anchorage) Douglas M. Clure, Anchorage Civil Defense; Mike Evans, U.S. Corps of Engineers; Dr. Perry Mead; Tay Thomas; Colonel and Mrs. Lyman Woodman; (Juneau) Bill Pelto, Department of Commerce and Economic Development; (Seward) E. G. Skinner; Arizona—(Scottsdale) Charles Montooth, Bruce Pfeiffer, The Frank Lloyd Wright Memorial Foundation; California—(Berkeley) Rick Clymer, Roy Miller, William M. Roberts and Russell Sell, University of California at Berkeley; (Half Moon Bay), Arthur Zich; (Los Angeles) Ralph Wright, American Red Cross; Peter Malin, University of Southern California; (Menlo Park) Dr. Henry C. Berg, Tom Burdette, Dr. John Derr, Jacquelyn Freeberg, Dr. J. H. Healy, Dr. Reuben Kachadoorian, Edna King, John Langbein, Dr. David McCulloch, Dr. Carl Mortensen, Dr. Robert Page, Dr. George Plafker, Dr. Barry Raleigh and Dr. Robert Wallace, United States Geological Survey; (Oakland) Thomas E. Curran, Oakland Museum; (Pasadena) Dr. Clarence Allen, Dr. Don L. Anderson, Dr. John Davidson, Ken Graham, Dr. George Housner, Dr. Kate Hutton, Dr. Hiroo Kanamori, Peter MacDoran, Dr. Karen McNally, Dr. Dennis Meredith and Dr. Kerry Sieh, California Institute of Technology; (Redwood City) Robert Reitherman, Scientific Service, Inc.; (Sacramento) Dr. Roger Sherburne and Dr. Tousson Toppazada, California Division of Mines and Geology; (San Francisco) Martha Kennedy and Waverly Lowell, California Historical Society; J. Richard Monaco, Monaco Labs; John Maounis, National Maritime Museum; (San Mateo) Christopher Arnold, President, Building Systems Development, Inc.; (Stanford) Roxanne Nilan and Dr. Amos Nur, Stanford University; Colorado—(Boulder) Dr. Herbert Meyers and Dr. Carl Von Hake, National Geophysical and Solar-Terrestrial Data Center, EDS-NOAA; Dr. Carl Kisslinger and Susan Tubbesing, University of Colorado; (Denver) Marge Dalechek, United States Geological Survey; (Golden) Waverly Person, Earthquake Information Center, United States Geological Survey; Washington, D.C.—Robert N. Sockwell, AIA Research Corporation; Elizabeth Hooks, American Red Cross; Dr. Charles Thiel, Federal Emergency Management Agency; Dr. Yoshiaki Shimizu, Freer Gallery of Art; Dr. William Melson, Department of Mineral Sciences, Museum of Natural History; William Petrie, National Academy of Sciences; Tom Callen, The Smithsonian Institution; Idaho—(American Falls) Elt Davis; Maryland—

(Greenbelt) Dr. David E. Smith, Goddard Space Flight Center; (Silver Spring) Dr. Charles A. Whitten; Massachusetts—(Cambridge) Dr. William Brace, Massachusetts Institute of Technology; Dr. Richard J. O'Connell, Harvard University; (Westboro) Ed Levine, Weston Geophysical Research Inc.; Missouri—(St. Louis) Dr. Otto Nuttli, St. Louis University; New Mexico—Harold Clark, Albuquerque Seismological Laboratory; New Jersey—Dr. F. A. Dahlen, Princeton University; New York—(Mount Vernon) Steve Burgard, *The Daily Argus;* (Palisades) Dr. Larry Burdick, Ellyn Schlesinger-Miller, Dr. David Simpson and Dr. Lynn Sykes, Lamont-Doherty Geological Observatory; Ohio—(Columbus) Dr. Shunji Mikami, Ohio State University; South Carolina—(Charleston) Jack Rutland, Gibbes Art Gallery; Virginia—(Fort Belvoir) Dr. Frederick Camfield, Department of the Army Coastal Engineering Research Center; (Reston) Kurt Dowd, Dr. Gregory Gohn, Dr. Robert M. Hamilton, Dr. Walter Hays and Dr. Mark Zoback, United States Geological Survey; Washington—(Tacoma) Austin Post, United States Geological Survey. **In West Germany:** West Berlin—Heidi Klein and Dr. Ronald Klemig, Bildarchiv Preussischer Kulturbesitz; Axel Schulz, Ullstein Bilderdienst; Bochum—Dieter Knippschild, Ruhr-Universität, Sektion für Publizistik und Kommunikation; Erlangen-Nürnberg—Dr. Alice Rössler, Universitätsbibliothek Erlangen-Nürnberg; Köln—Professor Dr. L. Ahorner, Geologisches Institut der Universität zu Köln; Dr. Hella Robels, Wallraf-Richartz-Museum; Munich—Christine Hoffman, Bayerische Staatsgemäldes-ammlung; Rudolph Heinrich, Deutsch Museum.

The editors also wish to thank the following persons: Fareed Trabulsi, Algiers; Mirka Gondicas, Athens; Enid Farmer, Boston; Nina Lindley, Buenos Aires; Ann Shakespeare, Caracas; JoAnne Reid, Chicago; Dorothy Slater, Denver; Larry Altman, Detroit; Bing Wong, Hong Kong; Tom Kaser, Honolulu; Marlin Levin, Robert Slater, Jerusalem; Tom Loayza, Lima; Cheryl Crooks, Los Angeles; Marcia Gauger, K. K. Sharma, New Delhi; Paul Taylor, Philadelphia; Cal Abraham, Santiago; Traudl Lessing, Vienna.

The index for this volume was prepared by Nicholas J. Anthony.

BIBLIOGRAPHY

Books

Birkeland, Peter, and Edwin Larson, *Putnam's Geology.* Oxford University Press, 1978.

Bolt, Bruce A., *Earthquakes: A Primer.* W. H. Freeman, 1978.

Bolt, Bruce A., ed., *Earthquakes and Volcanoes.* W. H. Freeman, 1980.

Bronson, William, *The Earth Shook, The Sky Burned.* Doubleday, 1959.

Clark, Sydney P., Jr., *Structure of the Earth.* Prentice-Hall, 1971.

Committee on the Alaska Earthquake of the Division of Earth Sciences, National Research Council, *The Great Alaska Earthquake of 1964,* Vols. 1-8. National Academy of Sciences, 1973.

Cox, Allan, ed., *Plate Tectonics and Geomagnetic Reversals.* W. H. Freeman, 1973.

Davison, Charles, *The Founders of Seismology.* Arno Press, 1978.

Dutton, Clarence Edward, *The Charleston Earthquake.* Government Printing Office, 1890.

Eiby, G. A., *Earthquakes.* Van Nostrand Reinhold, 1980.

Engle, Eloise, *Earthquake! The Story of Alaska's Good Friday Disaster.* John Day, 1966.

Fried, John J., *Life along the San Andreas Fault.* Saturday Review Press, 1973.

Fuller, Myron, *The New Madrid Earthquake.* Government Printing Office, 1912.

Gelman, Woody, *Disaster Illustrated.* Harmony Books, 1976.

Grantz, Arthur, et al., *Alaska's Good Friday Earthquake, March 27, 1964, A Preliminary Geologic Evaluation.* Government Printing Office, 1964.

Halacy, D. S., Jr., *Earthquakes, A Natural History.* Bobbs-Merrill, 1974.

Hallam, A., *A Revolution in the Earth Sciences.* Oxford: Clarendon Press, 1973.

Herbert-Gustar, A. L., and P. A. Nott, *John Milne: Father of Modern Seismology.* Tenterden: Paul Norbury Pub. Ltd., 1980.

Hodgson, John H., *Earthquakes and Earth Structure.* Prentice-Hall, 1964.

Iacopi, Robert, *Earthquake Country.* Lane Publishing, 1971.

Jacobs, J. A., et al., *Physics and Geology.* McGraw-Hill, 1974.

Kendrick, T. D., *The Lisbon Earthquake.* London: Methuen & Co. Ltd., 1956.

Lane, Frank W., *The Elements Rage.* Chilton Books, 1965.

Leet, L. D., *Earth Waves.* Harvard University Press, 1950.

Mallet, Robert, *Great Neapolitan Earthquake of 1857.* London: Chapman and Hall, 1862.

Marx, Robert F., *Port Royal Rediscovered.* Doubleday, 1973.

Motz, Lloyd, ed., *The Rediscovery of the Earth.* Van Nostrand Reinhold, 1975.

Mydans, Carl, *More Than Meets the Eye.* Harper, 1959.

Oakeshott, Gordon B., *Volcanoes & Earthquakes/Geologic Violence.* McGraw-Hill, 1976.

Ouwehand, Cornelis, *Namazu-e and Their Themes.* Leiden: E. J. Brill, 1964.

Pawson, Michael, and David Buisseret, *Port Royal, Jamaica.* Oxford: Clarendon Press, 1975.

Penick, James, Jr., *The New Madrid Earthquakes of 1811-1812.* University of Missouri Press, 1976.

Phinney, Robert A., ed., *The History of the Earth's Crust.* Princeton University Press, 1968.

Press, Frank, and Raymond Siever, *Earth.* W. H. Freeman, 1978.

Richter, Charles F., *Elementary Seismology.* W. H. Freeman, 1958.

Rikitake, Tsuneji, *Earthquake Prediction.* Amsterdam: Elsevier Scientific Pub. Co., 1976.

Sawkins, F. J., *The Evolving Earth: A Text in Physical Geology.* Macmillan, 1978.

Sullivan, Walter, *Continents in Motion.* McGraw-Hill, 1974.

Tazieff, Haroun, *When the Earth Trembles.* Harcourt, Brace & World, 1964.

Thomas, Gordon, and M. M. Witts, *The San Francisco Earthquake.* Stein and Day, 1971.

Uyeda, Seiya, *The New View of the Earth.* W. H. Freeman, 1971.

Verney, Peter, *The Earthquake Handbook.* Paddington Press, 1979.

Vitaliano, Dorothy B., *Legends of the Earth.* Indiana University Press, 1973.

Wilson, J. Tuzo, ed., *Continents Adrift and Continents Aground.* W. H. Freeman, 1976.

Wood, Fergus, ed., *The Prince William Sound, Alaska Earthquake of 1964 and Aftershocks.* Government Printing Office, 1966.

Wright, Frank Lloyd, *An Autobiography.* Horizon Press, 1932.

Periodicals

Agnew, Duncan, and Kerry E. Sieh, "A Documentary Study of Felt Effects of the Great California Earthquake of 1857," *Bulletin of the Seismological Society of America,* December 1978.

Aki, Keiiti, "Progress in Japanese Earthquake Prediction Research," *Earthquake Information Bulletin,* November/December 1978.

Benioff, Hugo, "Earthquake Source Mechanisms," *Science,* March 27, 1964.

Bingham, Roger, "Explorers of the Earth Within," *Science 80,* September/October 1980.

Byerly, Perry, "Earthquake Mechanisms," *Science,* May 20, 1960.

"China Discloses 1976 Quake Deadliest in Four Centuries," *The New York Times,* June 2, 1977.

"China, in Effort to Modernize, Puts New Stress on Science and Technology," *The New York Times,* July 14, 1977.

"China Predicts a Major Earthquake," *UNESCO Courier,* May 1976.

"China's Killer Quake," *Newsweek,* August 9, 1976.

"China's Secret Earthquake," *New Scientist,* October 4, 1979.

Derr, John S., "Earthquake Lights: A Review of Observations and Present Theories," *Bulletin of the Seismological Society of America,* December 1973.

Dewey, James, and Perry Byerly, "The Early History of Seismometry (to 1900)," *Bulletin of the Seismological Society of America,* February 1969.

"Do Earthquakes Give Advance Warning Signals?" *Physics Today,* July 1973.

Douglas, John H., "Earthquake Research: Rethinking Prediction," *Science News,* February 3 and 10, 1979.

"Earthquake," *National Geographic,* July 1964.

"Earthquake Disaster Drill Staged in 10 Prefectures," *The Daily Yomiuri,* September 2, 1980.

Earthquake Information Bulletin, March 1970 to December 1980.

"Earthquake Prediction Studies in China," *Physics Today,* April 1974.

"Earthquakes: An Evacuation in China, a Warning in California," *Science,* May 7, 1976.

Emmons, F. T., "Native Accounts of the Meeting Between LaPeruse and the Tlingit," *American Anthropologist,* 1911.

Evans, David M., "The Denver Area Earthquakes and the Rocky Mountain Arsenal Disposal Well," *Mountain Geologist,* January 1966.

"Exploring the Drowned City of Port Royal," *National Geographic,* February 1960.

"Foul Gas Preceding China Quake Called Sign of Methane Reserve," *The New York Times,* May 29, 1978.

"4.3 Million in Kanto, Chubu Regions Join in Disaster Readiness Drill," *Japan Times,* September 2, 1980.

Gilbert, G. K., "Earthquake Forecasts," *Science,* January 22, 1909.

Gorshkov, G. S., "Gigantic Eruption of the Volcano Bezymianny," *Bulletina Volcanalogique,* 1959.

Hagiwara, T., and T. Rikitake, "Japanese Program on Earthquake Prediction," *Science,* August 18, 1967.

Hamilton, Robert M., "Quakes along the Mississippi," *Natural History,* August 1980.

Hanson, Richard, "Tokyo's Programmed Earthquake," *Financial Times,* August 30, 1980.

Hillmar, K. E., "The Hand That Rocks the Earth," *Oceans,* July 1978.

"How a Stricken State Met Chaos," *Saturday Evening Post,* May 9, 1964.

"Japanese Cope with Quakes," *The New York Times,* August 17, 1976.

Kirishiki, Shinjiro, "The Story of the Imperial Hotel," *Japan Architect,* January/February 1968.

McKendrick, Neil, "The End of Optimism," *Horizon,* Spring, 1974.

Mathews, Samuel W., "The Night the Mountains Moved," *National Geographic,* March 1960.

Mooney, Michael, "Tsunami Coming," *Oceans,* September 1975.

"New Tools for Predicting Quakes," *The New York Times,* March 22, 1979.

Nuttli, Otto, "The Mississippi Valley Earthquakes of 1811 and 1812," *Bulletin of the Seismological Society of America,* February 1973.

"Prospects for Earthquake Prediction Wane," *Science,* November 2, 1979.
"Quakes in Search of a Theory," *Mosaic,* July/August 1976.
Raleigh, C. B., et al., "An Experiment in Earthquake Control at Rangely, Colorado," *Science,* March 26, 1976.
"Recurrent Intraplate Tectonism in the New Madrid Seismic Zone," *Science,* August 29, 1980.
Reid, Harry Fielding, "The Lisbon Earthquake of Nov. 1, 1755," *Bulletin of the Seismological Society of America,* June 1914.
Reithermann, Robert, "The Seismic Legend of the Imperial Hotel," *AIA Journal,* June 1980.
Richter, Charles, "Earthquakes," *Natural History,* December 1969.
Rikitake, Tsuneji, "The Large-Scale Earthquake Countermeasures Act and the Earthquake Prediction Council in Japan," *EOS,* August 1979.
Sieh, Kerry E., "Prehistoric Large Earthquakes Produced by Slip on the San Andreas Fault at Pallett Creek, California," *Journal of Geophysical Research,* August 10, 1978.
Smith, Robert E., and Robert L. Christiansen, "Yellowstone Park as a Window on the Earth's Interior," *Scientific American,* February 1980.
Stokes, Henry Scott, "Earth Tremors in Tokyo Stir Fear That Big Quake Is Due," *The New York Times,* October 20, 1980.
"Tangshan Quake; a Chinese Report," *Science News,* September 1, 1979.
Thomas, Tay, "An Alaskan Family," *National Geographic,* July 1964.
"Tracking Down Ancient Tremors," *San Francisco Chronicle,* April 17, 1980.
"Tracking Temblors," *Wall Street Journal,* September 26, 1974.
"Tracking Tremors," *Wall Street Journal,* April 18, 1979.
"When Do Earthquakes Occur?" *New Scientist,* February 12, 1976.
Wright, Frank Lloyd, "In the Cause of Architecture," *Western Architect,* April and November 1923, February 1924.
Wood, Harry O., "The 1857 Earthquake in California," *Bulletin of the Seismological Society of America,* 1955.
"WWNSS: Seismology's Global Network," *Science,* October 15, 1971.

Other Publications
"Earthquake Prediction Research in Japan," Coordinating Committee for Earthquake Prediction, Japan, November 1, 1975.
Ganse, Robert A., and John B. Nelson, "Significant Earthquake File," National Geophysical and Solar-Terrestrial Data Center; National Oceanic and Atmospheric Administration, Boulder, Colorado, 1979.
"Prediction of the Haicheng Earthquake," American Geophysical Union: Transactions, 1977 (Haicheng Earthquake Delegation Report).
"Protecting Yourself in an Earthquake," Planning Section, Disaster Prevention Division, Tokyo Metropolitan Government, March 1981.
Sieh, Kerry E., "A Search for Great Prehistoric Earthquakes along the San Andreas Fault, California," California Institute of Technology, 1980.
"Some Recent Earthquake Engineering Research and Practice in Japan," The Japanese National Committee of the International Association for Earthquake Engineering, Tokyo, July 1980.
Wallace, Robert, "Gilbert's Studies of Faults, Scarps, and Earthquakes," U.S. Geological Survey.

INDEX

Numerals in italics indicate an illustration of the subject mentioned.